It was my privilege to be Janet Williamson's Pastor at the Free Methodist Church, Peterborough, Ontario from 1995 when she started attending until my retirement in 2016. The Peterborough Free Methodist Church supported Janet and her children through their battles with cancers and continued to undergird her with loving support after her children's deaths. Both Eric and Tanya's deaths had a profound effect on both me and our congregation. In spite of horrific tragedy, Janet Williamson was able to see and experience the faithfulness of God through the death of both of her children. You will be encouraged and inspired by her remarkable story!

—*Lloyd R. Eyre, Senior Pastor, Peterborough Free Methodist Church, 1984-2016*

I know Janet Williamson's story well and am therefore so pleased that she has taken the incredibly bold step of writing it down. Some experiences are unique to the individuals involved. However, the lessons and understandings about life and of God gained in such furnaces as Janet relates, are not quickly found in normal circumstances of life. Janet's book can advance our understanding as she shares her life and the incredible journey the Lord brought her and her children through. A phrase she mentioned in one of our many conversations on the subject was to… "look for Gods face not His hand". So many of us, myself included, want God to do something for us when He wants to do something In us. We want Him to move His hand in help. He wants us to see His face smiling on us, assuring us of His presence in our trials. Many more such lessons, some deeper than others but all fashioned in the furnace of a life of faith and trust in God. I heartily recommend this book for ordinary people, for believers and unbelievers, for church members and for pastors and workers.

—*Rev. Archie Murray, Author, Lobo, Ontario, Canada*

When I met Janet at Christ for the Nations Institute in 1983 she was already talking about writing Eric's miraculous story of victory over cancer, but little did we know that there was ever so much more life to live, trials to be faced, and things to learn before this victorious story could be written. Two years after we met, Tanya was also diagnosed, but this family kept walking in faith, believing God for miracles – and God provided over the years as they lived with joy and trust in good times and in the shadow of the valley of death" (Psalm 23:1). Janet is an amazing mother who raised two amazing children whose goal was to glorify God in everything. This is their inspiring story of living victoriously with an eternal perspective. May your faith grow as you read the story of these giants in the faith.

—*Carolyn Hink, Virginia Beach, Virginia, USA*

GOD OF THE VALLEYS

Mysteries along Life's Journey

JANET WILLIAMSON

GOD OF THE VALLEYS
Copyright © 2022 by Janet Williamson

Unless otherwise indicated, scripture quotations are taken from The Holy Bible, New International Version® NIV® Copyright © 1973 1978 1984 2011 by Biblica, Inc. TM Used by permission. All rights reserved worldwide. • Scripture quotations marked KJV are taken from the Holy Bible, King James Version, which is in the public domain. • Scripture quotations marked ESV are taken from The Holy Bible, English Standard Version, Copyright © 2001 by Crossway, a publishing ministry of Good News Publishers. Used by permission. All rights reserved. • Scripture quotations marked NCV are taken from The Holy Bible, International Children's Bible, New Century Version, Copyright © 1986 by Sweet Publishing.

Please note that current conventions for grammar and punctuation have been used in the editing of this book as per the Chicago Manual of Style.

Printed in Canada

Soft Cover ISBN: 978-1-4866-2221-4
Hard Cover ISBN: 978-1-4866-2180-4
eBook ISBN: 978-1-4866-2222-1

Word Alive Press
119 De Baets Street Winnipeg, MB R2J 3R9
www.wordalivepress.ca

MIX
Paper from
responsible sources
FSC® C103567

Cataloguing in Publication information can be obtained from Library and Archives Canada.

Dedication

THIS BOOK IS dedicated to the glory of God, with thanksgiving for His loving faithfulness and my two beloved, cherished children, Tanya, born in 1973 and Eric, 1975. They loved God, fully engaged in a life that spilled over with joy, humour, and kindness to others. They taught me how to do the same. This book is also dedicated to my dear father, Robert Williamson, who was always an active part of my life and his grandchildren's lives. He demonstrated his love in quiet, practical ways, was always present at special celebrations and was always faithful to support us through every health crisis with helpfulness and love. He is now in heaven united with his grandchildren, having received Christ, November 10, 2020, at the age of ninety-seven in answer to my children and my prayers!

In addition, this book is also dedicated to Dr. Harold Reents and his dear wife Patty Reents, whom I met at Christ For the Nations in Dallas, Texas. Dr. Reents was an instructor, academic dean and served in other positions. Dr. Reents and Patty Reents were my spiritual parents for decades, mentoring me spiritually, and are referred to as my beloved Mama and Papa Blessing in this story. Dr. Reents, affectionately known as Papa Reents, joined my children in heaven on November 17, 2020.

Contents

Acknowledgements

ALL MY THANKS to God, who kept bringing me back to my promise to my children to write our stories. God answered my prayer and gave me perseverance and reassurance that His timing is never too late. I thank Him for all the hope and strength I found in the Scriptures, and through many special people that helped to keep me focused on Him. Sharon Mehew, Linda Lake, Patti Burton, Karin McCrae, Ishbel Bryan, and Susan Taylor—my friends for decades who were a rock of spiritual strength and practical help. I also thank the many friends from church, especially Pastor Lloyd Eyre and the Free Methodist Church and the different circles of my life. Thank you for walking this journey with me and for the richness of your friendship, and the generosity of your kindness.

I would like to thank my father, Robert Williamson, whose love and support were constant throughout my life and his grandchildren's lives. I would also like to acknowledge and extend a special thank you to my close and loyal friend from Christ For the Nations Institute, Carolyn Hink, who has walked with me on my journey with God for many decades and sacrificially gave numerous hours of time to read my manuscript and offered helpful suggestions that I incorporated. I would also like to acknowledge my first cousin Babs Snelgrove and my friend Elizabeth who carved out time in their busy schedules to read my manuscript and offered insightful comments that I applied. Equally important, I want to acknowledge my beloved children Tanya and Eric, who urged me before they died to write their stories, and now, I have. The details are taken from my copious journal notes, and most of these are their words verbatim.

Prologue

GOD'S MYSTERIOUS WAYS are overshadowed by His promise to never leave or forsake us (Hebrews 13:5), even when life is a crescendo of crises with increasing challenges. I found God's love, peace, and joy as did my children, Eric and Tanya, as they each endured cancer, surgeries, medical complications, chemotherapy, radiation, and multiple hospitalizations. Our lives were entrusted to a faithful God as we faced every challenge with faith and courage. This story is about God and our journey with Him. Proverbs 3:5–6 instructs us to 'lean not to our understanding but to trust God.' Why do some people turn to God in difficult times while others run away from Him? Another mystery.

Even though we weren't exempted from suffering, God provided us with grace and peace to move forward, our lives sprinkled with blessings of humour and abiding joy for the gift of life. Gratitude is directed to God and to those He placed on our paths. My prayer from the beginning of my son's first battle with cancer at age four, and for the sequent challenging years that our family faced was, "Lord, please do not ever let my children's suffering cause them to turn away from You. That would be more than I can bear (1 Corinthians 10:13). Lord, please give us the grace to love You, to know You, worship You, serve You, walk with You and talk with You, all the days of our lives no matter what the cost."

PART ONE

Eric's Journey Begins

TO LAUNCH OUR story, Eric will speak in his child-like voice and from his viewpoint. Eric aptly describes our family's dependence on God to overcome unforeseen difficulties. As the story unfolds, the narrator's voice will transition to Mom's.

ONE
Eric Reflects!

GREETINGS! MY NAME is Eric; I was born September 19, 1975, and I was the apple of my mum and dad's eyes, as was my sister Tanya, two years older. From the outset, it was clear I wouldn't be a sleeper. Mummy observed that, along with a budding passion for music, I could complete complex puzzles with my sister by the time I was one, and I began reading and spelling phonetically at three. As I grew, I memorized many of the books my sister and I shared. Storytime was learning time. My sister and I eagerly answered Mummy's probing questions to test our comprehension.

In 1974 my parents purchased a modern, cozy bungalow on a quiet street in Peterborough, Ontario. I was born in Peterborough, whereas my sister was born in a city close to Toronto called West Hill.

My speech pronunciation for soft sounds like 'th' was delayed with frequent ear infections and a mild hearing impairment. Mummy was studying Early Childhood Education part-time, so she quickly realized I was missing developmental milestones. She set me up with Miss Jackie, a lovely woman who introduced me to speech therapy. It was all fun and games as far as I was concerned. Yes, I loved to play games, and Mummy would convert a request into a game and trick me into compliance when I was stubborn.

When my sister was six years old, she invited Jesus into her heart and was, *born again* followed by my copycat decision: "Me too! Me too! I want to be born again too!" Mummy instructed me to repeat the same words Tanya had prayed— to confess I was a sinner and that Jesus died and rose from the grave to save me. It was a big event to invite Jesus into my little four-year-old heart. And now it was bursting with God's love. With Jesus living in my heart, I insisted that Mummy read the real Bible to me. Now her morning devotions included me, sitting at her feet, attentively absorbing God's Word. I became very curious about heaven and how to get there.

A few months later, in early spring, our family attended a special gathering after church. I thought I had eaten too many sweets and complained of a severe tummy ache. As the pain escalated, Mummy took me to the doctor, but he was unconcerned. She carefully watched over me with great concern as I writhed in pain, and she prayed continually while searching the scriptures for comfort and encouragement. The words of God helped her. *"Trust in the Lord with all your heart and do not lean on your own understanding. In all your ways acknowledge him, and he will make your path straight"* (Proverbs 3:5–6, ESV).

Another doctor appointment, a diagnosis of dehydration, and I was admitted to the hospital to receive IV fluids and have tests done. That night, Jesus appeared at my bedside dressed in a white gown with a glowing halo all around Him, and He placed His hand on my tummy.

The pain went away. I was discharged and eager to get on with life. Upon arriving home, I asked Daddy to remove the training wheels from my bicycle, and I practiced with great determination until I learned to balance and ride independently. My parents and I were elated!

However, my tummy ache returned with a vengeance, and again the doctor dismissed my symptoms. Mummy was concerned and took me back to the doctor many times until the doctor refused to see us. In all, I saw eight doctors, two of them paediatricians. They all agreed that my symptoms were psychosomatic— faked for attention, and that Mummy was an overprotective, annoying parent harassing the doctors for nothing. Regardless of what the doctors said, I knew Mum believed me when I told her that my tummy ached, and I expected to go to heaven to see Jesus soon.

The doctors kept saying that I was fine, that I only had a virus, so I tried hard to act fine, but I was exhausted. My tummy hurt so badly I couldn't eat. When I wasn't whimpering from the pain, I only wanted to sleep. I developed a stiff neck and couldn't move my head, so Mummy rushed me to the hospital. The doctor wondered if my neck was broken and ordered x-rays. No problems were found, so I was fitted with a neck brace and sent home.

Mummy prayed continually out loud to Jesus. She took the words of 1 Peter 5:7 seriously where the scripture instructs us to cast all our anxiety upon Him. Mummy was giving it all to Jesus night and day. I was confused about what was happening. Pain was my constant companion, and I would forget simple things. Searching for answers, I asked, "Mummy what's this?" pointing to the fridge. She told me. I asked again, "Mummy, what's this?" pointing to the floor. She told me. I pointed to many things and asked the question, "What's this?" I was baffled, "Mummy, how come I used to know these things and I don't know them anymore?"

Her eyes were wet with tears, and her cracked voice revealed how perplexed she felt, "I don't know Eric, I don't know." Proverbs 3:5–6 kept coming back reminding us not to lean to our own understanding but to trust in the Lord with all our heart. And we did!

Before long, I was sleeping twenty-one hours a day. Mummy used to play rhyming word and spelling games with me because that had always been my favourite pastime. But I was no longer interested. As my energy waned, she read dozens of books out loud to keep me awake. She was deeply troubled, though her face glowed with the peace of God that passes all understanding (Philippians 4:7). Mummy and I had peace during this turmoil.

My weight plummeted at age one. I was a skeleton. Every time she called different doctors, they got cross and told her they had patients who really needed care and she should stop calling. But Mummy wouldn't give up.

I told Mummy again and again, "I am not faking my sick tummy, I am going to see Jesus real soon." And she believed me.

On a hot June day, about six weeks after my symptoms began, I became clammy, cold, and comatose. Mummy scooped me into her arms and begged for help at the hospital emergency department. Suddenly there was a buzz of doctors examining me, and they told my mum that I had no reflexes and didn't respond to pinpricks. My pupils didn't respond to light but were fixed and dilated, all indications that my brain was swelling. At this point, they thought I was dying, and an ambulance transported me to Sick Children's Hospital about 150 kilometres away. On route, Mummy read encouragement from the Bible, until the evening light made it too dim to read. I woke up and whispered, "Sing me Jesus songs. Sing me Jesus songs." And she did.

Hours later, when we arrived at Sick Children's hospital, I drifted in and out of consciousness. Sometimes, when I was awake, I didn't recognize my mother and became very angry. I would suddenly switch back to recognizing her and cried that I loved her and wanted to give her warm fuzzies. Then without warning, I would abruptly become angry again and tell her I wanted to give her cold prickles. I was quoting what I remembered from a Christian storybook that taught children to give warm fuzzies and not cold prickles to people. When I arrived at the Intensive Care Unit, now in a coma, the sterile sound of the heart monitor's intermittent beat reverberated through the silence. Mummy put her ear to my lips when I woke up, and I whispered, "Jesus you can heal me. Please heal me. Mummy don't worry about me. Jesus will heal me."

When Mummy told the nurse my confession of Jesus, the nurse grinned. Mum drew the nurse's attention to the heart monitor. Was it malfunctioning as the numbers darted from thirty-five to 180 and everything in between? After the consultation with the neurosurgeon, it was determined that my erratic heartbeat was one of the reasons he wouldn't operate. Other vital signs were also unstable. The neurosurgeon prepared Mummy for my death. Wrapped in a cocoon of God's loving grace, the words of death wouldn't penetrate her heart. She clung to Jesus as her lifeline, believing that He would heal me.

Unexpectedly, I woke up and my vital signs stabilized. I asked for food. The neurosurgical team began to immediately prep me for surgery, and I was ushered into an operating theatre for eight hours of surgery. That was Sunday, June 22, 1980.

After surgery, the neurosurgeon came into the waiting room, still wearing surgical scrubs and smiling in amazement. He didn't understand why I was alive. He told my mother that there was a left-hemispheric tumour the size of a grapefruit, and after they removed part of my skull, the tumour burst with the first incision into the brain matter, and he caught the explosion of disease in a basin. He removed parts of my brain responsible for speech, movement on the right side of my body, memory, and vision. He couldn't understand how I was able to sit up in the recovery room and announce, "I want my Mum!" Later he would always refer to me as *the most unusual case*—because medically I shouldn't have lived.

When Mummy came to my side in the recovery room, I tried to sit, but the nurse urged me to remain horizontal to prevent swelling, so I cried out, "Mummy, pray for me! Pray for me!" and before my mom finished her prayer, I was resting peacefully. After I recovered in the ICU, I was transferred to the neurosurgical ward on 5G. All the little children in my ward had brain injuries. Mummy stayed with me all day and as late into the evening as permitted. Some of the nurses were nice and understood my suffering. Some didn't and told some of the really sick children to stop crying or they would get another operation. My mother kept quiet and was worried about leaving me, so she stayed until I was asleep every night. Sometimes Mummy was so tired she rested her head on the side of my crib and one nurse would sharply reprimand her for contaminating my bedding and threaten to ban her from coming to see me or staying so long. In all of this, Mum stayed meek and apologetic, inconspicuously sleeping on the lobby couch, dashing to my bedside at the crack of dawn before I woke up. She was always there to take care of my needs, washing me and helping me to the bathroom. For twelve days she persisted, being present during my waking moments, to protect me from impatient nurses. Lines of fatigue and sleep deprivation etched themselves into her face. She prayed constantly for my healing, my sister, my daddy, the children with brain injuries, and she prayed for strength and grace to walk every moment with Jesus. I held her hands and prayed the same prayer with her—for all the children and for my healing too. Mummy had been trying to have me discharged into her care and applied for a Care-by-Parent Unit in the adjacent nursing dormitory. Approval was given to move me to this less restrictive and more community-based environment after I recovered from a setback, an abdominal hernia that needed repair.

The first week after surgery my sister, Tanya, and Daddy came to visit, and they took me for walks in a wheelchair around the hospital. My parents took pictures, and I smiled. I was happy to have my family close to me, but at the end of the weekend Tanya and Daddy had to go back to Peterborough, and that made me sad.

After the weekend, our morning routine included taking a hospital taxi to Princess Margaret Hospital (hereafter referred to as PMH) to meet the oncology and radiation specialist followed by casting preparations for radiation treatment the next week. The attending doctor marvelled at my gross motor and fine motor abilities before directing my mummy's attention to the illuminated CT scans. My mum gasped in disbelief at the size of the tumour before surgery. He explained why radiation to both hemispheres of my brain was imperative. Sadly, this radical radiation regimen, while extending my life, would have grave long-range repercussions that would challenge my life. The doctors agreed that my survival and recovery was a miracle but added that I was still in need of more miracles. My mother listened courteously to the gravity of my medical future, a prognosis of six months after radiation. She guarded her emotions, permitting her heart to entertain only a parade of Biblical miracles that inspired her to trust and focus on Jesus's healings.

At the end of the week, my heart swelled joyfully with the arrival of my father and sister, and that joy didn't waver even to bedtime preparations. The day had been filled with wonderful fun, memorable experiences, which included a visit to the hospital park, crawling through the grass with my sister, capturing grasshoppers, and corralling them only to release our hopping athletes for race competitions, giggling as we kept them on course. I was full of humour when I competently demonstrated to my daddy and sister how I could catch a ball with my right hand. Tanya was my biggest fan, applauding my ambitious accomplishments, understanding the limitations that could have been mine except for God's intervention. My dad and sister sealed our day with kisses and hugs. We prayed and sang Christian songs, curled up on my mummy's lap, my arms clinging to her neck, clutching my stuffed toy, the sweet fragrance of Jesus permeating the room. I prayed aloud from a sincere heart. "Jesus, I got a sore back, and it always hurts, and I have a sore nose, it's always bleeding, and I have a sore bum. You can heal it. You can do it. Just make me better please, in Jesus's Name, Amen." My prayers were candid, and I already knew that Jesus was living in my heart with all His power.

It was another enjoyable family time the following day. Mummy arrived first, so we began the day with my favourite game, rhyming and spelling words. I impressed my mum with a safety proposal. I knew the drill. If I get lost, find a policeman—and to demonstrate my competence and confidence, I spelled my name, address, and phone number, pulling from memory the safety strategy, assuring Mummy that I was well prepared to enter kindergarten in the fall. Mummy felt exceedingly grateful to our Lord Jesus for this evidence that my cognitive ability had been preserved post-surgery. As well, my gross motor capability had not been damaged and I was able to competently catch all the balls that Mummy threw.

Then Daddy and Tanya arrived. Since Mummy had been apart from Tanya for two weeks, she needed to spend some special one-on-one time with her, and focus on hugging and holding hands while listening to her six-year-old little girl stories. Also, Mummy needed some spiritual food, so they took the subway to a church.

On their return, we revisited the grassy park to hunt grasshoppers on our knees, but this time my sister climbed up on Daddy's back and I straddled Mummy as we combed through the grass, our parents now prancing ponies, creating happy memories. My sister went to supper with Daddy while Mummy borrowed a wheelchair. As we strolled around the block, we chanted above the noisy traffic, "Going on a lion hunt, going to catch a big one, I'm not afraid…" and "Five little monkeys jumping on the bed, one fell off and bumped his head, Mama called the doctor and the doctor said, no more monkeys jumping on the bed…" Everything about the day was perfect. My parents lifted deep-felt whispers of thankfulness heavenward.

Grandpa arrived with treats, and Tanya and I thanked him with hugs as we scurried off to play. He had stopped by to see me and to tell Mummy about a job interview the next day, and she reminded him to thank God. As evening approached, our blissful day was over, and it was time for my dad and sister to bid goodbye and drive back home to Peterborough. Many hugs and kisses were exchanged, and they disappeared through the closed elevator doors. We turned our attention to my little patient friend, also a four-year-old, struggling with a 40–degree fever. My mother led his mother to our Lord Jesus, so Mummy spent time consoling her with encouraging prayer and scripture, compassionately holding her in her suffering. After my story and snuggle time, I passionately prayed aloud for my brain, my sore penis, stomach, my sister, Daddy, and all the sick children in the hospital. Mummy hadn't seen me happier, brighter, or more content in a long time.

Radiation treatment began on Monday, July 7, 1980, and I was so happy to wake up and see Mummy there. Nothing mattered! When I opened my dreamy eyes, she told me that my face had the glowing gentleness of an angel, and I embraced her love.

Mummy casually reviewed the day's plans after breakfast while colouring in my book. At PMH our first stop, Betatron radiation to my brain's left hemisphere was followed by Picker 2 cobalt for the right hemisphere. The radiation specialist explained that I would receive 5250 rads in twenty-eight consecutive treatments, the maximum dose short of killing me. When Mummy asked about the risk of radiation exposure, the specialist explained that the high rads of radiation would lead to problems. Mummy researched the diagnosis in the hospital library. She researched my bleak prognosis after the doctor diagnosed my tumour as a glioblastoma grade 4 malignancy, with a life expectancy of six months post-radiation. The neurosurgeon had said that there were no long-term survivors, and the textbooks concurred with the doctor's dismal prognosis. Nevertheless, Mum chose to cling to Jesus for a full healing and recovery. Here I was at my first radiation treatment, curious about all the dials and gadgets and asked many questions that the technicians pondered seriously and answered honestly. The first treatment was uneventful.

Then, back at the hospital, we played bouncing-ball games, practiced my eye-hand coordination, (so that my right-hand catch became my signature skill), ate lunch, had a nap, went to the playroom, painted at the easel, and had more outdoor adventures. Mum chatted with other moms, my grandpa visited, my aunt and uncle came bearing gifts and lots of chatter and laughter continued until bedtime. Then we sang Jesus songs, had Bible reading, stories, cuddles and prayers, and finally sleep.

The next morning when Mummy arrived, my roommate and I, a preschool recipe for mischief, had filled our water guns, squirting the walls and each other with serious effort. Mummy was happy that I was being a kid and not a patient, so we entertained her for a while with our childish play.

We taxied to PMH for my second Picker 2 cobalt treatment and then down to Betatron for radiation. The technicians marvelled at my bravery and fearlessness when I flashed my famous heart-melting smiles at them, chirping with inquisitiveness and observations. Mummy explained that I drew courage and strength from my faith in the Lord Jesus. Grinning, I nodded in agreement. My effervescent smiles and articulate observations won me favour, and they invited me to push the buttons to move the giant mechanical arm of the immense radiation machine at both Betatron and Picker 2. I asked about the mechanics of the equipment, and my childlike wonder charmed the technicians.

I was also very curious about stairwell echoes and probed with Mummy how much furniture I would need to fill the stairwell to absorb the sound bouncing off the walls. I wondered if a couch and the garbage cans could be sufficient to silence the echoes. We would explore more scenarios later.

After treatment, my neurosurgeon was making his rounds with his team of resident doctors, so I boasted proudly, "I can catch a ball with one hand. Do you want to see?" Mummy threw the ball and I caught it with ease. The neurosurgeon was startled—I wasn't limited in my gross motor skills especially on the right side which should have been paralyzed. The neurosurgeon always called me, '*his most unusual case.*' Mummy asked him if after Friday's treatment we could go home to Peterborough for the weekend, and when he agreed, I exclaimed, "I can see Tanya and Benji!" I cheered, clapping my hands, elated with the thought of hugging my sister and my dog. The neurosurgeon was amused with my childish delight. However, Mummy was puzzled by my episodes of uncontrollable laughter.

I was finding silly things really funny, and I couldn't stop laughing. At other times I was just very friendly. We meandered to the cafeteria to discover Grandpa eating supper with a doctor whom I cordially greeted, "Hi, how are you?" My uninhibited preschool sociability spilled over. Everyone dressed in hospital green scrubs, or a white lab coat was friendly to me, and it being a children's hospital, most adults were dressed that way. The doctor smiled, winked at me, pulled from his pocket two tongue depressors, and handed them to me. "Oh, thank you, thank you!" I politely beamed with gratitude and showed Mummy and Grandpa my prize.

Soon it was time to prepare for bed. Every night we had a routine of rocking-chair cuddles, prayer, Bible stories, and Jesus songs. However, this night I was distracted by the dying flowers. I found them exceptionally funny and exploded with laughter. Mummy silently pondered these outbursts.

The next day and the day after, my treatment routine was established. My cheerfulness and unabated fearlessness gave no evidence of intimidation despite the colossally massive machines, which won me the privilege of pushing the buttons that operated the giant monsters. Mummy shared her faith at every chance, and we prayed together about everything.

The next day at Betatron, I read the print above the coloured light symbols on the machine, amazing the radiation therapist, "Can he read?" Mummy said I'd learned to read phonetically spelled words when I was three, and I had memorized the words on the symbols, so they were now sight words. I loved reading and spelling games. To demonstrate my interest, I showed the technician the book tucked under my arm and explained that I was like the main character, a curious monkey, and that was why I asked so many questions about the machines. Apart from wearing a head cast and there being big machines with lots of buttons making weird noises, I was oblivious to the destruction of radiation. I was exuberantly looking forward to our bus trip home to Peterborough after the morning's radiation.

Since I was determined to ride my two-wheeler at the first opportunity at home that weekend, the neurosurgeon addressed me exclusively by holding up three fingers and saying, "Three-wheelers only." I groaned. The other doctors looked surprised and laughed, not expecting this wee guy to be able to balance on a bicycle.

By mid-afternoon of July 11, 1980, we stepped off the bus in Peterborough and were greeted by Tanya. Home at last! We hugged her tightly while smothering her with kisses. I was delighted with a card signed by the neighbourhood kids. I immediately accepted their invitation to dash through the sprinkler with my preschool buddies, getting soaked until my toes looked like dried prunes. When Daddy arrived home and suggested some father-and-son time, we scurried off fishing. Mummy used the time to give Tanya undivided attention, listening to her concerns while playing with toys with her. That evening after our prayer time we sang an echo worship song that Tanya and I loved. The lyrics were about us his servants, blessing the Lord in God's holy house. Tanya was so happy! I was so happy! Mummy and Daddy were so happy! But some unexplainable changes were happening—I was having extreme mood swings from hysterical laughter to abrupt anger. Sometimes I'd forget a word and substitute a rhyming word like when I asked for the "look" instead of the "book." On many levels, my ability to understand and reason had sharply decreased since the start of radiation treatment only five days before.

The second week of radiation I was staying with Mom in the hostel Care-By-Parent Unit with other moms and kids. I taxied every morning to PMH, chatting happily at both radiation stations, with never-ending questions and comments. At a follow-up examination, the doctor focused on my memory. Mummy was concerned that I forgot words, and I often described the forgotten word using hand gestures or charades but most often with outbursts of anger and frustration expecting her to know what I was thinking. The doctor indicated that radiation was the culprit, and in time things should improve. After my appointment, I complained of sharp pain in the front of my head, which grew worse as the day progressed, so Mummy took me to Sick Kids Emergency. The doctor suggested that the head pain might be the radiation treatments shrinking the remaining cancer.

At the hostel, while preparing for bed and listening to the Christian tapes, my nose spontaneously bled profusely. The flow of blood would temporarily clot through nose pinching only to abruptly start again. Concerned, Mummy phoned the emergency doctor because it had taken over an hour to clot, but the doctor said it was safe for me to sleep and to bring me to the Emergency if it bled again. Mummy stayed up late to make sure that the bleeding had stopped and used the time to hear the story about another mom's child with cancer.

The next morning as we taxied to PMH, stormy skies suddenly opened with loud, crashing thunder, flashes of zigzagged lightning, and drenching rain, which led me to explore flood possibilities like Noah and his ark.

After Betatron and Picker 2 cobalt, and my morning entertainment of pushing buttons to move the big machine, it was back to Sick Kids. To pass some rainy-day time, I wanted to slip into the gift shop and agreed to just *window shop*, until a water gun captured my heart. Mom stood her ground against my tears and rage and steadfastly refused to give in to my drama, holding firm to her words that today we would only *window shop*. When I settled down, I was happy to play a game of *follow the leader*, leading Mom around the hospital corridors. "Eric, how come you are such a happy boy?" Mummy playfully asked while I was smiling.

"Jesus makes me happy!" I replied proudly as my short stature grew tall.

My sister had been feeling unwell all day with a fever and a headache. Mummy spoke with Daddy and suggested he ask our church leaders if Tanya should see a doctor or just rest since my father was at a loss as to what to do. I talked to Daddy and described every detail about the underground tunnel from the hostel to the hospital that I had discovered and told him I would be coming home on Friday, only three days away. At the moment, Mummy thought that I seemed brighter, able to think through complex matters, like understanding Friday was in three days. At other times, she noted that I struggled to understand simple directions.

This morning, I refused food and complained of a tummy ache, but by the time we arrived at PMH at Betatron, my spirits lifted when the radiation therapist permitted me to push buttons as before. Mummy shared her faith in Jesus again when the technician marvelled at my intelligence and curiosity. She shared how our church prayed for my healing and that she believed God would continue to sustain me with His healing love, power, and grace. The technician's eyes were as wide as saucers as she saw Mummy's confidence in Jesus.

Back in the taxi, Mummy tried unsuccessfully to rouse my interest in lunch despite ongoing abdominal pain. She brought me back to the clinic at Sick Kids, feeling desperate to learn the source of this dreadful pain, and the attending doctor was also concerned but attributed it to the radiation treatment, reassuring Mummy that if it persisted after treatment, they would investigate the symptoms further. For now, they offered me medicine. Mummy spoke boldly to the doctor that she believed that Jesus would completely heal me. He asked her if she was getting enough Christian support, and if not, he would introduce her to supportive Christians with whom he was connected. He and Mum shared the power of God, and Mum shared that she was thankful for the fellowship of believers back home who were prayerfully supporting us. As Mum thanked him for attending to me, she said goodbye and he called back loudly, "Goodbye and God bless you!" Mum was so blessed that his parting words were a confident Godly blessing that people could hear. Mum returned the blessing and felt part of the bigger body of Christ, reasoning that there were many born-again believers strategically placed on our path by God to communicate His loving presence.

After Mum gave me a dose of medicine, I was able to ignore the pain and engage in the rest of the day's planned fun as we set out for Centre Island in Toronto. My grandpa and my aunt arrived, and both wished my mother a happy birthday and presented her with thoughtful gifts. Mummy had almost forgotten that this was July 16th, her twenty-seventh birthday. Her concerns had been so focused on my health that other events were unimportant. I was glad we could have this special outing to be a birthday blessing for her. I was captivated by the ferry boat and the life jackets suspended on the ceiling. I had many questions as I tried to learn everything about this new world. Once on the island, we were drawn to the amusement park where I rode the merry-go-round, the cars, and the trains with Mum. I was also attracted to the zoo animals. My grandpa was delighted to engage my young mind and pointed out facts and stories about the animal habitats. It was a splendid afternoon, but later Mummy and I felt sad when we learned that my sister had a fever that was getting worse.

Every day my tummy felt sick, so to encourage me to eat, my mother played fun contest games with me. When she wasn't coaxing me to eat, she prayed out loud. Sometimes I added my prayers and Mummy paused for me to pray. "And Jesus, we lift Tanya up to You and ask You to heal her. You can make her better. We love You and we pray in Jesus's Name Amen." My voice was firm and carried authority, power, and certainty that Jesus was able to perform my prayer request.

My tummy pain led to another visit to the oncologist, and a specialist was called in to review my symptoms. They were bewildered and attributed my pain to radiation. Mummy had been noticing that my behaviour was changing along with my speech. I would say the opposite or completely ignore people until reminded to respond. She observed that I was steadily having increasing difficulty with cognitive processing. I required much repetition to follow directions, and at times I had extreme mood swings. Nevertheless, most of our time I remained passionate about my activities and appreciated the visits with family and new hospital friends with whom Mummy often prayed. Mummy gave another mom whom she had led to the Lord my cassette tape, 'The Bread of Life' which was scripture to music, and invited her to pass it along to other parents.[1]

Later at the hostel, Tanya phoned me. When she reported that she was feeling better, I cheered at the top of my lungs, "Well, praise the Lord!" This delighted my mum as she realized God had cradled a genuine love for Him in my heart. When we had visited Grandpa earlier, he had let me play his piano, and I made up songs to worship Jesus. He gave me a special flashlight that was generator-powered, so I told Tanya and Daddy all about the marvellous flashlight that used no batteries.

---

[1] M. Parks, David Culross & Stamps-Baxter "He Is the Bread of Life," Side 2 song 6 on *Bread of Life*, Singspiration, Division of The Zondervan Corporation, 1978.

By the end of the second week, Friday, July 18, 1980, I was feeling grumpy. I resented that we had to dash to PMH for treatment and then had to hurry to catch the bus home. My disagreeable behaviour continued at home where I spoke harsh, critical words to my sobbing sister as she crumbled in Mummy's arms. Mummy validated Tanya and helped her feel less insecure and adjust to the many changes in me and our disconnected family life. My mother's frequent prayers heavenward were that God would give her the correct, gentle words to comfort me and my sister, just as James 1:5 urges the believer, *"If any of you lacks wisdom, you should ask God...."*

When we attended church on Sunday morning, Mummy was attentive to Tanya who seemed to disappear into the shadows, as attention was showered upon my recovery. At every opportunity, Mummy tried to be a conduit of God's love and peace, focusing attention on Tanya who felt lost and forgotten. Despite my rejection of her, Tanya's devotion to me remained strong.

In week three of radiation, I was noncompliant, and I flopped around like a rag doll while at the hostel, so Mum had to dress me. There was no relief from tummy pain, and the smell of food was nauseating. She recognized the reality of my suffering as she prayed, and her eyes filled with tears, helpless to relieve my anguish. To make my day worse, the hostel receptionist announced that we would be moved to another unit with a crib. When I heard the word, *crib* I protested loudly. I did not want to sleep in a crib! All the way to the cafeteria I cried and complained. I would refuse to sleep in one. Mummy coaxed a half-bowl of cereal into my tummy in spite of my pain by playing the food game. When we arrived at PMH, the radiation therapist observed that my hair hadn't fallen out. She looked worried. My mother tried to reassure her that Jesus had intervened. Even the neurosurgeon was amazed that I was neither paralyzed nor speechless, and perhaps it would be amazing again if my hair didn't fall out.

After treatment, Mummy took me to the radiation specialist and told him about my persistently painful stomach and asked if the malignancy could have spread, but the doctor reassured her that brain tumours don't spread to other body parts. We spent the afternoon at High Park with Grandpa. It was stifling hot, so to quench my thirst I stuck my tongue out as I darted in and out of the park sprinklers, catching the water spray, and got soaked to the skin. The outing briefly distracted me from the incessant pain, but back at the hostel I was soon on the toilet crying in extreme discomfort, "It will never heal! My tummy will never heal!" Mummy held me while she softly prayed for healing and comfort. I was defiant and irritable when we went for supper.

The thought of eating was more than I could deal with. The eating game didn't work some days.

The remainder of the week brought more treatments and pain. I woke with stomach aches and headaches and went to sleep with no relief. Mummy held me and sang to me, but nothing helped. Memory loss was worse by the day, and then to add to my misery my scalp ached as my long, curly blonde locks fell out in thick clumps that covered my sheets and pillow. Mummy didn't realize that the dark discolourations on my scalp were radiation burns. The large horseshoe-shaped area where they removed part of my skull bone had permanent metal staples just under my sensitive skin. There were so many changes going on that Mummy frequently whispered to God, asking Him to increase His grace and patience so that she could accommodate my expanding needs. Her gentle responses validated my feelings, and her deep well of compassion gave me a glimpse of how her heart ached for her little Eric!

That week I no longer had fun pushing the buttons or asking questions at radiation treatment. I wouldn't even smile for the therapist. Mummy told her I was in a lot of pain.

My mother tried to cheer me up by playing 'I Spy' in the waiting room, but I had trouble remembering the words, and I angrily clenched my fists, gritted my teeth, and tried to regain control by inhaling deeply. Although Mummy tried to capture my interest, to distract me out of this gloomy mood, without warning I would erupt in anger, furiously targeting her. At other times I would show calm, rational maturity, like when I wanted to buy a surprise gift of a water gun for my sister, but they were sold out, and I was okay with waiting until the next day to get one.

Mummy was torn between her concern for me and Tanya's ongoing, unexplained fever. She couldn't be in two places! She phoned the church's Disciple Leader who told her that her place was at home looking after Tanya and Daddy and to trust the Lord to guide the nurses to care for sick kids like me while she fulfilled her marital obligation as a supportive wife at home. Mummy cried her heart out and wondered why it couldn't be the other way around, to trust Tanya and Daddy to the Lord and stay with me. I was only four years old and suffering so intensely. She submitted to their decision because she was afraid that if she disobeyed, something worse might happen to me. As a new Christian, she still had a lot to learn about God and didn't understand that He would never threaten a child with harm.

She contacted the neurosurgeon and explained about Tanya's illness, and he agreed to readmit me to the hospital. I cried and screamed that I'd be alone and didn't want to be readmitted. Mummy prayed for wisdom, then gently tried to phrase the decision in four-year-old terms. She said that she had been with me day and night for a long time, and she needed to take turns, so now she had to give Peterborough a turn for a few days. I understood the concept of taking turns so that quieted my separation anxiety. Mummy didn't tell me anything at all about Tanya, only Peterborough gets a turn because she didn't want me to feel insecure that Tanya's sickness was more important than staying with me.

I slept peacefully in the hospital crib that night, and my mother came, as promised, to take me for radiation before returning to Peterborough. Before she left, I showed her the long, yellow strands of hair on my pillow. I partially accepted the loss of my hair after her explanation that hair falls out like teeth do at age six and that I would grow back adult hair. I thought that explanation was reasonable since I knew my sister had adult teeth, and I thought she had adult hair too. Mummy and I had no idea that the radiation would destroy my hair follicle cells and I would never again grow hair. Before she left for Peterborough, she reminded me to pray to Jesus and to never forget that I wasn't alone. She prayed that God would protect me from the sharp tongue of the nurses, and she arranged for my grandfather and other relatives to visit during her absence.

TWO

Jesus Calms the Storm: Mummy's Voice

LEAVING ERIC IN the hospital was the hardest decision, and it tore my heart apart. I arrived in Peterborough shortly after noon on Wednesday, July 23, 1980, and I borrowed my husband's car to pick up Tanya. Later, when I drove back to my husband's workplace, I noticed him with a woman and glimpsed their closeness. I felt uncomfortable, but when I discussed what I had seen with him he dismissed my concerns and became defensive. Our teenage marriage had been unstable from the beginning, and after the children arrived, he would leave and return as he pleased. He had been back with our family less than a year since our last separation. Eric's health crisis made our collapsing relationship weaken even more. I had no energy for marital conflict. My crisis-oriented prayers were all focused on my preschool son as he suffered radiation side effects, and our six-year-old daughter with a chronic, fluctuating fever.

Tanya had been feeling abandoned, and our bond needed nurturing. After supper, we sauntered to the park, played on the swings, slithered down the big slide together, and caught crayfish at the pond. We returned to the park the next day and strolled hand in hand, skipped in the pleasure of being together, and felt liberated in the breezy, summer morning winds. We chased each other and lived entirely in the moment. Her willingness to assert her preferences regarding her desires spoke volumes about her renewed confidence, security, and contentment. Our day continued to soar with mutual laughter and activities that she had initiated, thus giving her some control over her young life that had now become completely unpredictable. We rode our bicycles to the plaza bowling alley as she had wanted. We didn't have bicycle locks, so we held hands and prayed over the safety of our belongings trusting Jesus. After bowling, we walked downtown. We rested and chatted in the cool shade of several towering trees when she got tired.

At her suggestion, we continued our jaunt to the library where we checked out her choice of interesting books. She was eager to hear them, so we sat on the grass outside the building and snuggled arm in arm as I read two books aloud. We walked downtown to catch the bus home, tired from a day well spent. Tanya was still savouring every moment and asked for us to colour together with her special markers. She was exceptionally happy; a day with Mummy was just the remedy for her feelings of loneliness and abandonment. She went to bed after hugs, kisses, prayers, stories, songs, and cuddles, without any complaints. It was the best day with my little girl.

Nevertheless, all day I had been silently praying for Eric. My sister-in-law called to update me about Eric's day and said he had had a fever and slept most of the day. I called again, and the nurse reported that they were working to reduce his fever. Feeling anxious about Eric, I prayed and committed his care into the hands of Jesus.

Early the next morning, a church member phoned to lift me up with a scripture from Job *"I will maintain my innocence and never let go of it; my conscience will not reproach me as long as I live"* (Job 27:6). The scripture encouraged me to hold fast to Jesus, the source of all righteousness. *"I know that you can do all things; no purpose of yours can be thwarted"* (Job 42:2). She was urging me to focus on how the Lord sees Eric and not on the circumstances. God had a plan that would be accomplished. She explained that even though Job was left with nothing, the Lord restored everything, even more than before (Job 42:10). It confirmed what God had been speaking to me, thus boosting my faith, spurring me to confess and praise God for healing rather than being discouraged by the radiation side effects. *"The Lord blessed the latter part of Job's life more than the former part"* (Job 42:12). I was optimistic in the Lord and expected good things for Eric's future.

Additional encouragement came when we received a card in the mail from friends in another church, assuring us that a prayer chain was active for Eric's complete recovery. What a blessing to know that the body of Christ from many churches was interceding! I wasn't sure what God was doing in my life with all the challenges, Eric's ongoing suffering, Tanya's chronic illness, and my unstable marriage.

Despite these hardships, I yearned to study God's Word by attending Bible College as a family. The application and booklet for Christ for the Nations Bible

College in Dallas, Texas, had arrived, and I scanned through it. I prayed, "Lord, is it possible that you will heal my son, and our marriage, and as a family, we will travel to CFNI to study your Word?"

Later, my neighbour visited and asked me what would happen if the Lord didn't completely heal Eric? I couldn't entertain doubt. I was convinced that God would make Eric defy a natural human outcome. God makes impossibilities possible! Eric was already miraculously alive! I shared how the radiation department marvelled at his precociousness, and the doctors had labelled him as *a very unusual case* to explain his miraculous recovery. I prayed to Jesus Christ constantly, took everything in stride, dealt with every new challenge prayerfully and cognitively, addressed unforeseen challenges, all the while casting all my cares on Jesus, trusting in His faithfulness to see me through. I felt unshakable confidence in Jesus. I realized that God had given me the greatest gift: faith to cling to Jesus.

As we drove back to the hospital on Friday, we were unsure if Eric would qualify for a weekend pass because of his fever, but his temperature had returned to normal by the time we arrived. I brought him to the cafeteria to see his family. Tanya complained her head hurt, so my husband took Eric up to his 5G ward, and I brought Tanya with me to buy a thermometer. Tanya had spiked a fever. I went back to the ward and told the nurse that even though she was on medicine, Tanya was running a high fever. The nurse confirmed that Tanya's contact with Eric could have been detrimental to his condition. Immediately, I prayed that the healing power of God would cover both my children.

My husband took Tanya to my father's flat in Toronto, and I stayed in the hospital with Eric, who was depressed and short-tempered. He would ask a question and would irritably accuse me, saying, "You're lying! That's not the right answer!" Then he would cry and strike out physically. I prayed for him, and when I was finished, he added, "And dear Jesus, every time I touch my stomach it hurts, and every time I pee my penis hurts, and dear Jesus every time I turn my head it hurts. Just heal those three things, in Jesus's Name." My poor baby boy! Every part of his wee body hurt. I held him as closely as he permitted. I returned to the nurse's station and asked if there was any mention of a bladder infection because he had complained of pain urinating. A urine sample had been sent to the lab. I told the nurse of his neck pain, which she attributed to radiation side-effects. I went back and rocked with Eric. He snuggled on my lap resting in the medley of worship songs and children's songs. I left him awake at 10:00 p.m. in good spirits.

Tanya was still feverish when I arrived at my father's flat. This had been going on now for two weeks even though she was on medication. Why would her temperature be normal and then spike? I couldn't understand! Then, I remembered that Proverbs 3:5–6 instructed me to trust God when I did not understand.

Tanya recovered from chronic fevers and Eric continued daily radiation until August 14, 1980, when he completed the twenty-eight treatments. The final weeks became harder and harder for both of us. We both knew that each treatment was harming his body, increasing his abdominal pain, and causing further brain trauma. But the doctors held no long-term hope of survival, even as we clung, never wavering, to our hope in Jesus Christ. The radiation caused extensive memory loss, and for the rest of his life, he would struggle with expressing his thoughts though he knew what he wanted to say.

In addition to permanent hair loss, the radiation had other, life-altering effects: severe burns on his scalp developed into blisters oozing with pus. The radiation burned his ear canal, eardrums, and inner ear, which resulted in progressive hearing loss—he became profoundly hearing impaired in one ear and so severely hearing impaired in the other that he required a hearing aid. The radiation damaged his pituitary gland, an organ essential for normal growth, so he remained the size of a five-year-old for years, until he was treated with synthetic growth hormones as an adolescent. Through it all we trusted in Jesus, read God's Word, prayed earnestly, sang worship songs, and daily lived in the moment as though it were the last, full of love, laughter, and no regrets. I soon realized that God had given Eric two special gifts: a gift to memorize scriptures and Christian lyrics, and a gift to love His Word.

Post radiation, my husband's attraction to the woman he had defended as a *friend* developed into a romantic relationship. Three months after Eric's treatment, our marriage collapsed, and the church leaders held me partially responsible for my husband's infidelity (since I was unavailable at home to meet all his *needs* while tending to Eric in hospital for two months). Even as a baby Christian, I knew that I was responsible to choose to pray and seek God. However, the choices and actions that others made were solely their responsibility, so there were no excuses to evade responsibility, nor could we blame God or others for the choices we made.

I learned quickly that the Christian life was walking with Christ as one fights the work of the evil one, knowing fully that the believer was equipped in Jesus for the battle. I chose to deflect the leader's judgement that I was responsible for my husband's actions, and instead to accept Christ's extended hand, holding me in the midst of their harsh words. I prayerfully basked in God's total peace—I had obeyed Him through my constant, loving presence with Eric in the hospital, protecting my son from potential neglect due to understaffed, overworked nurses. I had even intercepted his confusion of abandonment in a sterile, cold hospital. God gave me the grace to understand the extent of a child's *needs*, juxtaposed with adult *needs*, a point of view the church leaders wouldn't understand.

After my husband left, I was the only separated woman in the church. I was ostracized by some and was eventually banned from the fellowship. Being expelled from this church was a blessing in disguise. It transferred my devotion, and I became fully focused on Jesus. I was without spousal support and had a five-year-old son who lived beyond his six months prognosis. Eric still suffered severe radiation-related side effects. As well, I had a seven-year-old daughter who was trying to process all the unexpected changes that had occurred in her world.

We moved from our comfortable middle-class neighbourhood to a war-time shack with a leaky roof, a flooded basement filled with stagnant water, a non-functioning furnace, and electrical problems. Every room was overrun with mice, and there were cat feces embedded in the floor and a toilet that hadn't been properly vented. Sewer gas contaminating our breathing air was a real danger. But through it all, I had an uncanny peace! I can't explain it! It was a gift from God! As a family, we laughed, found humour and silver linings in the least of things, prayerfully read scripture together, sang worship songs daily, and felt blessed. We had Jesus in our hearts and the assurance of the scripture to trust the Lord, not my understanding, and to follow his straight path (Proverbs 3:5–6). Not only did He make our path straight, but He showered us with unspeakable joy and glory along that path.

His mercies extended to me were like a bridge to extend to others. As on my knees in daily prayer and with ardent desire, I beseeched the Lord's help to forgive the church leaders who had expelled us. God's grace prevailed until I knew in my heart that I had forgiven the church authority. The new church to which God had led me embraced our single-parent family with open arms and filled us with Godly love. Through the pastor's television ministry connections, God opened the door in 1981 to share Eric's testimony of Jesus's love and healing faithfulness on a national television program called 100 Huntley Street. The feedback answered my prayers to glorify and honour Jesus.

When Eric started kindergarten two weeks after completing radiation, the children in the upper grades made fun of his bald head and would bang on his helmet or pull it off to laugh and mock his baldness. This went on day after day after day. One morning, as Eric dressed in a costume for a special class play, he checked his character makeup in the mirror and my five-year-old reflectively said, "Mummy, I don't know why the kids at school make fun of me because I am bald. It is just like this costume. I am different looking on the outside, but I am the same person inside." Words of wisdom!

From the age of five, even though his height remained the same and his hair didn't grow back, Eric grew in wisdom. His caring heart expanded, and his faith and love for Jesus matured him into a mighty prayer warrior, filled with love and compassion for hurting and disadvantaged people. In the years to come, Eric continually modelled what real life was all about as he lived it daily. If Eric could turn to Jesus for every little challenge, if his sister Tanya could be as diligent to seek God for her answers, I could do no less than to encourage them to love Jesus, walk and talk with Him through every circumstance of life, no matter the cost. That became my daily prayer.

Eric thrived beyond the doctor's prediction that he wouldn't survive more than six months. After three years, our new church pastor, Eric's neurosurgeon, oncologist, ENT specialist, endocrinologist, our family doctor, and many others, affirmed that yes, we could pursue moving to Dallas, Texas to attend Christ for the Nations Bible Institute (CFNI). As a single-parent family, our hearts were united to study God's Word and to grow deeper in our love for Jesus as we each had developed an ardent desire to serve Him. We spent hours together in fervent prayer, over every detail and challenge, as we enjoyed sitting at the feet of Jesus. Whenever I failed, Eric would chide me gently, "Mummy, did you pray first?" Eric had learned that when he had trouble with finding the right words to express himself, he could pray, "Jesus you know the word that I want to say, can you tell me please?" Then the word would pop into his mind to complete the thought he wanted to communicate. He was a child who demonstrated a *child-like* faith for me to follow. He rapidly developed wisdom beyond his years as he trusted Jesus as our provider, our first line of defence, our protector, our Father, our peace, and our joy. Eric often quoted Philippians 4:13, *"I can do [everything] through him who gives me strength."* We would need the armour of God to overcome the obstacles that lay ahead (Ephesians 6:10–20).

THREE
Adventures on the Journey: Time in Dallas

ERIC AND TANYA'S testimony of our two years at CFNI beautifully described how God was with us while we were there.

When I was eight years old, my mum, sister, and I packed one small suitcase each and boarded a bus to CFNI in Dallas, Texas. As soon as we arrived, we moved into campus housing, and I had many attacks of the devil, that were numerous health crisis that could have discouraged our family, but we cleaved to Jesus. Mummy kept teaching us that every time we worship God in our suffering, it was like stepping on the devil's face, so we spent much time stepping on the devil's face.

I wanted to be baptized, but prone to ear infections because of radiation, I avoided water. But I trusted God's protection, was baptized in the campus swimming pool while declaring to the world that my old life was buried and raised to new life in Christ. Mummy could see a tumour inside my ear canal. The doctor at the free clinic in Dallas used an instrument to show her the tumour size, then made an appointment for me to see a specialist. Mummy asked the CFNI students and faculty to pray, and when she brought me to the specialist, he said the tumour had vanished! How we praised and thanked Jesus!

We had lots of other challenges, but Jesus always took care of them. Living in a one-bedroom cozy apartment on campus, Tanya and I wrote scriptures on large sheets of paper, which we used to decorate our walls to remind us of God's ongoing faithfulness and provision. Bedtime, we would have *Family Altar* where we sang worship songs, read scripture, prayed, and asked and answered questions to draw us closer to Jesus. One day I told my mother that Tanya and I needed more spiritual food. Just as we eat three meals every day to feed our bodies, we need to read the Bible at least twice a day for spiritual food. Mummy agreed, so we had Family Altar before school and again before bed.

Tanya's voice was equally heard and respected as we met new challenges at Bible College. Her story is told in her words as follows:

My brother and I adapted well to CFNI, and soon after we arrived in late June 1983, I found my best friend. There were more than sixty kids in the family-housing section, and my best friend also had a younger brother, and her mom was a single parent too. My friend enrolled in a Christian school in the fall, and I prayed that God would permit me to attend there too, and Mom agreed.

Mom saw that Eric's faith in Jesus was bold, outspoken, and demonstrative, whereas mine was reserved and quiet. When we were together as a family, people noticed Eric, his small stature, his bald head, and his spiritual precociousness. Mom was careful to include me in conversations, recognizing my strengths, and saw how attending a Christian school built my faith. God helped develop my strengths and a passion for science so that I excelled at the annual Science Fair competition, ultimately winning a ribbon for my theme and presentation.

One day at the Christian school, while watching the children play soccer, I was hit in the face. When Mom arrived to take me to the clinic affiliated with the school, she explained that Satan would like us to be upset because of my injury and that we had a choice, to be upset or to step on the devil's face by singing worship songs to Jesus. We chose to sing all the way to the clinic. After the doctor told us my nose wasn't broken, as suspected, and the swelling would subside, this helped further build and advance my faith in Jesus.

In the second year at CFNI, Mom and my best friend's mom had no extra money for Christian education. My best friend and I were still together in the public school Eric had attended the previous year. Public education was a lower standard than private school, so my friend and I always completed our work first, and we were offered enriched program opportunities.

Just before Easter, my mom had an appointment for Eric at Dallas Children's Hospital clinic. That morning, Mom had discovered blood in my stools, and she had decided to include me to ask the doctor a question about my health. It had been going on for several weeks, but I hadn't said anything because I thought it was from the awful lunches provided in the school cafeteria. I had no discomfort, but Mom had noticed my energy level was down, and I needed more sleep than usual.

Blood tests were immediately ordered when blood in my stool was mentioned. The results alarmed the doctors who said that my haemoglobin was comparable to someone seriously injured and haemorrhaging, and about to go into shock. Child Protective Services stepped in and ordered my immediate hospitalization. After Mom explained that we were attending CFNI in Dallas and wanted the faculty and student body to pray for me, they permitted Mom to do that. I wasn't afraid. I felt the love of Jesus, expressed to me through memorized scriptures and the love of the many people in our lives that exemplified Jesus's love in action.

On Good Friday, 1985, I was eleven years old and had major surgery to remove a malignant tumour in my colon. The medical team was in a buzz to come up with a post-surgery treatment plan since they'd never had a child with colon cancer at Dallas Children's Hospital. Some on the team advised immediate radiation, but another group disagreed and insisted on chemotherapy. Mom was conflicted. She prayed passionately for a sign from God to know how to proceed. The Christian surgeon was confident he had removed all the cancer and told Mom that if I had been his daughter, he would not recommend radiation or chemotherapy. God's peace led Mom to accept his words and to decline treatment. While I healed from surgery, I had to live with a colostomy. My large intestine, called the stoma, was attached to the outside of my body and emptied into a bag. This was often challenging to manage.

My discharge was delayed because of a bladder complication. When I couldn't urinate, I had to have a catheter. Weeks post-surgery, Mom learned how to catheterize me in the morning before school, after school, and before bed, so that I could be discharged from the hospital and resume a normal life. About a month later, my bladder recovered enough that I was able to void without support. Being a child, I resumed my normal activities of swimming and playing sports, much to my mother's concern. I felt well trusting Jesus!

We stayed in Dallas after Mom graduated from CFNI, and new experiences continued to grow our faith in Jesus. We were committed to a missionary team, living in Fort Worth, while maintaining our connection to our Dallas church. We would borrow a vehicle to attend the mid-week service in Dallas. Mom knew the precise amount of gas needed for the round trip so filled the tank and off we drove. During service, she deposited her remaining change on the collection plate. After the message, the pastor recognized the grieving family of the latest victim of a serial killer in the area. Mom lingered after service to chat with church friends, before heading out to the freeway. The Dallas highways had a web of convoluted, complicated exits, and Mom was directionally challenged. Worship music from Mom's lips lulled Eric and me to sleep.

After a series of wrong exits, the tank was on empty, and Mom was hopelessly lost. Praying fervently for direction, she exited again and found herself on a deserted, forlorn, dark country road. She pulled into a lane where vicious barking dogs lunged and leapt at the car. Startled, Eric and I woke up to learn that Mom had been driving on an empty tank for a long time and she had no money for gas. And she was lost! She decided we'd sleep in the car and work out a solution in the morning. At Family Altar, we had been reading scripture about unity, and I adamantly declared that we were *not* in unity and should trust God to supernaturally put gas in the tank, and immediately leave this laneway. So, we did. At the next driveway, I felt safe and agreed to sleep in the car.

A stranger knocked on our window and told us it was *not* safe, and the serial killer's latest victim had been killed nearby! It was 1:00 a.m. when he and his wife escorted us to a gas station, filled our tank, and led us back to the highway on the correct route to Forth Worth. Elated that God had sent an angel to guide us home, we exuberantly thanked God. When the gentleman pulled over at our exact exit, our repeated thank you felt insufficient to Mom to express her gratitude. But when she asked to repay him, this mysterious angel insisted that his only concern was for our safety, and he drove away into the night. The Bible tells us that it might be an angel when we entertain a stranger (Hebrews 13:2). When Mom couldn't memorize his license plate, I suggested that we receive this angel's kindness as a gift from God.

God clearly showed us His loving provision with absolute control in all circumstances. The missionary team we were on included teachers, Bible translators, a water purifier expert, and other skilled professionals. Obviously, our health challenges would prevent us from going with them to Mozambique, but they invited us to attend the six-week orientation as prayer support to encourage them. The greatest blessing for us came when one of the team members gave Mom their old Volvo car to drive back to Canada when our student visa expired at the end of summer. Mom drove it on the highway as a test run. The muffler fell off, and we were left stranded. A police officer escorted us back to Fort Worth, and our lame vehicle limped into a muffler shop so we could determine the cost of repairs.

Eric spotted a tall Texas man with a trendy cowboy hat, fashionable jeans, and fancy cowboy boots, waiting to be served there. So, he sauntered over to the gentleman and boldly asked him if he loved Jesus. At age nine, Eric was direct and not very polished in his witnessing as he showed off his badge with the words, *I love Jesus.* The stranger told him that he, too, loved Jesus. Eric freely offered his testimony and told this gentleman all about the missionary ministry, our commitment as prayer warriors for the team, and our efforts to get back to Canada until the muffler fell off. The distinguished Texas cowboy approached Mom to ask the repair cost and how much she would need for gas to return to Canada, and I think Mom told him about $50.00.

The next day the Mozambique Team Leader approached Mom and praised God for His provision. The stranger had dropped by the church and offered a substantial financial gift for the team and another one for us to *fly* back to Canada. The stranger's gift fortified the Missionary Team—God would provide for their needs while in the war-torn areas of Mozambique. Most importantly, it bolstered our faith that Jesus would always provide for us (Philippians 4:19).

FOUR
Eric Finds His Purpose in Life

RETURNING TO CANADA, I (Eric) was ten years old and I was assigned to a small class of children with learning challenges. My memory was poor, and my hearing had deteriorated, such that I couldn't hear the teacher even with a hearing device. In the second year, my teacher felt I was failing in every area of the curriculum, and she repeatedly told me I shouldn't come to school because I wasn't capable of learning. I loved school in Dallas, but now I didn't want to go. I told my mum, "The teacher thinks I am stupid, but I'm not; I just learn differently. And I can't hear her. Will you teach me?"

My mummy was working for the School Board as a Teacher's Assistant, and they threatened she would lose her job if she withdrew me from the educational system. Besides, it was the law for children to attend school. At Family Altar, we prayed earnestly for God's guidance and courage. With God's help, Mummy came up with a plan. She created a curriculum for me, found a babysitter during her working hours, and when she arrived home from work, she would homeschool me until 11:00 p.m. My mum changed my bedtime, so I slept from 11:00 p.m. until 11:00 a.m., and I'd be awake for only four hours before she returned home from work. She would leave a list of school-related work for me to accomplish independently, especially math, since it was my strength. In the evening, she would teach me to read using a tactile approach with the Bible, combined with other memory modalities, such as auditory, visual, writing, and kinaesthetic. I loved the Bible, and it became my primary textbook for reading. As I learned to read it independently, I developed a personal prayer and Bible time with the Lord.

After much prayer, God made a way for me to be assessed in Toronto by a paediatric neuropsychologist. She tested my scholastic aptitude and confirmed that brain damage had left me with several learning deficits. However, I had a solid, tactile memory and average intelligence in many areas, contradicting the Public-School Board's test results. After six months of home-schooling, Mummy proposed that I return to the public school for the last two months before summer break and submitted recommendations from the paediatric neuropsychologist to the Public-School Board. They retested me, and my score results confirmed that I had improved several grade levels in math and language. The School Board accepted my progress as evidence that I could learn academically and implemented the paediatric neuropsychologist's recommendations. All of this drew us closer to dependence on Jesus and nurtured our faith.

While I was homeschooled, Mum recognized that I could play the piano by ear, even though I was deaf, so she found a special piano teacher, Sue, who taught me many piano pieces. Playing by ear, God gave me the joyful ability to fill our home with many 'Jesus songs.'

Also, during the months of homeschooling, Jesus answered my biggest prayer. I had yearned for hair and prayed faithfully every day for my hair to grow back. I didn't get my prayers answered for the regrowth of my natural hair, but I received the next best thing. Since I really wanted natural hair, which cost thousands of dollars to have a tailor-made wig from Thailand, Mummy got funding from charitable organizations to make two full wigs. They were beautiful and were of mostly real hair, and they looked so natural that nobody could tell I was wearing a wig. I was so thankful to Jesus and the sponsors that I wrote them all letters to express my heartfelt gratitude. I felt like a new man. Now that I had hair, I was sure I wouldn't be teased by the children when I returned to the public school.

The new school that Mummy found for me had the best teacher ever. I could perform math skills competently, but I had difficulty expressing how I derived the answer with my language deficit. However, my new teacher praised my accomplishments and focused on my strengths. I made new friends, and I was involved in many activities, including church groups, a bowling team, a cake decorating course, and a paper route to earn my own money. I had a bank account, and as an avid saver, I purchased my own VIC 20 computer, a new bicycle, and electronic toys. My prayer time with Jesus was strong as the Lord enabled me to memorize His Word. It seemed like my life was becoming normal, and Jesus had done it all!

Close to Christmas, I noticed blood in the toilet. Even though the local paediatrician regarded it as nothing to worry about, Mummy knew something was amiss. She decided we would create happy memories by vacationing in Florida for Christmas break. While there, we enjoyed the love of relatives, the warmth of the white sandy beach, and the excitement of Disney World, all while earnestly praying for God to bring healing.

On our return home, Mum immediately called the surgeon at Sick Children's Hospital in Toronto. I got a new diagnosis of colon cancer. I refused to have the operation to remove all my large intestine because I vividly remembered my sister's suffering and numerous complications following her second colon cancer surgery. Soon after, we were watching a movie about the birth, death, and resurrection of Jesus. When Jesus was tortured and nailed to the Cross, I turned to Mummy and said, "I hope that when I am suffering after surgery, I can be like Jesus."

Colon cancer was painless, with the only symptom being blood in my stools, so I asked Mummy if I could have a goodbye party before going into the hospital. I invited three of my best school buddies to come over for a GT snow-racing party. We raced down the steepest, fastest hill in Peterborough on our sleds, climbed back to the top, to race down over and over again as freshly falling snow made the hill icier and faster, projecting us like missiles. We howled with delight, enjoying the moment. Then it was back to my house for hot chocolate, homemade pizza, and a boy's sleepover with movies and treats—too much fun for sleep that night. Mum took lots of pictures, so I could fondly recall this recent event while I was recovering in hospital.

The surgeon removed my large intestine. He pulled the end of my small intestine through the hollow cavity to connect with my rectum and created an ileostomy that would function while I healed from the surgery. I adjusted to the nuisance of cleaning and changing the bag, knowing it was temporary. Minor complications delayed my recovery, but I was soon back to school. The kids in my class were kind, and my teacher, Ms. Lake, was the best.

My sister was hospitalized a short time later, and Mum had no one to take me to school, so she asked my teacher for some lessons. Ms. Lake was a gentle, kind person, and she offered the best solution, which was that I would stay overnight at her house, and she would take me with her to and from school each day so she could continue teaching me. I was so excited! My teacher's daughter, Tammie, also wore hearing aids, so with that in common, we connected strongly. She was like my big sister, and I relished teasing and annoying her as she playfully took me under her wing. It was so cool to get to see Ms. Lake in the morning with curlers in her hair, then drive to school with her and learn my lessons all day with her. God always provided for my every need in very unexpected ways. Mum and Ms. Lake remained friends even after I graduated from elementary school to the next level.

The intermediate level was hosted in a segregated high school section where my sister attended and Mum worked. My small class roster included eight male students with learning challenges and one class bully. I was the brunt of cruel jokes because I was so small. At thirteen, I was still the height and appearance of a five-year-old, and the other boys joined the bully's taunting, abusing me. They would shove me into the locker, securing it tightly, or do karate sidekicks just a fraction of a hair short of kicking me in the head. My mother made every effort to have the boys disciplined but to no avail. The threat of severe physical injury to me prompted Mum to contact a lawyer, and she presented her concerns in writing to the School Board. God had given me a great sense of humour, so I thought I could win the bully over with humour and kindness if I just tried harder, but it didn't work.

One day at lunch, while the teacher was absent from the class, the bully did the unthinkable, the most disparaging action you could imagine. After mocking me and threatening me physically, he and his circle of followers grabbed my wig to pull it off as I sat transfixed at my desk. Unsuccessful, the bully spat on my wig. Terrified, I dared not move and hardly breathed. I desperately prayed in my heart to Jesus for help while the bully continued with his contemptuous behaviour, ridiculing, calling me demeaning, derogatory names. Then the most humiliating thing of all: the bully spat in my face! The gob of saliva dripped down my cheek. I was terror-stricken, petrified that any tears or response would antagonize him more to abuse me further. I did not flinch; I dared not blink and sat frozen, speechless. The other boys were also horrified, stepped back, and urged the bully to leave me alone.

I ran to the bathroom, where hot tears cascaded down my burning cheeks and mingled with the spit as I splashed fresh water on my face. A kind teacher found me broken and weeping and escorted me to the library. My mum worked nearby with special needs students at the high school level and was immediately at my side comforting me with her love and prayers.

A crucial meeting was organized, which included the principal, school social worker, school psychologist, Board appointed Special Education Consultant, special education teacher, the bully's mother and father, the bully, Mum, and me. The bully was arrogant, showed no remorse, and owned his behaviour with condescending pride, while the bully's parents excused and even defended their delinquent son's behaviour. They actually asked the committee to transfer me to another school to prevent further injury, since I was deemed a *fragile student*. Mum and I were shocked but had been praying for the bully, and now I felt grieved and empathetically sad that the bully had two parents who didn't love him enough to help him stop hurting people. The bully was given an ultimatum—keep a distance from me, or he would be removed from the Intermediate Division and, since he was of age, placed in the high school part of the building.

He didn't heed the warning and was promptly removed, banished from the intermediate section of the school. The bully had a scheduled math test in the high school program and was assigned to Mum's class for study support. When Mum approached him and offered him strategies to learn so that he could earn a high grade, the bully was taken back by my mum's willingness to support him. He said to my mum, bewildered and astonished, "You are going to help *me* to get better marks in math? Why?" Mum explained that she could teach him learning strategies to help him effectively recall math material for higher marks. He was attentive to Mum's instructions and appreciative of her assistance, and indeed he scored a high grade and returned to thank Mum for her help.

The bully had been told never to cross the barrier into the Intermediate Division where my classes were held, but he broke the rules. He crossed the line, found me at my locker, and with protective aggression declared, "Eric, if anyone ever bothers you, just tell me and I will beat them up."

I was surprised that God answered my prayers and softened the bully's heart, transforming him from my tormentor to my advocate and protector. Mum continued to work with him the remaining year, and his marks improved steadily, along with his attitude.

When the bully spat in my face and intimidated me with his physical aggression, jeopardizing and compromising my safety, I was beseeching God for the meaning to my life. I had so many challenges, and I was acutely aware of the extent to which my brain was damaged and the ongoing radiation repercussions.

"Why did God create me?" I asked Mum, "What's my purpose in life? I'm deaf, brain-damaged, and small as a five-year-old—I am bald and have to wear a wig, and I forget things. So why did God make me? What is my purpose in life?"

My mum and I made a list of all my perceived weaknesses and then another list of the gifts and strengths God had given to me. The gifts outnumbered the weaknesses, so Mummy asked me, "What do you think God wants you to do with your life, Eric? What do you like to do?"

"Mummy, I want to help people." God had given me a great sense of humour, the gift to play the piano by ear, a big heart for hurting people, and a desire to help the disadvantaged.

Thus began a journey with God, to find my purpose in Jesus and answer my *why* question. I knew Jesus had helped me *through* other people, but how could Jesus *use* me to *help* others? Mum and I prayed earnestly. The door opened for me to apply to volunteer at a nursing home, helping the elderly play Bingo, chess, and checker games, assisting them to and from the dining room, listening to their stories and entertaining them with my piano playing. During the following years, I added several more nursing homes to my volunteer commitment. By the time I was sixteen in 1991, I was nominated Volunteer of the Year for the Province of Ontario, and received publicity, a ceremony to receive a plaque, and an award for my commitment to volunteer service and overcoming my challenges in order to help others. When I found my purpose in life, I knew why God had created me. To help people. He had a plan that gave me hope for a future in Jesus (Jeremiah 29:11).

As the years passed, I had remained the size of a five-year-old. I wanted to grow! So, I talked to Mom about it, and she contacted the endocrinologist at Sick Children's Hospital to start Humatrope, a synthetic growth hormone. It only stimulated long bone growth, so my arms and legs would be lanky and my torso short. Growing pains accompanied the rapid growth, as altogether I sprouted twelve inches in height, six shoe sizes, needed new clothes every month, my little preschool squeaky voice deepened, and I developed facial hair. I was pleased with my unique mature appearance, and I was so close to my mother's height many people thought I was age twelve, not five. My wig was wearing out as well, and we were offered funding to have a more mature wig made to compliment my adolescent growth. Everything that happened seemed like God was watching over all my needs, and I drew very close to Jesus in scripture memorization, daily prayer, and singing worship songs. I was so thankful to my Father God, for indeed, *"Every good and perfect gift is from above..."* (James 1:17).

In 1993, two years after I received my Volunteer of the Year Award, cancer returned as lymphoma. I had no large intestine, which had been removed, so to have cancer in the small intestine was unprecedented. I underwent rapid weight loss and was unable to digest food. When the surgeon examined me, I was too incapcitated for an operation. I was put on intravenous feedings (TPN) injected into the port-a-cath, a central line implanted directly into my heart artery. Moreover, this was used to inject me with a cocktail of potent, toxic chemotherapy drugs, which began in February ending in July. Mom remained with me in hospital as my health precariously declined before it finally improved. The horrible side-effects of the chemo drugs were that they burned the lining of my rectum, which led to painful chronic bleeding. I developed life-threatening sepsis that spread to all my organs, worsening my failing health when my temperature spiked to over forty Celsius. Typically, people don't survive when their temperature rises that high or when infection invades a weakened body. As I steadily declined, Mom prayed earnestly, as did my sister and many church members, including churches back in Peterborough. I later learned that no patient in the hospital had survived a sepsis infection as widespread as mine.

Chemotherapy depleted my red blood cells, white blood cells, and platelets, thus leaving me neutropenic and susceptible to fever and infections. This required that I be put in isolation with high doses of intravenous antibiotics until I recovered sufficiently to start the next cycle of chemotherapy.

I slowly regained my strength, but I was never again able to think quickly. Even though my thinking processes were slower, I cultivated my sense of humour, and amusing antidotes rolled off my tongue with little effort, entertaining my mom and sister. I attributed the recovery of my humour as one of God's many gifts. The second gift that God restored to me was my ability to play the piano so that whenever I was able, I would go to the hospital teen room to play worship songs to Jesus.

Nearing the end of the last chemo cycle, the doctor prepared me for surgery, but I explained to Mom that I was exhausted. I wanted to refuse surgery because if God wanted me to live, I would be with Him, and if God wanted me to die, I would still be with Him. *"If we live, we live for the Lord; and if we die, we die for the Lord. So, whether we live or die, we belong to the Lord"* (Romans 14:8). Mom listened and prayed, pouring out her heart to Jesus and me—her desire was for me to live and serve the Lord here on earth for His glory.

Nearing the end of my treatment, not expected to live, I was granted my heart's desire through the Wish Foundation of Canada. I remember when they phoned and asked me where I wished to go, Tanya had whispered in my ear, "You wish to go to Maui," and obediently, I repeated her words verbatim to the official representative on the phone.

After I hung up the phone, I asked Tanya, "Where's Maui?" When she told me Hawaii, we all jumped for joy!! God had granted my wish to see a volcano, and we joined our hands and hearts in prayerful gratitude. The Wish Foundation provided us with air transportation, a beautiful resort on the beach, a car, a wheelchair, and spending money for a week. It was my greatest leap forward toward recovery, and the first time in six months, I would be disconnected from my NG feeding tube, a tube that went through my nose to my stomach that delivered nourishment on a steady basis for life support. Now in Maui, I was excited to be alive, to enjoy solid food and a host of new adventures.

The morning we arrived, Mom drove to the Haleakala Volcano summit to grant my wish to see a volcano. We arrived at 3:00 a.m. huddled inside the viewing hut so we could watch the sunrise. However, a volcano has no predictable weather patterns; it's all chance, so we bundled with blankets wrapped around our shoulders as the rain and fog choked the anticipated sunrise. But that didn't dampen our enthusiasm or deter us. We returned on another day, mid-afternoon when the sun was shining, and together we climbed the summit of the Haleakala Volcano. Mom took photographs of Tanya and me sporting our victory climb. We absorbed every waking moment on the island, enjoyed the cultural tradition of a Luau, and admired the enchanting graceful Hawaiian dancers and the daring male fire dancers. We ventured on a boating excursion for snorkelling near a bird sanctuary off the coast, and on another adventurous day, we parked the car, stripped off our clothes, bathing suits beneath, and spontaneously swam in the waves of the warm coastal waters. We drove to a pineapple plantation, to a historical museum, and the highlight of our week was Tanya's 20th birthday on August 12th, where we ate a lobster dinner in her honour, along with a helicopter ride over the island to experience a bird's eye view of the majestic mountains and rushing waterfalls. The week was filled with a familial bonding time for Tanya, Mom, and me making spectacular memories. Our vacation adventure was pure joy.

When I returned to Peterborough, we learned that the biopsy was cancer-free, and the surgeon withdrew the recommendation for surgery. It was an answer to our prayers. No more hospitals. No more treatments. Soon it was time to return to school, but my energy level hadn't recovered enough for me to meet the demands of school. Instead, I attended a few courses and picked up another volunteer position in another nursing home. I felt that my time and energy divided among the nursing homes was my calling and fulfillment of God's purposes for my life, *"being confident of this, that he who began a good work in you will carry it on to completion until the day of Christ Jesus"* (Philippians 1:6). God had called me to help people, and that was what I was doing.

I turned twenty-one in 1996, and my sister invited me to move from Peterborough to London, Ontario, to live with her. At the same time, she suggested that our mom move to a developing country to get some classroom teaching experience. Mom had graduated from teacher's college, but the door was closed to hiring elementary teachers in our province. She applied for a grade one teaching contract in Bucaramanga, Colombia.

I was happy with the prospect of living with my sister and the opportunity to reestablish our sibling bond. Growing up, I admired my sister, cherishing her consistent kindness. I would often express my appreciation by reserving a portion of my paper route money to surprise her with a treat, reminding her that she was the best sister and my angel sent from God to help me with my troubles. Tanya was my defender and would often include me in her circle of friends, mindful of my cognitive challenges and physical limitations.

Oh, the memories of my sister and I growing up together! I remember when my sister was twelve, and I was ten; it was Expo 86. Tanya convinced me that it would be the coolest experience to go to the World's Fair in Vancouver, Canada. I was totally on board with her plan that Mom could drive. Mom reminded us that she had a highway phobia and could barely drive through the congested highway traffic to Sick Kids in Toronto, much less over three thousand kilometres to Vancouver, British Columbia. Tanya and I begged Mom to try, and even if we didn't get out of Ontario, it would satisfy us that Mom had tried. After all, she would always tell us that the effort counted, not the results.

So, we packed up our little rust-eaten Lada car with cans of spaghetti for food emergencies, our tent, camping gear, our little cockapoo and her kennel, a knapsack of clothing, and with a $1,000.00 in Mom's pocket for the month, we set out. Wow! We anticipated an amazing adventure! The first day Mom drove merely two hundred kilometres before she needed to call it a day, and we praised her accomplishment. However, Tanya did the math and realized it would take fifteen days to reach our destination and another fifteen days to return, using up our entire vacation time of thirty days. We needed a strategy to keep Mom focused on driving so we could cover more distance each day! We sang worship songs, played "I Spy," counted specifically coloured cars, and told *remember when* stories as Mom focused on driving, forgetting her fatigue. We would convince her to pass by rest stops. When we did stop, Mom would recline the seat and instantly be sound asleep. Tanya and I would take the dog for a walk and explore the rest area until she woke naturally. Then, with renewed energy, she could drive farther. The second day we covered twice the distance, and by the third day, Mom was driving with our support and encouragement through the night. We enjoyed an interlude of fun-filled adventures with my cousins in Manitoba, and from there, we rolled on, pushing forward toward the flat, boring prairie horizons that put Tanya and me to sleep. Mom also fell asleep… while driving! A truck's blaring horn startled her back into her lane, and she pulled over to the shoulder to finish her nap. Tanya and I reinforced our efforts to stay awake to keep Mom awake.

As we approached Calgary, we slowed to a crawl in heavy traffic, as the famous Calgary Stampede was in town. We all agreed that stopping there was well worth our while. However, when Mom found out how expensive the tickets were, she sadly turned away from the ticket booth. But then the ticket master called Mom back and advised her to get the cheap standing-room-only tickets because the best seats in the house would likely be empty as the wealthy ticket holders rarely came. It worked as she had predicted, and we thoroughly enjoyed the show from fantastic seats! How we praised God for such a wonderful treat!

Continuing west, it was a good thing we had a sense of humour because Mom's poor sense of direction got us lost time and again. It was a standing joke that 'Mom was lost once more.' Tanya and I would pray to Jesus to help her find her way back, and He always obliged. We were excited to see the mountains appearing bigger with each passing mile. Mom pulled over for a nap at a rest stop. Refreshed, she drove back onto the Trans-Canada highway, and Tanya and I snickered. In a matter-of-fact tone, Tanya said, "Mommy, I think you are going the wrong way."

Mom insisted, "No, dear, I'm sure we are going the right way." Tanya and I continued to giggle, trying to convince her we were going the wrong way. But Mom was adamant and kept driving.

"Mommy, aren't we supposed to be going to B.C.?" Tanya asked, and Mom agreed. "Then Mom, why are the mountains behind us?" Mom broke out in a roar of laughter at her obvious mistake, and still chuckling at herself, turned the car around to face the imminently majestic mountains.

We explored Lake Louise and Banff, rode the tramcar to the summit of Mount Norquay, and hiked back down the mountain to the parking lot, sore from the steep climb. We slept in the car, and the next day we pulled the car over to watch curious deer along the road. We detoured to the Athabasca Glaciers. We climbed to the summit, where we threw snowballs at each other and even built a snowman. We ventured to the lookout to see Mount Robson and Mount Terry Fox, named for the famous athlete who ran across Canada on a prosthetic leg, to raise money for cancer research.

After two and a half adventurous weeks, we arrived in Vancouver. Mom bought a three-day pass to Expo 86, and each day we came early and stayed late, taking in every pavilion, attraction, amusement, ride, and event that the World's Fair had to offer. Each day was filled with amazing new escapades, and every day we held hands as we gave thanks to our Father God that He had allowed us to enjoy such an incredible time as a family. After three days, we headed home.

Tanya learned that the sun sets at 1:00 a.m. in Jasper, so we drove through the late evening arriving after midnight to check it out and were enthralled. She also learned about the gigantic West Edmonton Mall, which encompassed several blocks, and decided it was a must-see. Mom drove through the night while Tanya and I slept in the car so that we could see this phenomenon. It was more spectacular than we'd imagined, containing an amusement park with a Ferris wheel, other rides along with an Olympic size skating rink and a swimming pool. My favourite was the wave pool with tube slides that snaked down a slippery waterfall to the churning waters below. So much to see under one roof!

Mom drove through the night again to make it home on time except for stopping for a few cat naps. She was a focused driver, praying and singing worship songs, stopping to refuel, and doing jumping jacks to keep herself alert. We were grateful and prayed our thanksgiving to God for giving us such memorable experiences. We agreed that this was the best family trip ever! In later years, we would take more trips: Cuba, Hawaii, New Brunswick, another trip to Dallas, Missouri, Kansas, the Grand Bahamas, and several trips to Florida. Memories! So many great memories!

Back to the present. As a young adult living with my sister, she taught me how to disagree without being disagreeable and present my case persuasively. She explained that when someone wants something, one should know what the benefit will be and be able to clearly defend the reason in an amiable and diplomatic way without infringing on the rights of others. Mom would say that Tanya could defend and argue her case so convincingly, without emotion, that she should be a lawyer.

I recall when our dog Esther was in heat, tied to our verandah when a neighbour's dog off-leash decided to mate with her. Esther had already had two planned litters with a purebred, and Tanya felt that she shouldn't be bred again, and definitely not to a stray mongrel. After consulting the vet, the only option was to spay our dog immediately. First, Tanya researched the city by-laws regarding liability for owners whose off-leash pet came onto our property and learned that they were responsible for any veterinarian bills. She approached the dog owner and tactfully asked him to pay half the cost. He refused, so Tanya calmly informed him, "I'll see you in small claim's court, and I will be suing you for the full cost of the vet fees and my legal and court fees." She left with no further discussion, and later that day, the owner's wife dropped by with the money. Tanya was in high school taking a course in law enforcement, practicing her skills using logic and facts to present her case succinctly, and she was successful at it.

Living with Tanya in 1997 while Mom was teaching in Bucaramanga helped me feel like an independent adult at age twenty-one. She was involved with her church Young Adult Group, and they embraced me with acceptance and understanding. Her friends would playfully tease me, just like guys do, and I would jokingly tease them back as *one of the guys,* feeling like I belonged. Sometimes I grew wistful with missing Mom, but Tanya would remind me of the freedom I had living with her, and nostalgia for the familiar past with Mom would dissipate. Our mother kept in touch by phoning and sending us a weekly fax.

Tanya planned to visit Mom in May after she finished her university term. I was happy to return to Peterborough and help my piano teacher, Sue, cut her acreage of grass, using the riding lawn mower, and live with her until Mom and Tanya returned.

Less than a week after Tanya left, living with Sue, I had a grand mal seizure. I was taken to our family doctor, who called Mom in Colombia. She flew home the next day. I had just been admitted to Toronto hospital when Mom arrived.

FIVE

Countdown to the End of Life's Journey: Mom Speaks

IT WOULD BE an oxymoron to say that this story was about living with death or joyful suffering. On the contrary, it is the story of our journey with God, of Jesus in us providing joy through the scriptures amid suffering, with the emphasis on Jesus. Paradoxically, we learned that suffering unites us with God and doesn't isolate us from Him. Suffering had the power to break the chains of despair and pull us from the pit. It was suffering that refined us without destroying the heart. Suffering called us into a strong voice of worship rather than muting our feeble cry. Suffering served as a beacon of faith that illuminated the path to our Lord—suffering identified us with Christ (Philippians 3:10).

It would be much later that God clarified the passage 2 Timothy 4:7–8 that I had pencilled in the margin, "*For Eric.*"

I have fought the good fight, I have finished the race, I have kept the faith. Now, there is in store for me the crown of righteousness, which the Lord, the righteous Judge, will award to me on that day—and not only me, but also to all who have longed for his appearing. (2 Timothy 4:7–8)

Eric longed for His appearing. He fought the good fight by calling on the power of Jesus to shield him in the battle. The battle was crouching at my doorstep too.

Sometimes, in the middle of the battle, it felt like the fight was too long, and I, too weary to endure. Nevertheless, quitting was never an option for me.

In Christ, we could never give up. In Christ, we were clothed with the whole armour of God (Ephesians 6:10–19). Our weapons for this fight were not of this world. We demolished strongholds and took captive our thoughts to make them obedient to Christ (2 Corinthians 10:4–5). It was through our weakness that we found His strength. Jesus's protective words were that His power was made perfect in our weakness (2 Corinthians 12:9). It was unbelievable the degree of power that was reserved in Christ. And to top it all, His power rested on us, and we could rest in His power, *"I will boast all the more gladly about my weaknesses, so that Christ's power may rest on me"* (2 Corinthians 12:9). The great Apostle Paul stated confidently that when he was weak, it revealed his *real* strength, and that strength was in Jesus.

Strength found in weakness seemed counter-intuitive, but it was an abiding principle of truth with Jesus. The stronger we became in ourselves, the weaker we grew in Christ. Does that assurance of strength in Christ only apply to Paul? No, it applied to every believer. It applied to me.

Therefore, if I fought the battle and died, would dying be giving up? Eric had many conversations with me about dying, and he told me that we all had to die. In some ways, dying might be interpreted as giving up. Did Eric give up? When we die to self, is that giving up? Or when we die to selfish desires or die to self-soothing relief from suffering, are we giving up or giving it over to Jesus? Giving something over to Jesus is quite different than giving up Jesus. If giving up is abandoning Jesus, we would miss His love and power; whereas, giving up to Jesus is humbly giving one's life over to Him and His victory. Dying in Christ was giving one's life over to Jesus for eternity, and our eternity started at salvation when we died to sin through Jesus's shed blood on the Cross. Christ hid us in His righteousness because the wages of sin would always be death (Romans 6:23). We don't pray for suffering, but when it comes, and it will come if we are Christians, we transfer our suffering and our burden to His broad shoulders with God's grace.

It was simple, but it was also complex. God didn't exempt Eric from physical suffering. God didn't exempt Tanya from suffering. God didn't exempt me from suffering. For me, there was no suffering on this planet greater than that of a mother watching her child die. Suffering and death were real—but more real was the love, grace, power, and peace of God in our lives. The One who began the work of salvation through suffering will complete it when Jesus reappears (Philippians 1:6). For Eric, the completion of Jesus's work in him was on September 6, 1997. For me, God was continuing His work to conform me into the image of Jesus until He comes again or my physical death.

Friday, August 22, 1997 was three months since my return from Colombia and almost three months since Eric had had surgery for his newly diagnosed brain cancer. Now to jump forward, I have chosen to continue his story at the end of his life; and will fill in details from those earlier months later.

Eric was extremely weak. He asked me to read the Psalms and listen to the CD, "God Will Make a Way."[2] Our family doctor made a house call. She felt that Eric's time was near. Tanya had come home from work exhausted and fell asleep snuggling her brother. She was alarmed to discover the extent to which his irregular shallow breathing had become worse in one day. Tanya hadn't been feeling well. She was working two jobs, and her heart was breaking as she daily watched her brother's frail health decline. She and I talked, hugged, and prayed for him frequently.

Eric slept most of the next two days. During the moments when gospel music played "Holy Ground,"[3] he stirred, attentive to the words, and whispered, "Mom, I used to play that on the piano." The lyrics were about praising God, angels, and being in God's presence.

Yes, indeed, Eric could play most Christian songs and hymns on the piano. Eric spoke again with appreciation, "Mom, you do one thing right. You play music for me." He loved the worship song, "If You Could See Me Now" that talked about heaven, no more pain, and a beautiful place with golden streets.[4] Eric longed for heaven.

When he was awake, I changed his clothing and sheets; and helped him to the toilet. I accidentally touched his sensitive arm. "Don't you love your son?" he implored.

I apologized profusely and reaffirmed my love for him. He used it as an opportunity to tease me and told me all the things that I did right.

Even in his weakened state, he surprised me by recalling detail. For example, he had watched a video a few weeks previously, but this afternoon, when I replayed the same movie, thinking that because his eyes were closed, he wasn't awake, a scene in the film caught his interest. "That man dies, and the black man dies because he can't swim." Both statements were accurate. Despite his brain tumour and dying body, I was amazed at his short-term memory and ability to recall.

---

[2] Don Moen, "God Will Make a Way," Track 9 on *God Will Make a Way*, Hosanna! Music, Integrity incorporated, 1997, CD.

[3] Geron Davis, "Holy Ground," Meadowgreen Music Co. Capital CMG, 1983.

[4] Don Moen, "If You Could See Me Now," Track 6 on *God Will Make a Way*, Hosanna! Music, Integrity incorporated, 1997, CD.

When Tanya arrived home from work, we had our first argument. It was stressful for Tanya to have her tiny apartment filled with my clutter, belongings, and habits while helping care for her dying brother. She'd been working two jobs so that she had virtually no downtime. She was exhausted. Eric, disturbed by our disagreement, mustered up the energy to intervene. "I don't like it when you and Tanya argue. I would rather go to the hospital and have you visit than for you and Tanya to argue. There's nothing difficult in life. When you trust God, nothing is too hard. When you have Jesus in your life, on your side, there's nothing difficult in life."

Eric's lecture was right on the mark, but Tanya had to hurry off to her second job from 5:00 p.m. to 9:00 p.m. So, he prayed for me, "God, give Mom understanding for Tanya and wisdom to say the right words. God, please make a way to give Mom the right words." I was repentant. I had missed the grace of God. It said in Ephesians 4:7, *"But to each one of us grace has been given as Christ apportioned it."* That was why the Apostle Paul told us that His grace was sufficient (2 Corinthians 12:9). I needed to stay on my knees in prayer until I was in tune with His grace.

When Tanya returned home at 9:30 p.m., Eric's first words were about going to the hospital and concern for his sister. "I don't want Tanya to be unhappy." Tanya and I took the time to talk and resolve our differences. We hugged and exchanged words of forgiveness and affection before she went to spend time with Eric. I had failed to appreciate the intense pressure on Tanya. I, too, was feeling the strain of it all as I surrendered all to Jesus in humble repentance. The peace that God had showered upon us returned, for He was our peace (Ephesians 2:14).

Eric's body was weak, but his sense of humour was strong. Before bed, I obtained Eric's permission to brush his teeth since I had neglected them due to painful gums and teeth. He laughed, not realizing he was quoting from Isaiah 6:5, *"I am a man with unclean lips."*

I laughed with him and corrected him as I began to brush his teeth gently. "No, you are a man with unclean teeth." We both giggled unreservedly.

I tucked him back into bed, and he repeated, "I am a man with an unclean mouth." I reminded Eric that his mouth was clean. Eric said, "Isn't that taken from the Bible? I am a man with unclean lips?"

"Yes, it is from Isaiah." I nodded.

"I believe that's from the sixth chapter." Eric piped up. I asked him if he wanted me to look it up in the Bible, and he said yes. Sure enough, the scripture was indeed from Isaiah chapter six. I read aloud from verses one to eight.

Every time God restored Eric's memory for a spiritual purpose, to glorify Him, I was awestruck at His majesty and power. Imagine, being able to recall a specific book and chapter in the Bible, notwithstanding physical death at his door. I was reminded that his spirit was very much alive on the many times Eric would tell me, "Read on! Read on! My body is dying, but my Spirit is growing." So true! So true!

For the next few days, Eric slept most of the time. During his short, wakeful periods, his eyesight deteriorated noticeably, and his eyes vibrated vigorously. I mentioned the vibrations, and he said, "That means I'm having a seizure. At least I'm aware of it." Eric was aware of a lot. He noted that we were reading Psalms when I reached for the Bible. We read from Psalm 11 to Psalm 34 but paused at Psalm 20, and in verse four, it said, *May he give you the desires of your heart…"* I turned to Eric and asked, "What are the desires of your heart, Eric?"

"Serving God!" Eric firmly replied in a strong voice, no hesitation, no time to process my question.

Every other time I asked Eric even a simple question requiring a yes or no, he paused to process and ponder his answer. He had slept most of the day except for when I read scripture.

That evening when I prepared Eric for bed, every movement led to excruciating pain in his leg. Eric pleaded, "Mom, why do I have to suffer?" I took that question to heart and prayed it aloud as I gently washed Eric and changed his clothes and sheets. He was cooperative even though morphine wasn't relieving his intense pain. Although he had slept most of the day, he had requested that his Christian music be played continuously. The cough Eric had been exhibiting the last few days was sounding more like a rattle in his chest.

The following day the pain in his legs increased, and he was blind. I offered him morphine, and he vomited. I read aloud up to Psalm 71. Eric did not speak nor answer my questions unless I asked, "Do you want me to read the Bible?"

And he would always answer, "Yes, please."

A couple from Peterborough, now pastoring in London, came by with their new baby and guitar to sing worship songs while Eric slept. There was a serene enveloping presence of God in the peace of music. After prayer and goodbye, the family left only to be followed by another couple, a pastor and his wife who came to pray for Eric. Becoming conscious of the presence of prayer, Eric whispered, "Pray for my mom. She needs a job." Eric was selfless, always concerned about others. All day Eric slept, Christian music constantly playing, becoming more alert when his sister arrived from work and making every effort to capture his sister's smile with his sense of humour.

The next day Eric's blindness continued while his speech was laboured and selective. He said "yes" to questions of interest like, "Do you want me to read the Bible?" or to play specific Christian songs. By mid-morning, I had read aloud up to Psalm 86. He couldn't be aroused until Tanya arrived home that evening, and for brief periods she was able to elicit a small response from him. His temperature spiked to 39.5 Celsius, and his pain spiked as well; he was unresponsive to increasing doses of morphine. It felt like Jesus was there, carrying Eric home, but I wept sorely to see his suffering. During the night, I cried and cried as my child moaned in pain, his breathing shallow. I read aloud up to Psalm 94. When I read Psalm 91, he awoke and asked me to read it again and again. Eric rested peacefully while I read. As soon as I stopped, he would jerk, moan, and cry out in pain. When I sang Christian songs aloud the lurching would subside, so I sang worship songs throughout the night. I wept and asked Eric to forgive me for all his pain and suffering and he whispered, "Yes, I forgive you." He squeezed my hand. I continued to sing Christian songs.

The night of pain blended into the day, breaking with more ongoing leg pain, grunts of discomfort, and blindness. The family doctor called to increase his morphine and apply a morphine patch to deliver a steady dose. She offered no explanation for the excruciating leg pain and was especially concerned about his high fever. Eric only spoke a few times, but his words indicated that he was fully conscious of his surroundings. All day I played music, and when one tape finished, I asked him if he would like to hear another, and his answer was always a gentle whisper, "Yes, please." When music wasn't playing, I read scripture. Even though his skin was sensitive, Eric gave me a hug and many kisses, and it pained him to do so. I asked him if he would like me to start Acts and return to the Psalms later. "Yes, read," he replied. Partway through one of the chapters, I started singing the scripture, and then one praise and worship song after another. After a lengthy worship time, I returned to reading the scriptures. I read up to the stoning of Stephen, and Eric spoke, "God's presence is in this room." He reached up and hugged me and kissed my cheeks. His arm vibrated with tremors, and he kept repeatedly wiping his face. The side effect of morphine was decreased respiration, tremors, and itching, all of which Eric had been experiencing. He was so weak.

My weeping heart was broken as I crooned, "You are going home soon, my love."

"Yes, I know. I'm so tired. I'm so tired," Eric whispered.

Eric's twitching settled as I sang more worship songs. He gave Tanya goodbye kisses on her cheek. We had a very close family time. Eric asked for his album, scripture to music called "*The Bread of Life.*"[5]

His breathing was laboured and intermittent, his lungs rattled with mucous, his eyes blind, he was burning with fever, and he was in a semi-coma. I was convinced that Jesus was taking him home that night.

At 3:00 a.m., Eric awoke and asked to use his "throne" (commode). I reminded him that he hadn't been out of bed for days and his legs lacked strength. He surprised me when he replied in a complete sentence, "I can do all things through Christ who strengthens me. Can't you give me a chance? I can do all things through Christ who strengthens me. Right now, you don't think I can get myself to my toilet. You don't think I'm able to do it?" As I transferred Eric to the commode, I was in awe at the power of God at this physically impossible transformation from a coma to alert and articulate in only a few hours.

His determination was so remarkable. "Eric, do you know that God is with you?"

"Of course, God is with me," Eric replied firmly.

Tanya awakened, thinking perhaps he had died while she slept, then wanted to help with him. She was astounded! Eric was coherent and spoke to her about many things. Then he said, "Tanya, you look like an angel. You are my angel, and I am Mummy's angel."

Eric spoke in complete sentences, and he remained focused while asking and making appropriate comments. His vision had been miraculously restored and he proved it by copying Tanya's hand gestures. They shared their special childhood memories. Eric's memory and speech were perfect! "Tanya, what time are you home from work tomorrow?" He was disappointed but certainly understood when she told him she would be working both jobs and would be home only to eat and change for the next job. But in this I was witnessing a miracle of healing!

The next day Friday, August 29, 1997, Eric woke up alert, and he wanted to go the distance to the bathroom. When I said it was impossible, he replied, "Nothing is impossible. Just believe I can do it." He resolutely struggled to get out of bed. While he insisted that he could do it, I helped him. His mind was very clear. Back in bed, he soberly instructed me. "Before I die, I want all my favourite songs on one tape. You can play it at my service." Immediately I started recording the songs he named, searching through our tapes and CDs to locate each title.

---

[5] M. Parks, David Culross & Stamps-Baxter, *Bread of Life*, Singspiration, Division of The Zondervan Corporation, 1978.

Eric reflected as I fulfilled his request, "Mom, when Jesus was on the Cross, I was on His mind." So true, and I found the tape with that song. Then he added, "Every time I had cancer or was suffering, I was on His mind." He was filled with gratitude for his Saviour's death and resurrection, recognizing the saving work of Jesus on the Cross plus the privilege of knowing Jesus as his Lord anew. Eric burst into worship singing from his heart with thanksgiving to God as instructed in scripture (Ephesians 5:19).

When I found his rainbow song, Eric said something I would treasure the rest of my life: "Mom, I want to be your rainbow. When I die, I am going to ask God to turn me into a rainbow. Then every time you see a rainbow, you'll remember me. The job of a rainbow is to help people, and you are one of them. When I die, I'm going to give you all my tapes. I love you, Mom. I love you, Mom." And he hugged me. Eric's functioning hand was shaky, and he played with my hair and held onto my arm. "My soul is in God's hands." He told me repeatedly as if I was slow to learn, and he was correct. He impulsively kissed me and hugged me more. As I recorded his songs, he recited many of the encouraging lyrics as if they were his own words.

When Tanya returned home from her first job, she snuggled her brother while he informed her, "I am going to ask God if I can be an angel. Then I could do a job for you or volunteer in heaven. I could help people."

"What kind of job would you like?" Tanya asked.

"I would like to do the job of a rainbow," Eric said, reflective and serious.

"What do you mean?" she probed further.

Eric asked, "Do you want me to explain it better? Doing the job of a rainbow is helping people in the world that need help, and you will be one of them. I'd like to be the one who does a job in heaven. I think the angels do come down. Remember the last book in the Bible? Maybe I could do the job of the angels like in the last book, Revelations. When you are on Jesus's side, you can do all things. And there would be nothing too hard for me to do. Maybe I could be the angel, the leader for praising God. I have felt kind of like a leader since a child. I could be a leader of praise and worship, leading the song with the children who have died." Eric expanded on the wonderous possibilities with childlike faith as he babbled on, "I will take a rechargeable battery and a camera and take a picture of heaven and put it through the mail so you can see it." Eric spoke more about what he thought heaven would be like. Then he added to his thoughts, "To be able to go to heaven, you've got to have love, joy, peace, patience, goodness, faithfulness and self-control. You've got to have all that fruit to go to heaven. You have to have all that before you hit the bucket." He was quoting the fruits of the Spirit from Galatians 5:22.

He continued, "Yes, before you die, the fruit of the Bible you have to have." Eric rolled over to his side, something he hadn't been able to do for a long time. I made a video to treasure how God miraculously intervened and gave Eric this momentary respite from the precipice of death. Eric asked for a baked potato. He hadn't eaten since Monday, and the day was Friday. He and Tanya fell asleep together, and when Tanya went off to work from 6:30 p.m., he slept.

When Tanya returned after 9:30 p.m., he again declared, "I can do all things through Jesus Christ who strengthens me. I can do all things in the Name of the Lord." Eric was determined to sit on his commode even though I first had to change his soiled clothing. He was so grateful, "Thank you for your help. Thank you for your cooperation." There was no mention of pain. Even when I brushed his teeth, he didn't mention pain. I lifted him back to bed. Eric was led to speak to God, "I pray that You will make a way for Mom to get a job. Lord, I pray You'll be in my life until the day I die, until I kick the bucket." Eric was asleep.

The family doctor called and was astounded to hear about Eric's rapid turn for the better, the return of sight, appetite, and even his language and comprehension. She had never seen such a comeback in a patient before. He stayed alert from 7:30 a.m. until 3:00 p.m. I prayed that Eric would never again suffer the unbearable, excruciating leg pains as he had earlier in the week, nor the blindness or loss of speech.

The following day, Eric woke up around 10:00 a.m. and didn't sleep for the entire day until midnight. Extraordinary! Fourteen hours of alert, focused energy! He wanted to sit on his "throne," several times too, with no complaint of dizziness, light-headedness, or pain! I washed his scalp and sponged bathed him without complaints of skin sensitivity. There were two large, raised masses on the right side of his skull. One cavity was filled with cerebral fluid leaking from his brain.

We watched a movie about a volcano erupting, and he remained attentive the entire time and made relevant observations and comments. He was eager to eat and, many times throughout the day, enjoyed making me laugh at every opportunity. When he made funny comments, I would ask, "Is that your sense of humour?"

"Take it any way you want," Eric replied with a chuckle. He made both Tanya and I laugh with his humorous witticisms. His voice was weak, but he articulated relevant thoughts coherently. We took photographs. Eric's vision was restored, and he held up his hand to interfere with the picture to tease us. He often repeated during the day, "Mom, I have so much energy! I have so much energy!" We were experiencing the power of God in the moment as we were so close to the Lord.

Before bed at midnight, Tanya took his pulse at sixty beats per minute. Eric prayed a very long prayer of blessings for Tanya, for him to continue to be energetic, and for a restful sleep. It was a prayer of thanksgiving—for friends, family, relatives to be saved, all those in his life who had helped him, and specifically for *Grandpa* to have an open heart to Jesus. Eric verbalized his thoughts clearly. It almost seemed that he was recovering, getting better, after those horrible, painful days the previous week. His improvement reminded me of times when he had been hospitalized for surgery or a health crisis and went from very ill to steadily regaining health and strength. What a miracle if he continued to improve progressively—if his legs regained strength and his left arm became useful. I fully knew that God was able. Eric told me several times that day when he asked to go to his commode, "Nothing is too difficult for God, and God can make a way where there is no way." His love for the Lord overflowed.

At 2:00 a.m., he awoke with leg pain. Morphine was administered, and when he insisted that he use his commode, Tanya awoke to assist. Hugging his sister, he said, "Tanya, thank you. I'll make it up to you." He sat there for over half an hour. He kept telling us how kind we were to put him on his "throne." Once cleaned with a change of clothing and back in bed, he said, "Thank you, Tanya. You can take $5.00 out of my account and buy Wendy's for you and Mom." Wendy's was his favourite fast-food take-out restaurant.

Tucked back in bed, Eric talked about going to the bank drive-through after church to get money from his account. He looked pensive, swept away in deep thought.

"What are you thinking, Eric?"

Eric reiterated his thoughts, replying, "Yea, I'm thinking how I am going to get to the bank tomorrow to take out $5.00. And I will give the rest to you and Tanya."

"What shall we buy?" I asked.

"Anything she needs," he replied, referring to Tanya.

"You are so generous." I praised his thoughtfulness.

"I'll just give myself something, a ninety-nine-cent thing and have a coke." He chuckled.

"You've got all this planned." I was impressed.

Eric laughed. "Yea, I don't mind enjoying myself for lunch. You can have anything that comes from Wendy's. I know one thing you want. Chilli! You're a chilli lover!" I agreed with him and turned the lights out. It was quiet until his voice pierced the darkness with his blessings, "Good night. See you in the morning."

"Good night. I love you," I affectionately replied.

"I love you more," Eric responded.

Teasing, I argued, "No, I love you more."

"The reason I said I love you more is that I couldn't live without you." He was serious. I reached over and hugged him and again told him how dearly I loved him.

He was reflective. "Mom, in a way, I am rich, and I am poor. I am rich to know God and poor in this world. We should know God and trust God, and that makes us rich." Yes, indeed, I agreed with Eric.

The following day when Tanya was at work, she phoned to tell me that Princess Dianna had died. When she got home, we discussed at length the fragility of life. We watched the television coverage of the accident. Withdrawing from the newscast, Eric asked that I read aloud from the Bible, specifically from Acts. His prayer for us was even more meaningful when he closed with his signature remarks, "Lord, make a way for Mom to get a job. Lord, give Tanya a good sleep and money so she can pay for her books. Bless her. Make a way where there seems to be no way. Bless my sister in a special way. Do a miracle in her life, Lord. Bless Mom in a special way. Always let her know that You are right beside her, Amen."

I awoke at 5:00 a.m. to find Eric was also awake. He asked, "Mom, did I wake you up? I don't want to disturb you." Eric was so conscious of the needs of others.

On September 1, 1997, Eric awoke at 10:00 a.m. requesting his "throne." He remained bright, cognizant, perceptive, in good humour, and affectionate all day. He hadn't mentioned pain, for which I was exceedingly thankful. My relationship with God grew deeper day by day as He walked with me along with Eric. Our Father God was walking with each of us separately and collectively as a family. Individually, we were aware of His awesome love, power, grace, and strength. This experience was a suffering beyond anything I could ever have imagined. Our family's trial compelled us to bend our ears to listen to the heartbeat of God. It was a unique depth of suffering with Christ, a deeper intimacy with Him.

The palliative care nurse dropped by. Flabbergasted, she hugged Eric. "What a miracle! I would not have believed it had I not seen it!" she exclaimed. She took his pulse, a steady eighty-eight beats per minute. She said that on her last regular visit, Eric's pulse was 120 beats per minute and erratic. She was convinced earlier that Eric was close to death, but now she believed he might see his birthday on September 19.

Eric chimed into the conversation. "This year, my birthday is on a Friday." How did he remember that? I recalled that on August 19 he had commented that it was exactly one month away from his birthday, and he had asked me what day of the week it would be. He easily remembered my answer!

While I was joyful in the moment, my memory slipped back to Eric's horrible days—days of severe leg pain, intensified by tremors so that he would cry out, the uncontrollable eye convulsions, the fixed dilated pupils unresponsive to light, and his blindness. At times, he was unable to speak—and when he did speak, it was painfully laboured, marked by shallow, intermittent breathing, rapid heart rate, paralysis, and a high fever. Watching Eric's decline had been heartbreaking beyond words! The suffering had been unbearable. There were times that I cried out to God in raw surrender, desperately trying to understand why God was allowing Eric, who loved Him so much, to go through so much intense pain and suffering that had no apparent purpose.

It amazed me that through all that pain, Eric never lost touch with God but laboured through it. By His grace, he emerged stronger than before in his faith and love for Jesus. If Eric hadn't complained, who was I to dare to complain? Today I was thankful! Today we expected and hoped that he would enjoy his birthday in nineteen days. I embraced the gift of today. That was all God asked of me, to live one day at a time. Eric taught me this by constantly singing the lyrics to the Marijohn Wilkins and Kris Kristofferson song, "One Day at a Time."[6] Jesus had given an extension of life called "one day" for Eric and me to live and to treasure together.

I had just finished taping a special song while Eric slept, snoring soundly. His breathing was steady, regular, normal. He had a day of twelve glorious hours of attentiveness. We enjoyed hours of home videos, remembering the past summer and all the wonderful people in his life that we saw again in the videos. He was so at peace. Ephesians 2:14 tells us that Jesus is our peace. Jesus was very present. Eric was so serene, so sweet, it almost seemed unnatural. Today he thanked me again for the little things that I did. He thanked me for the food, for putting him on the "throne," for meeting simple needs.

---

[6] Kris Kristofferson and M. Wilkins, "One Day at a Time," *One Day at a Time*, California: Mega Records, 1974.

The following day Tanya's university term started. When she returned home from her classes, we discussed Princess Dianne's death and the vulnerability of life. The Bible reminds us that our life is but a mere breath, a fleeting vapour, that no person is immune to death, not the rich, or famous, or powerful, not anyone (James 4:14). We needed to live every day as if it were our last, filled with the abundant life that Jesus offered (John 10:10). I was so thankful that God had allowed us as a family to live a life of blessings, rich in love, where there were no regrets, no *if only,* and no looking back. Life in Jesus! Even Eric stated clearly that he had fulfilled his desires in life, "to know God more and to help people." His heart's desire was constantly tuned into God; indeed, he knew God intimately and had helped people beyond imagination.

The night before, Eric was awake and pensive. I asked, "What are you thinking, Eric?" Tanya had gotten up to help him during the night, and he was thinking of ways to bless her. Only God can keep our minds and hearts focused on the essentials, the things that matter, to love God and others.

On this night, Eric reminded me as I tucked the blanket under his chin. "Good night, Mom. I couldn't live without you. I couldn't take care of myself without you. It takes two to have fun. It takes two to work as a team to help each other. We've got to help each other. You help me, and I help you."

With each of his statements, I injected words of affirmation, "That's right! That's right!"

"You help me in one way, and I help you in another." Eric continued his thoughts.

"Explain. What do you mean?" I was curious.

"I help you in one way with my sense of humour, and you help me when I need help." Eric was lighthearted.

"That's true," I agreed.

I wanted to savour his every word of hope, love, and encouragement. Eric never stopped caring. I was so blessed. Thank you, Jesus, for Eric.

He started his next day talking about the Lord. "I know Christ from the inside out. I wouldn't be talking if I didn't know Christ from the inside out."

While watching Christian television that evening, he commented during the altar call, "I've already been saved. I don't need to be saved twice." Before sleep, Eric's focused his prayers on Tanya and the man that gave him the print portraying Jesus carrying the little lamb. He identified with the lamb in the arms of the shepherd. He perked up, "I am ready to start to listen." He was referring to the Bible I held. He asked me to read more scripture, so I read aloud from Acts until it was time for lights out.

He awoke twice during the night to urinate in his homemade urinal. At 5:30 a.m., he awoke in a panic to go again but he had soiled his clothing by the time I got there. I repeated over and over, "I love you, Eric. I love you, Eric."

"Even when I make mistakes?"

"Especially when you make mistakes." I smiled.

His random chattiness was delightful. I welcomed it. I encouraged it.

"You're cute," I said after his monologue.

"Even when in the nighttime I ask to go to my throne?"

"No," I laughed, "you are not cute then." Eric chuckled with me.

The following day he insisted he wanted a tub bath. Tanya was helping get him ready when his leg pain came back. It didn't prevent him from the enjoyment of basking in a warm shower streamed over his frail body.

He laughed and prayed before our nightly scripture reading, "Dear Lord, I pray that You will open the door for Mom to get a job, a teaching job. Bless Tanya, give her a good night's sleep and to wake up refreshed. Bless Tanya, let her be able to do all her studies. Help us have a good night's sleep and for me not to wake up Mom in the night and wake up refreshed. Lord, keep me feeling good for a week. Bless Mom in a special way. Keep me up in energy. Keep me full of energy for the end of the week, Lord. I pray that You will bless my mom in a special way." Even though he repeats the same prayer, it is fresh and to my heart, like the first time spoken.

The following day when I was feeding Eric, I dropped some food on his chin. He laughed, "What are you trying to do? Dress me up like a clown?"

I laughed with him and said, "You're cute."

"Well, I won't stay cute forever," Eric responded quickly, still trying to make me laugh with his uncanny sense of humour. Eric's humour was the antidote to impending sadness.

His energy deteriorated rapidly. I tried to wake him up at 1:00 p.m. to eat. His eyelids were heavy, but he obediently took sips as I brought the straw to his lips. Eric went back to sleep until 3:00 p.m. when I woke him, and he said he didn't understand my language. He complained that he was cold. I added a third comforter; nevertheless, his hands, chest, and feet remained cold. Later in the evening, I woke him again.

He whispered, "I'm wiped out. I'm wiped." He grunted, "I'm not feeling well."

I tried to determine if he was in pain, but he didn't respond. I offered him sips of liquid and questioned him again, but with no response. "Do you understand my words, Eric?"

"Not really." He murmured.

I knew what Eric loved most. "Eric, do you want me to read to you? Maybe if I read the Bible, that will help you feel better."

"Yes, maybe," he whispered.

I read the last few chapters of Acts. Each time I asked if he would like to hear the Bible, he muttered, "Yes, please." He never answered that question with any other answer.

He was most alert, and a broad happy smile stretched across his face when we talked about heaven and going to sleep to wake up in the arms of Jesus. He had a glimpse that only he could see. He beamed with pleasure when I said God would look at him and welcome him, saying, *"Well done, good and faithful servant!"* (Matthew 25:21).

"It sounds wonderful." Eric's voice was strong and peaceful, and several times while I spoke, he injected, "I can't wait till I get there. I can't wait till I get there." With tears streaming down my cheeks, I started singing the scripture song that he and all the angels would be singing before the Lord, "Holy, Holy, Holy Lord, God of Hosts. Heaven and earth are full of Thy Glory. Hosanna in the highest. Blessed is He who comes in the Name of the Lord. Hosanna in the highest" (Matthew 21:9).

Eric smiled and agreed it would be nice to go to heaven to worship God all the time and be in a place where his legs would never hurt.

That day we received a card in the mail from his family doctor. I'd given her a copy of Eric's testimony. She wrote: "It was so wonderful to read the story of your life. What an inspiration! I consider it such a blessing to know all of you. Sincerely, D. Ferman." Her words perfectly captured the purpose of Eric's story, to inspire and to bless people. That had been his heart's desire, and I believed that God would accomplish that for years to come after Eric went to be with Jesus.

On Friday, September 5, 1997, I woke Eric at 8:00 a.m. His eyes vibrated while his facial muscles twitched for a minute. He was blind when in seizure, and his vision returned when it subsided. His leg pain returned with a vengeance, and he moaned as I administered more morphine. I called the doctor to see if it was safe to keep increasing his dose. She instructed me to give him as much as necessary to keep the pain under control. She gave me the palliative care doctor's contact since she had planned an out-of-town weekend.

Eric was asleep, and I snuggled beside him while his favourite worship song was playing, my hand on his chest, his hand over mine. Eric moaned, "I'm wiped. I'm wiped. I'm just wiped." He repeated it at least a dozen times. I tried to comfort him, but he was too exhausted to care. I was ever so aware of his infrequent breaths and then sharp inhalations as if to catch up on lost air. He had such peace, such a quiet and submissive spirit. I prayed aloud for him, released him to the loving arms of our Lord Jesus Christ, holding his peaceful body close, a steady heartbeat and quiet shallow breaths. I repeated how much Tanya and I loved him and reminded him to always remember that, and he acknowledged my request with, "I will, Mom."

I asked him if he wanted me to play the album, "The Bread of Life," all scripture to music. "Yes,"[7] he replied. I sang along as it played, and as the evening progressed, it was as if the Holy Spirit brought to memory every scripture song I had ever sung to glorify Him—and ushered Eric into His presence.

His eyesight was gone, albeit his hearing was acute. The television minister that night preached about heaven and eternal life. Was this God telling me that Eric was going home to meet our sweet Jesus tonight? Or would he linger on for some time, sleeping and losing strength until he slept his way into eternity? Eric had had a dream several weeks before that this could happen, and he would wake in the arms of Jesus. In response to the television minister's message, Eric quietly spoke, "He will never leave us or forsake us" (Hebrews 13:5).

Before bed, Tanya did her nightly ritual, "Love you, little brother," and a kiss good night.

"Love you, big sister. Good night," Eric whispered. He kissed Tanya on the cheek. I too gave him a close snuggle and kissed his cheeks and expressed my words of love as I constantly did during the day. Eric pursed his lips and kissed me. I knew it took a lot of effort and concentration.

"Do you want me to play the Bread of Life?"[8] I asked Eric.

"The Bread of Life," he repeated in a clear, articulate whisper. His last words on earth were a call for Jesus, the Bread of Life (John 6:35). Then he closed his eyes and fell asleep.

Saturday, September 6, 1997, Eric was in a coma as morning dawned, moaning in pain. I lifted him and held him in the rocking chair while praying.

---

[7] M. Parks, David Culross & Stamps-Baxter, "He Is the Bread of Life," *Bread of Life*, New Dawn, 1979.

[8] M. Parks, David Culross & Stamps-Baxter, "He Is the Bread of Life," *Bread of Life*, New Dawn, 1979.

I called the doctor, who came immediately and administered more and more and more morphine to bring his pain under control. She handed me a supply of morphine to give every hour. Tanya and I curled up on the bed with Eric, exhausted from a sleepless night. I read aloud his favourite Bible books—James, Ephesians, Philippians, and 1 John, passages from Psalms, especially Psalm 91, which he had memorized, and Hebrews 11. I prayed and then asked Eric to wait for us to be awake at his side before going on to Jesus. With our arms over Eric's chest, we fell asleep holding Eric, my dearly beloved son and Tanya's loving brother, as he lay peacefully resting and breathing quietly.

I awoke with a start, wondering if I had missed the time for his next morphine injection. With Tanya at my side and the syringe in my hand, Eric slipped away into the arms of Jesus. His strong heart beat on for over a minute after his last breath, my ear to his chest, listening, as it gently faded away. Eric's earthly journey ended. Eternity had begun!

Although we all knew it was coming, I couldn't contain my anguish and wailed for over an hour. My sorrow had been bottled up for months, and now it was spilling over onto the lap of Jesus in a torrential flood of tears. Tanya wept in her own private way. We bathed and dressed Eric as we prayed together, then after three hours, we called the funeral home.

After Eric's body left Tanya's apartment for the funeral home, the day, which had been sunny, suddenly turned dark and stormy, with thunder, lightning, and heavy rain that streamed from the sky like a floodgate of my tears springing forth. I remarked to Tanya, "Isn't it like God to welcome Eric home with all the angels rejoicing?" Eric had told us he wanted God to turn him into a rainbow, and you can't have a rainbow without the rain.

On the day he died, three hundred kilometres away near Peterborough, friends saw magnificent double rainbows. Eric had requested that God turn him into a rainbow, and the job of a rainbow was to help people. His words reverberated in my heart. Only Abba Father could paint the weeping sky with brilliant colour against the backdrop of sunshine, as a symbol of the hope in Him and the promise that He would help me to learn to live with my grief.

The next day, I called the funeral home. The director told me that as he drove down the street, the lightning had struck the streetlamps, and the street went dark, as if Eric was being formally ushered into eternity. Eric's doctor called to say that around the time Eric died, she had been looking out over London from her hotel balcony, observing the flashes of lightning and hearing the roar of thunder. Impressed, she had told her mother, "Isn't it like God to welcome Eric home with a firework display of lights?" When she called and told me, I was awestruck all over again, because her words echoed mine spoken at the precise time. God loves us so much! God is personal! God is in control!

PART TWO

Eric's Legacy

PART TWO OF our story is told in Mom's voice. Strolling down memory lane and reminiscing is written in italics. As well, the dialogue exchanges are verbatim from Eric and my words as recorded in my copious notes and journal entries. Part Two is very repetitive and Eric's many quotations are recorded to emphasize the positive words he left with me to encourage my future walk with God. It is intended to invite the reader to walk daily with us to the end of Eric's journey on earth and to experience Eric's devotion to God in his child-like ways.

SIX
Eric's Legacy of Hope for The Journey

AS OUR JOURNEY with God continues, let us return to May when Eric was diagnosed with his last brain tumour. What was Eric's journey like from when I left Colombia in May 1997 until he went to heaven on September 6, 1997? What legacy of hope did he leave for me to share with others so that it would *help people* as he had desired? Let me take you back to the beginning of the last leg of Eric's life with Jesus and the many *words* he left behind to help me to follow God no matter what the cost. May Eric's words also inspire you to follow Jesus wherever He leads.

It was Thursday, May 22, at 5:30 a.m. in Bucaramanga, Colombia when Tanya came to visit, and we found ourselves sitting on the ground at the airport praying for it to open. Bucaramanga was known to cancel flights and shut down the airport for indefinite lengths of time for no apparent reason. It was a volatile country, and in the past five months, while I was teaching grade one there, buildings had been bombed. Once, we had to evacuate our school due to a bomb threat. Initially, I was intimated by the strong military presence, with machine guns pointed at civilians. There was no peril greater than separation from God, so I quickly realized that earthly weapons were an insignificant threat. While earnestly praying the previous night, God made it possible for us to fly back to Toronto just hours after the phone call from our family doctor about Eric's grand mal seizure. He would be admitted to a Toronto hospital later in the day.

At the Toronto hospital, the neurosurgeon confirmed that there was now a tennis-ball-sized brain tumour in the right hemisphere that required immediate surgery. How would this affect Eric's ability to think and talk? His left hemisphere had been damaged at age four by a left-sided tumour the size of a grapefruit, and now his right hemisphere was invaded by another sizeable tumour. His current ability to speak and walk was evidence of God's intervention, but I was heartbroken that he had to go under the scalpel again. Humbled by the grace of God, encouraged by Eric's confident reliance on Him, I was clinging to God's Words in Jeremiah 30:17, *"But I will restore you to health and heal your wounds,' declares the Lord."*

The neurosurgeon granted Eric a weekend pass at my request if we returned Monday morning for the surgery. My dad drove us to his flat in Toronto for a weekend together as a family. That evening as I wrote in my journal, I heard the soothing melody of Eric's voice lifted in a new song floating from room to room: "My soul is in Your Hands! My soul is in Your Hands!" Eric peeked out from the bathroom. "Was it David who had a heart after God's heart?"

"Yes, why?" I asked, wondering about the reason behind his question.

"I think I am slipping because I haven't read the Bible for a couple of days," Eric spoke solemnly. As previously described, Eric's life had been devoted to scripture and trusting God. From the time of his first brain injury, he had struggled with poor memory until God gave him the ability to read and memorize scripture and worship songs. How could he now suggest such a thing?

I reassured him that his heart after God was that of David and Job; Eric worshiped God in all circumstances, always running to God and never away.

"You mean in my heart I have always loved God?" Eric asked to be certain.

"Yes," I replied.

He nodded and moved on to other thoughts, "I think I might be in a wheelchair for the rest of my life. It's going to be embarrassing."

"For you, Eric?" I pursued his concerns.

"Yes," he replied.

I knew what he needed to hear. "God will give you grace."

He agreed. He further assessed his future. "I think I am in the wrong hospital. I might never be able to walk."

"Are you worried about the operation?" I sensed a more profound, unspoken question.

"Yes, how much life am I going to have left? It seems like most of my life has been taken away—first, a brain tumour, my intestines, then another cancer. Now, another brain tumour. What next? My life is like Job. Most of it has been destroyed, like the devil would do. But God returned twice as much to Job, ninety-nine percent destroyed by the devil. I think the devil thinks I'll fall away from Jesus. You can take ninety-nine percent of my life, but you can't take my love for Jesus. I started with nothing, and I take away nothing. Job's wife said, 'why not blame it on Jesus?' but Job worshipped God. I'm going to fall on my face and worship God. This is going to get me closer to doing it."

He had a gift from God to see the bright side of everything consistently. Even with the challenge of his uncertain future, he was rejecting the devil's attack while seizing the opportunity to love and worship God. Eric had frequently stated, "The devil can put cancer on me, but the devil can't take away my love for Jesus." His words would resonate in my heart every day for the rest of my life.

His impromptu singing blossomed into a voice with authority, "Stand up if you love Jesus, stand up and be identified!" He sang it over and over, paraphrasing Ephesians 6:13–14. Pausing, he spoke further about his life with great wisdom. "There are risks in life that we have to face. I'm risking a big one this time. A whole piece of my life. I'm putting all my faith in Jesus."

He spoke convincingly about Jesus. I responded by saying, "If you put all your faith in Jesus, He won't disappoint you, Eric."

He paraphrased my words using Hebrews 13:5, "Yes, He won't fail me or forsake me. Mom, there's a rainbow at the end of time with Jesus waiting for you."

Eric reminded me that Jesus would be waiting for us at the end of time with a beautiful rainbow as written in Revelations 4:3, "...a rainbow that shone an emerald encircled the throne."

His reflections continued, "When I had my brain tumour on my left side, how much did I lose, about one-third?"

Reticently, I mumbled, "A lot."

Eric persisted, "How much? More than a third? I hope I don't lose all my hearing. I have a feeling I'm going to need a hearing aid in my right ear. It's greater than my left hand, left leg, left ear. They questioned me about my hearing in my right ear, but...."

Eric sometimes had difficulty selecting the correct word and would go through a string of related words until he found the right one. He had forgotten that a hearing aid would not help the profound deafness in his right ear.

He continued pondering what lay ahead. "After this cancer, I will probably get a stronger hearing aid. I don't know how I got a hearing aid in my left ear when the left controls the right." He doesn't realize he is completely deaf in the right ear. Eric surmised, "It was probably the radiation. I'll probably have to retake radiation. How much radiation did I take the last time?"

I told Eric the number in rads, and it satisfied his questions. For devotions later, we recited Psalm 91 together as a family. This Psalm had become our anchor in Christ before surgery. I clung to verses 14 to 16 for our family.

"Because he loves me," says the Lord, "I will rescue him; I will protect him, for he acknowledges my name. He will call on me, and I will answer him; I will be with him in trouble, I will deliver him and honour him. With long life will I satisfy him and show him my salvation." (Psalm 91:14–16)

Eric's voice filled every nook and corner in my father's small flat with prayer as he reiterated the words of his surrendered heart to God. "God, You created me in the beginning. I started with nothing, and I end with nothing. I have no choice but the choice to follow Jesus and trust Jesus, and the devil can't take away my trust in God. Fear not, for I am with you, says the Lord. I called you by name, now you are mine. When you walk through the water, I will be with you. In Jesus's Name. Amen." Strengthened by scripture, he quoted several more verses, wondering: "Maybe I won't be able to speak. What side of the brain is speech?"

My son was trying to anticipate the possible outcomes of the radical brain surgery scheduled in two days. I couldn't give him a definite answer so explained the complexity of speech as best as I could. "The problem is we don't know how many functions the right side of your brain took over after the damage to the left side at age four," I replied with uncertainty. At age four, the neurosurgeon had been unable to understand why Eric could speak after the brain's speech, movement, and vision areas had been removed. Now that the tumour was in the right hemisphere, the surgeon had already prepared us that Eric would lose the ability to speak after surgery.

Eric loved to talk. I couldn't imagine him unable to speak, for he articulated his thoughts and appreciation with words. He loved the gift I had given him from Colombia, a clay figurine curled restfully in a mighty hand. He told me, "Mom, that hand reminds me of a symbol of God's love."

Had God already intervened in his life? I had noticed that even without the hearing aid, his hearing was so sharp he could sometimes hear me whisper to Tanya. Then he tapped the table with his left finger, the side of his body still affected by the grand mal seizure earlier in the week. "Hey, that medicine is really working. I couldn't do that before. Yes, but the medicine won't last. I guess after the operation I won't be able to do that." He tried to sound logical.

"Yes, are you worried?" I wanted to keep the door open for him to explore any questions.

"No." Eric smiled. "Not after our talk. God is in control."

He led us in singing a song of confidence and hope, committing himself into the Lord's care. *"The Lord is my strength and my shield; in him my heart trusts, and I am helped; my heart exults, and with my song I give thanks to him. The Lord is the strength of his people; he is the saving refuge of his anointed"* (Psalm 28:7–8, ESV). Worshipping as a family had always been the glue that bound us together in Jesus's Name.

Eric quoted from John 14:6 to encourage himself in the Lord, *"Jesus said, 'I am the way and the life.'"* He continued to reference other passages: "He who believes in Me, though he be dead, yet shall he live. Jesus has the most power. He said Lazarus come forth. He has power to raise Lazarus from the dead. He has the most power, and the devil can never take the power of my love for Jesus." We continued to encourage each other with more scripture verses.

My father and I decided to take the kids to our favourite restaurant. On the way, Eric broke the silence, paraphrasing Philippians 1:6, "Mom, I am confident of this very thing, that He who has begun a good work in you, He shall perform it until the day of Jesus Christ." Extemporaneously, as a family, we burst into singing the scripture together to glorify our Lord Jesus with our lips, cementing us in our love for God and each other.

The highlight on Sunday was attending church to sing worship songs. Eric woke up several times during the night singing, "Welcome, Jesus! Welcome, Jesus!" I made cereal first thing in the morning, and Eric sang out again to Jesus between mouthfuls of food, "Welcome back, Jesus. I miss you when I sleep. Welcome back." Numerous times he excitedly proclaimed, "I can't wait to go to church! I can't wait to go to church!" He just loved to sing worship songs. It was still too early, so he went back to bed, still singing songs of praise.

Suddenly his excitement reignited, and I asked, "What are you so excited about?"

Eric grinned. "Church! I get a chance to praise God! *Sing to the Lord a new song; sing to the Lord all the earth. Sing to the Lord, praise his name; proclaim his salvation day after day. Declare his glory among the nations, his marvelous deeds among all peoples"* (Psalm 96:1–3). He was singing his own tune to Psalm 96. He always overflowed with joy singing scripture. Later in church, Eric sang his heart out in complete surrender to his Lord. Was he constantly worshipping God with the expectation that he would not be able to speak after surgery?

The weekend passed, and it was time to return to the hospital. Eric was alert, bright-eyed, and reminisced about his conversation with his piano teacher, Sue, who had visited the previous day.

Surgery was scheduled for the following day, and to pass the time, Eric repeatedly sang scriptures and choruses he had memorized. He quoted the last part of Isaiah 43:19 *"…I am making a way in the wilderness and streams in the wasteland."* He continued, "God will make a way where there is no way. Mom, God will make a way for you." He spoke reassuringly, "That's what He promised to do. When the situation looks impossible, don't worry, Mom. God will help me." Eric was trying to reassure me; he was so poised in God's love, passionate about God's power, and resting in God's peace. His confidence was contagious. He further encouraged me, my heart attentive to his every word, "Mom, trust in the Lord for a miracle. He will make a way when there is no way. God will make a way for you." In harmony with God, he explored a possibility, "I wonder if I'll still be able to play the piano? I believe God is going to give me twice what the devil took."

I listened then responded softly, "I pray you won't suffer, Eric."

"Maybe I'll suffer like Job, and the Lord will give me back twice," he responded quickly. We prayed together hand in hand. Eric prayed for the ability to play the piano after surgery. Delving into more questions, he asked, "I wonder how big this tumour is?"

"It's the size of a tennis ball," I answered honestly.

Eric contemplated the information while summing up his current limitations prior to surgery. "The only thing damaged so far is the movement of my arm." He made a concentrated effort to move his fingers ever so slightly but without success.

I explained that the tumour was in the frontal lobe. He didn't realize that the frontal lobe was where personality functions were located. Jose Vega MD. PhD reports that frontal lobe damage can cause "weakness on one side of the body or one side of the face, falling, inability to problem solve or organize tasks, reduced creativity, impaired judgment, reduced sense of taste or smell, depression, change in behaviour, low motivation, low attention span, easily distracted, impulsive or risky behaviour."[9]

---

[9] Jose Vega, MD PhD., "An Overview of Frontal Lobe Damage." *Brain and Nervous System Very Well Health*, Medically Reviewed by Claudia Chaves MD (October 14, 2020), www.verywellhealth. com/the-brains-frontal-lobe3146196).

SEVEN
Living Life While Preparing for Journey's End

ERIC WAS OUT of ICU in three days and discharged on Monday, June 2, 1997, six days after surgery. He astounded the neurosurgical team as he bounced back to health and demonstrated precise speech and sound thought processes. However, there were disruptive chemotherapy side effects. I pencilled in my Bible margin, Sunday, June 8, 1997, Genesis 32: 22–31 and 2 Peter 1:3–9 "stay close to God to know His will, re: radiation." I was wrestling with God if radiation was necessary following chemotherapy. The Genesis passage describes Jacob wrestled with God and was forever humbled with a limp, a reminder that God had touched him. In 2 Peter 1:9, there was a fitting reminder that the goal of my faith was the salvation of my soul! During this time, God was teaching me much from His Word and Eric's exemplary life.

Shortly after being discharged, Eric celebrated with others at the Volunteer Luncheon. His recent brain surgery showed the metal staples protruding from his skull. He confidently insisted he didn't need a chaperone while engaging in table conversation with the other volunteers. It was my cue to leave. Waiting for the *pickup* call, I reminisced about his reflective words the previous night and asked God about their meaning, "Mom, I never want to grow up. Why? Because grown-ups get too busy to pray."

He had wished to stay close to God. I had a sense in my heart that Eric would not grow up nor get too busy to pray. Every day he faithfully prayed for his sister, grandfather, friends, relatives, and me. I wondered if he would be here next June. I didn't know. He had no desire to grow up or grow old. I would cling to God to learn what He was teaching me in the moment.

He was exhausted when I picked him up from the Volunteer Luncheon and headed to his bedroom. In January, his sister had invited him to share her apartment in London while I taught in Colombia, so his bedroom was his personal space. I huddled next to him in bed as we listened to the gospel music playing in the background, and I whispered in his ear, "Eric, I love you."

"What percent do you love me?" he asked playfully.

"One hundred percent." My comeback was genuine.

"Is that the same as Tanya?" he pensively inquired.

"Yes," I simply replied.

Eric flashed a half-smile, "Sometimes I need to hear it, Mom."

He teased me further, so I pulled his pillow to my side of the bed, instructing him lightheartedly, "Share, share, share!"

"I share my sense of humour, so that's enough!" His laughter raised the roof, infusing every crack and cranny of the room.

Beside the scriptures in Hebrews 12:7–11, I had dated in my Bible 'Tues. June 24, 1997: No Interview for Job Posting # 12.' I had been struggling to find a way to support my family and had been praying about it. The scripture told me that God disciplined me for my good, and the harvest it produced would conform me to Christ. Even with today's rejection for a job interview, it wasn't an arduous burden—I was drawn to the notation in my Bible dated May 6, 1997, *"I will be a Father to you, and you will be my sons and daughters, says the Lord Almighty"* (2 Corinthians 6:18). I couldn't ask for more than to be a daughter to the Almighty God. I trusted that He would provide a job, and there would be lessons for me to learn in the meantime.

Tanya worked two jobs to support us, without complaint, while we lived together in her tiny basement apartment. She extended unselfish generosity and unconditional love, and I was thankful for such an extraordinary daughter who loved God and her family. Perhaps God was teaching me to be grateful for 'noble, right, pure, lovely and admirable things' (Philippians 4:8). It would be inconceivable that I would be unthankful when my mind was focused on those things. I was learning so much.

Canada Day! Tanya and her church friends made Eric welcome at the young adult's baseball and barbeque. To celebrate the day, Tanya painted maple leaf flags on everyone's cheeks. The outing exhausted Eric, but he was euphoric and delighted to have been able to enjoy it to the fullest.

We left Tanya in London and headed back to Toronto. We listened to Christian radio during the drive back to my father's flat, and the speaker spoke about lessons learned in the valley of life. I asked, "God, what are you trying to teach me in this dark valley?" There were lessons I needed to learn. Morning devotions had been from James 1: 1–12 where I had scribbled in the margin: "No teaching job, no truck to move, no house, Eric on chemo, finish cycle #1 tomorrow." I was encouraged by verse twelve, *"Blessed is the man who remains steadfast under trial, for when he has stood the test he will receive the crown of life, which God has promised to those who love him"* (James 1:12, ESV). The radio teacher had reminded me to listen to the voice of God, hear what He was teaching me and that everything that happened, every test and trial, was part of His bigger plan to know Him more, love Him more, to walk and talk with Him every day, no matter what the cost. That had been my constant prayer ever since this journey began nineteen years previously. The tapestry of our lives is beautiful to God as He sees the finished side, but we see the knots and disorganized threads on the working side and wonder what God is doing.

I continued to meditate on this while calling to mind Jeremiah 29:11–13 *"For I know the plans I have for you,' declares the Lord, "plans to prosper you and not harm you, plans to give you hope and a future."* I was reassured by the beautiful day and these wonderful words that we were God's workmanship, that He had a plan, our future secure in Him, and we were safe in His hands.

In an earlier conversation with Eric about his struggles, I had asked him, "If you could have anything in the world that your heart desires, what would you wish for?"

He paused momentarily as he pondered. He responded with softness and sincerity, "Mom, I would wish to know God more, and second, to help people."

His desire hadn't changed since his first brain surgery at age four. He could see with his spiritual eyes—God indeed satisfied the desires of his heart. His closeness to God was beyond my comprehension. And to help people? By just being himself, and without realizing it, his faithful and unselfish volunteer work in nursing homes for the past seven years had helped people. He had helped me.

Another time during our drive, I asked him, "Do you ever get angry with God?"

He spoke with boldness, poise, and assurance. "No, Mom! Job's wife told Job to be angry with God and blame God, but Job told his wife 'no.' It isn't God's fault. It's the devil. Mom, you know the devil can't touch me. He can put cancer on me, but he can't touch me. God has control over my life."

Before this, he had repeatedly stated this fact just as he would in the days ahead, "The devil can put cancer on me, but the devil can't take away my love for Jesus." Also, "The devil can't kill me. My soul is in God's Hands." Eric knew the reality of the scripture, *"You, dear children, are from God and have overcome them, because the one who is in you is greater than the one who is in the world"* (1 John 4:4).

Romans 8:38–39 was also real to him.

For I am convinced that neither death nor life, neither angels nor demons, neither the present nor the future, nor any powers, neither height nor depth, nor anything else in all creation, will be able to separate us from the love of God that is in Christ Jesus our Lord.

God seemed to be using Eric as my very own personal and wise teacher to remind me constantly to keep my eyes on Him, no matter what I would go through. Nothing would separate us from the love of God, and nothing was greater than God. I was so blessed and honoured to have Eric as my son!

Once we arrived in Toronto, he greeted his grandfather and begged to see the firework display at the Canadian National Exhibition grounds as if it were his last chance. Mindful that traffic would be congested, we decided to take the tram car and arrived in time for the grand finale. Even though the long trip tired him even more, he was delighted that we didn't allow his fatigue to prevent us from going. The look of joy on his face as he beheld the magical shooting lights that illuminated the sky in a magnificent display made the effort to be there worth it.

The next day, Eric went to the hospital for lab work, a doctor's appointment, and the last dose of chemotherapy for Cycle 1. He was given two weeks to recover his blood counts before starting the next cycle. He was pleasant even on the most painful, irritating, and dire occasions. A technician came to draw blood and ignored his advice about the best blood vessel to use. Her attempt failed as she probed deeper to find the target vein, causing Eric to squirm in pain. She apologized and then successfully tried the vessel he had recommended. He remained gentle and kind and simply thanked her.

It was a unique gift that my son saw the bright side of things in challenges and humour in dire situations. Eric was an eternal optimist and faced every trial by telling me, "Well, Mom, look at the positive side…" or, "Well, Mom, look at the bright side of things…."

My mind drifted back to the time when Eric had ridden his bike into my parked car and left an ugly scratch on the vehicle and his knuckles. Attempting to comfort him as I iced and bandaged his bleeding knuckles, he perked up, "Well, Mom, look at the bright side of things."

At that moment, I didn't see the bright side to his hand injury. "What's the bright side of this, Eric?"

He chuckled lightheartedly, "Well, Mom, at least it's not your hand." To that, we both burst into laughter.

On returning to London, I found Tanya was nursing a fever and had severe abdominal pain. A doctor diagnosed a kink in her intestines. She was also weighed down by apprehension about her brother's health, fatigue from working two jobs, and the financial stress of saving for her university studies and having enough for rent. The burden of providing for us complicated her life even more. Despite her physical pain, she was adamant she intended to work her second job that night because they were already short-staffed. She was a woman of her word, responsible to meet her obligations, and I was so grateful for her. Tanya's sacrificial love was truly a gift from God.

However, it was a tight squeeze in her small apartment, so when friends in Peterborough offered their home while they vacationed, I appreciatively accepted, and Eric and I made the move. There, Eric and I had a candid talk about life and death.

He spoke solemnly, "Mom, there's a whole lot of people going home. If I go first, Mom, you need to be careful." I asked him what he meant. I held back the tears that filled my eyes as I gave Eric my full attention. I wanted to reassure him that I was trusting God every step of the way, so he could freely speak about anything on his heart. Eric further cautioned me by saying, "Just don't give the devil a foothold. I'm not worried about dying." Previously, he had talked about going to heaven but not about dying. He continued, "I want to go to my Father's Home." He paused reflectively and asked, "Do you think I might go to heaven first, then Tanya, then you? If I go first, you must not give the devil a foothold." He was referring to Ephesians 4:26–27. Was he advising me not to be angry if he died? We talked about trusting God and keeping our eyes on Jesus to walk with us through the unknown. Why did he think Tanya would go next and me last?

The next morning, I read him verses from 1 Peter while he ate breakfast. Later, I asked him if he would like me to read more of the Bible, and he enthusiastically responded. "There's one scripture I would like to find, but I am forgetful!" He paused, motionless, centering all his mental energy on remembering. Then he suddenly recited a portion of the scripture he had committed to memory, "No weapon formed against me shall prosper!" he blurted out triumphantly!

I turned to Isaiah 54:17 and read it to him. He liked the wording in his version of the Bible, *"So no weapon that is used against you will defeat you"* (NCV). He reread it, mulling it over in his mind, then queried, "Is defeat the same as destroy?" When I agreed it was similar, he chimed, "The devil can't destroy me, and that means chemo can't destroy me." I agreed with his reasoning, and he asked, "Why?"

I reread the last line then paraphrased, "Because God has given you the victory."

His excitement grew, and his broad grin lit up the room. He suddenly wondered if he had a heart after God's own heart, and I reassured him that he had a good heart.

"Mom, sometimes I question myself." Pausing to collect his thoughts, he continued, "I wonder if I have a soft heart to God."

He sat quietly contemplating, scrutinizing his heart, then smiling, he shivered and lay down, softly drifting off to sleep.

The next day he stumbled, slurred his words, choked on his saliva, and the lump near his incision was swollen—the antithesis of healing and restoration. But Jesus wasn't finished with us. On the Cross, He said, *"It is finished,"* (John 19:30), but He wasn't finished with us. God had a plan to finish the work He had started in us. He was still working a deeper healing that went beyond healing the physical body. Everything happening in the moment pointed to the Cross. I made a doctor's appointment to check Eric's alarming symptoms.

I prepared supper at my housesitting home, and as he ate, he spoke, working out the possibilities, "Mom, do you think the brain tumour has come back?"

It had only been two months since brain surgery, and he was still recovering from the first cycle of chemo. I couldn't conceal my concern, "Yes."

Eric was silent and motionless, then responded with inner confidence and strength, "If I have to have more brain surgery, God will get me through it again. God will make a way where there seems to be no way."

I marvelled at how easily he rested in God's supernatural peace and assurance. God was his first line of defence. I remembered asking him recently what his choice would be if he could relive his life? Would he prefer to have no cancer, sickness, surgeries, and health struggles but know God the way most young people knew God—through prayer, Bible reading and church attendance? Or live the life he was living with all the cancers and sickness, and yet know God the way *he* does, intimately through his afflictions and suffering?

He didn't hesitate, "Mom, I would choose to have the cancers and know God the way I do." He had such a special relationship with God through his suffering that he wouldn't exchange it for anything. God was using Eric to teach me something *new*.

Tanya phoned, and it was a relief to hear her say she had recovered from her abdominal discomfort but still lacked her usual energy. However, her heart was with us, and she was concerned about the distance between us because she was in London while Eric and I were in Peterborough. She couldn't always see how her brother's health was doing and insisted that she wanted to be by his side if he needed her. I appreciated this protective bond with her brother but didn't want to add to her overwhelming burden of responsibilities. Waves of nostalgia swept over me when I casted my mind back to earlier days.

I'll never forget the moment when Tanya said to me, after I graduated from teacher's college and no jobs were available in Ontario, "Mom, if you want to get some teaching experience in another country, Eric is welcome to come and live with me. No one knows his challenges better than I do, and I have always been close and compatible with him." I knew she could handle this monumental responsibility on top of her full-time university studies, church involvement, volunteer commitment to research at the Cancer Regional Centre, and her paid part-time job.

She was aware that with Eric's short-term memory, he required reminders to take his medications. Tanya was truly the best choice for support, for she loved him dearly. She suggested it would be a chance for them to rekindle their childhood affections. Without hesitation, I flew off to Bucaramanga, Colombia, to teach an elementary grade while Eric was over the moon with delight to board with his sister in London. Tanya took the time to teach him the bus system so he could travel independently to his volunteer work in a nursing home. When Eric forgot how to make his bus transfer and it shook his confidence, he called her from a payphone. After she rescued him, the next day she insisted he board the bus again, and to ensure he made the correct transfer to reach his destination and support his emotional security, she drove behind the bus. Eric's confidence in navigating the city bus flourished. He never got lost again. Tanya understood what Eric needed to develop his healthy self-esteem, and she understood when to pull back so his confidence and independence could grow. What a remarkable sister and special daughter!

Once again, Eric was sleeping excessively, up to sixteen hours at a time. Lab work was normal, so the nurse concluded the brain tumour was the most likely cause and told us it takes two or three cycles of chemotherapy to destroy cancer cells.

As things progressed, so did his slurring speech, and his left hand became limp. He again inquired, "Mom, do you think the tumour is back?" Sadly, I nodded, yes. I asked him to squeeze my fingers with his weaker left hand, and he simply explained, "Mom, my left hand is dead." He was calm, and his observations were objective.

Later, while playing Christian music on the organ, he placed his right hand on the keys and let his limp left hand rest on his lap. He clearly sang the scriptures, *"The steadfast love of the Lord never ceases, His mercies never come to an end; they are new every morning; great is your faithfulness."* (Lamentations 3:22–23 ESV). He looked at me with new realization. He merely stated, "My left hand has forgotten everything. My left hand won't function." He then played and sang the hymn, "Great is Thy faithfulness, O God my Father, there is no shadow of turning with Thee. Thou changest not, Thy compassion they fail not, as Thou hast been, Thou forever wilt be. Great is Thy faithfulness! Great is Thy faithfulness! Morning by morning new mercies I see; All I have needed Thy hand hath provided. Great is Thy faithfulness Lord unto me."[10] He paid no heed to his ability or disability.

Eric wouldn't give up his Bible reading sessions and asked that I read to him from Deuteronomy, Joshua, and Judges. Eating had become a tedious chore, so I read his requested scriptures to encourage him while he ate. One session stands out. When he asked that I read the Gospel of John, I read nine chapters during each meal. Eric told me that although the tumour affected his movements, it hadn't affected his spirit. He understood every scripture. Whenever I asked him questions to determine his understanding, his responses were correct and relevant. I mentioned to him how marvellous it was that scriptural understanding came from the heart, which explained why his comprehension and long attention span for Bible reading weren't interrupted by declining health.

Through the corner of my eyes, I could see him use his right hand to help his limp left hand hold the knife. He casually commented, "The brain tumour is back." Eric wasn't disturbed. He spoke again of his confidence in Christ, "Mom, the devil can take my life, but he can't touch my love for Jesus." My heart and eyes overflowed again with tears of gratitude to our Lord Jesus, so blessed that my dear son was secure in his relationship with God. Eric was true to the meaning of his name, 'mighty warrior.'

While preparing for sleep after eating, he rummaged through his box of Christian cassettes as he sang the scripture in Isaiah, *"Yet you, Lord, are our Father. We are the clay, you are the potter; we are all the work of your hand"* (Isaiah 64:8). He continued to sing a cappella to the end of the scripture found in Jeremiah 18:6. The house filled with God's presence, refreshing my heart and soul with His power.

---

[10] Thomas Chrisholm, "Great Is Thy Faithfulness," Moody Bible Institute and Hope Publishing Company, 1923.

Tanya phoned, and we talked for an hour and a half. She and I had so much to share, and I listened intently to her work and friendship stories. My closeness with Tanya was special but also strained by the considerable distance that separated us. I knew she felt anticipatory grief, the possible loss of her brother, and the burden of earning enough money for the upcoming university year. We prayed together, casting all her cares upon God for her future, knowing His faithfulness would continue to sustain her.

We rose the following day, eager to embrace a new day, starting it with scriptures from John. Eric paused at John 13:34 to sing the scripture, worship flowing from him, "This is my commandment, that you love one another that your joy may be full...." We sang it over several times. When I read John chapter 19:33, he interrupted to comment. "You forgot to read the part of the one thief coming to believe in Christ while he was on the cross." I explained that each of the gospels had a different account and recorded different parts of the story. After our talk, I had forgotten where I left off, and Eric injected, "You left off at the part where they broke the legs of the other two people." How could he, with so much brain damage, remember a detail that I couldn't? He remained interested for hours as he absorbed the truths in God's Word. This had been a marathon of focus, a miracle of God! He was talking, thinking, remembering, and processing information with damage to both brain hemispheres! After an hour and a half of reading, I asked him if he would like me to stop, and he exclaimed, "No! Please read it all." Some of the scripture that he'd memorized he quoted verbatim as I read them aloud, smiling broadly, delighted to realize that the Holy Spirit was truly alive in him.

I reflected on his words throughout the day. He'd said that he always wanted to be a child in God's eyes. At lunchtime, he seriously asked, "Would you be sad if I went to heaven before you?"

I told Eric, yes, but I didn't want him to suffer to stay on earth. Then I asked, "What do you want to do?"

"I want to do what God wants me to do," he replied valiantly. Then he added, "Don't forget. I am a child of God. That is why I like songs about being born again."

I acknowledged his security in God. He switched to his memories at CFNI in Dallas and recalled his years from age eight to ten. Chuckling, he reflected on his childhood devotion to worshipping, "I was the loudest person singing in the choir." Indeed, he was, and I remember it well. People could hear Eric's little voice singing his heart out to Jesus clear across the auditorium.

His reflections morphed into a mini-sermon that epitomized his trust in a faithful God. His words left an indelible imprint on my mind and heart that I would perfectly recall in the future. "Remember, Mom, no weapon that is formed against me shall prosper. One thing the devil can't take away from me is my love for the Lord. It's the inside that counts, not the outside. I remember when I was reading Job that the wife said to blame it on the Lord. We are supposed to thank God. God isn't the one who makes us suffer. The devil! Blame it on the devil!" He had preached the same message to me several times before.

Eric delivered his mini-sermon with conviction and authority. I was a life-long learner, a spiritual student, and God had appointed Eric as my teacher. I clung to his words as he continued at length with his sermon, pointing me clearly to the Cross to find my safe refuge in the Lord while he exposed the schemes of the devil.

Although this day had been active with visits from friends, Eric slept most of the time. The next morning was challenging. He lost his balance, fell and bruised his hip, then choked on his breakfast, yet was happy to let me help him dress for church. However, he slept through the service, then throughout the day until bedtime. He awakened in time to read his Bible before going back to sleep. As he read, he asked, "Mom, who was the strongest guy in the whole wide world?"

"Do you mean Samson?"

"Yes!" Eric answered excitedly, "I don't know what book it's in. Maybe I can find it in my Bible." He flipped pages with his functioning right hand and found the story of Samson in the book of Judges. He asked me to read it as he attentively listened and smiled happily. After our reading, he prayed intuitively for me, my work situation, his sister's health, his grandfather's salvation, his friends, and for himself. As I fervently prayed for his healing, I contemplated whether God would restore him as He had in the past.

"Eric, do you think you will get better soon?"

"I do not have the answer. I do not have the answer," came his response.

Early the next morning, he was eager to read his Bible after breakfast. He pensively commented, "Mom, I think the devil is tricking you."

I wasn't sure what he meant, so I tried some guesses. "Are you talking about radiation or chemo?" Eric was on a different train of thought and brought me on board.

"No." He corrected my misunderstanding. "You need to keep reading the Bible to me, so my Spirit can grow." (He had said this to me before, "Mom, my body is dying, but my Spirit is growing.")

He recognized his hunger for spiritual nourishment. "What would you like me to read?" I asked.

"About how Moses was born!" he blurted out.

I read aloud to him for seventy-five minutes, Exodus chapter one to fourteen. Attentively focused and smiling constantly, he felt nourished and satisfied with his meal from the "Bread of Life" (John 6:35).

I held him close and repeated, "I love you, Eric. I love you."

"How much do you love me? More than anything in the world?" was his feisty comeback.

"Yes." I recognized the playful tone.

"Would you trade me for a car?" He continued to challenge my love for him.

I tried to convince him, "No. Tell me what I can do to prove to you how much I love you."

"You are doing it right now," he replied. His heart was so pure and sweet, so easy to love. I've asked the Lord from the day of his birth why He had blessed me with such a special child.

"Eric, may I give you a hug?" I asked, tucking him into bed.

"It will cost you a buck," he laughed. "I am expensive. I will make money off you." I think he enjoyed his sense of humour as much as I did. He delighted to make me laugh.

Tanya phoned to share her day's events and talk to her brother about having a special gathering of church friends in his honour. Even working two jobs, the geographical distance wasn't a deterrent for her. Over the phone, our mother-daughter hearts united in prayers for her concerns.

Eric slept most of the next day, and when he was awake, his mind worked overtime. That afternoon he asked, "Mom, who are the three men in the oven? What are their names in the Bible? You know, the ones in the oven that didn't die."

"Shadrack, Meshack and Abednego," I replied.

"Oh, yea!" Radiance beamed from Eric's eyes, "They were in the fire and then there were four, and God was in there." Eric started singing the scripture in Isaiah:

"Fear not, for I have redeemed you; I have called you by name, you are mine. When you pass through the waters, I will be with you; and through the rivers, they shall not overwhelm you; when you walk through fire you shall not be burned, and the flame shall not consume you. For I am the Lord your God...." (Isaiah 43:1b–3a)

He stopped singing and interjected, "Mom, that's for me. If I have radiation, I won't be burned. I think I am going to be walking through some fire and deep waters, but God is with me."

Eric's confidence in God was profoundly inspirational, and I was learning so much from him. He was not afraid to face the fires that lay ahead: cancer, chemotherapy, and radiation. To him, leaving this world to be with Jesus wasn't deep waters but rather living water to quench his spiritual thirst.

The phone rang. The nurse from the Toronto hospital called to tell us that the neurosurgeon was concerned about Eric's inability to use his left hand and had made an emergency appointment for a CT scan early the following day. Transportation was quickly arranged with a friend, and my father offered to bring us back to London. God was so faithful to meet all our needs.

When we arrived, the hospital nurse was delighted by Eric's good nature and kind heart as he gently directed her to the best vein to use for blood work. While he was on the stretcher waiting for the ride to radiology, he spoke softly, reflectively, and very clearly, "Mom, I think I am going to be leaving this world. I am going to see my Father."

"What do you mean?" I probed.

"I am going to kick the pail!" He hooted out loud, quickly correcting himself with more laughter, "I am going to kick the bucket!"

He cackled so contagiously that I also laughed, urging him to take deep breaths.

We calmed down again when the doctor returned to tell us the neurosurgeon was concerned about the paralysis in Eric's left hand, poor balance, drooling, and slurred speech, along with other alarming symptoms. He prepared us for the possibility of another brain surgery in which Eric would remain awake to minimize damage to areas of the brain that control movement, followed by stereotactic radiation. He also wondered if the ominous symptoms could be from the chemotherapy; perhaps the dose had been too potent for his small size.

While waiting after the scan, I reminded Eric to drink the recommended eight glasses of liquid to flush the contrast dye used in the procedure out of his system. His sense of humour kicked in to make me laugh again. "Just don't get me drunk." Chuckling, I told Eric that I write down all his jokes so I can recall them in the future. He was pleased that it meant that much to me.

The fluids flushed through him, and as I helped him to the bathroom, I noticed his wig had shifted. "Eric, your hair is twisted. Let me straighten it."

"Maybe my brain is twisted!" His quick reply was followed by more laughter. Later, while we waited for the CT results, he asked, "Mom, are you worried that

I might need radiation?" He knew the chemotherapy wasn't helping, and the doctor had suggested radiation after a few cycles of chemo.

"Yes," I replied.

Then Eric took the initiative. "Let's pray. God says if anyone needs wisdom, we should pray." He was quoting James 1:5. He grasped my hand and prayed for God's wisdom. After his submission to God in prayer, Eric ended his prayer and stated, "Maybe we won't have any choices." While he waited, he listened to Christian music and sang along, "One Day at A Time." The words resonated with our hearts, "One day at a time sweet Jesus is all I am asking of you...."[11]

More lyrics flowed from his lips, particularly the song that he wouldn't need his old body in heaven, and another song that described heaven as beyond the rainbow. For what was Eric preparing? For what was God preparing us? What was He asking us to do on this one day, today, that He had given?

We didn't have to wait long for the CT scan results. The neurosurgeon appeared from the viewing room with film in hand. He beckoned me to the doorway, declaring that he was sorry and repeated several times that the tumour was twice the size of the one he had removed only six weeks before.

Incredulous, it all felt surreal, as if I was locked into a time warp. How could this be? I told him that the original tumour was the size of a tennis ball. He nodded and repeated it was more than twice that size.

"Are you sure?" I hoped he might change his mind and correct a faulty conclusion. I asked about another operation, as the attending doctor had suggested earlier. He told me that the tumour would only grow back.

"Go and do the things Eric and your family would like to do. Eric only has a month. We will put him back on decadron, and he should regain some speech, left-hand movement, and balance. He may have a month or so." He couldn't believe how big the tumour had grown. His words shattered what remained of my devastated heart.

"Are you sure? Are you sure?" I cried, stunned, unable to grasp the significance of these dreadful words.

He regarded me with compassion. "You saw the first CT scan, come in, and I will show you." He placed the CT x-ray on the illuminated screen, and I gasped when I saw the giant mass covering what seemed like my son's entire brain. My eyes fixated on the image. I was stunned as I desperately tried to come to terms with this new and dreadful reality.

---

[11] Marilyn Sellar and Kristofferson K. Wilkins "One Day at a Time," *One Day at a Time*. California Label: Mega Records, 1974.

The neurosurgeon explained further, "The frontal lobe is the largest, and it is all tumour." He pointed out another area, all white, and said it was solid, and even still another location that was a gigantic cyst.

I felt Jesus's calm even while I was trying to absorb the enormity of the fact— what I had just viewed was my son's brain. After thanking the surgeon for his honesty, I walked back to Eric, where he was dozing on the stretcher.

When Eric awoke and saw me, he started cracking jokes, trying to be funny. My friend offered to fetch the clean clothes from the car. I took her aside and begged, "Pray for me. Eric has a tumour, and it is inoperable." I wanted to be strong for him. The tears spilled over and cascaded down my cheeks.

Eric placed his stronger right hand on my shoulder as I stooped to change his clothing. "Mom, why are you crying for me? Jesus will take care of me." His gentle voice was soothing. He knew God's faithful care and the truth of Jesus's undying, unconditional love. Through my tearful sobs, I could only tell him how much I loved him. Unbearable anguish and sorrow marked this day, the day the medical experts gave up, the day that Jesus wrapped us deeper and tighter in the cocoon of His Love and grace, July 15, 1997.

EIGHT
Making Joyful Memories While Saying Goodbye

THE FOLLOWING DAY, back in London, Tanya, her grandpa, and I discussed how we could create wonderful memories these remaining weeks. Dad had to return to Toronto but slated in a time when he would come again. Tanya's love for her brother had been beyond extraordinary, a constant champion and a big sister. I phoned my friend in Peterborough who willingly loaned us her video camera so we could record special happy memories with family and friends. While I was on the phone, Tanya snuggled next to her brother, whispering something in his ear.

Eric suddenly burst out, "Happy Birthday, Mom!" With no discussion, he decided to take us to our favourite restaurant to celebrate my 44th birthday. Tanya and I laughed because we both knew that Eric's decision to treat us was as much for his benefit. Eric insisted that his motivation wasn't purely selfish, pointing out that the staff in this restaurant would sing happy birthday and offer free dessert. Tanya gave me a pocket journal for a birthday gift. The pages of my current journal were full of anecdotes and memories. I hugged her with loving gratitude. When Eric asked me what I wanted for my birthday, I replied, "Your love, Eric." He hugged me, satisfied he was giving me my heart's desire. And he did!

I recalled that the drug decadron had caused severe pain in his legs and joints before surgery, which was a common side effect, and he was now back on that drug. I prayed that he wouldn't suffer this leg pain and would regain articulate speech, so I could cherish his every word. Words were the most important aspect of a person to me. The spoken word could bring healing, love, joy, and comfort. The most important words were the scriptures.

That night while preparing for bed, he started singing the song that talked about his body as an old house needing repair and no longer needed in heaven. The lyrics paraphrased the scriptures in Hebrews 3:6 that we are God's house if we hold on to our hope and courage in Him.

Another time, I remember talking to him about all his suffering, and he said, "I am like Jesus." Yes, indeed, Eric was certainly like Jesus. Again, as he lay in bed, he asked playfully, "Do you love me?"

"Yes, of course, I love you," I said, returning the tone of fun. "I love you one hundred percent."

"Not fifty percent?" Eric pursued.

"No, one hundred percent." My reply sparked more banter. His sense of humour was refreshingly delightful each day as we continued our simple verbal jesting.

Another night as I reminded Eric that I loved him, he playfully inquired, "Do you love me more than anything?"

"Yes, Eric," I replied.

"You're a good mother." He smiled.

"You are a good son, my only son, my blessing from God from the day you were born." This was no joke. I was serious.

He responded, "You are the only mother I have, and Tanya is my only sister." We talked about the time on earth that he had left. Eric reflected, "You mean, I have one month before the brain tumour takes over? That's bad news." Eric spoke in a matter-of-fact tone. "Mom, one month is like two minutes to God" (2 Peter 3:8). His calm, peace and deep insightfulness fit my definition of a miracle.

Earlier, before Eric's bath, he had spoken wearily, "I'm tired. I want to hit the bucket." Then he laughed and corrected himself, "No, kick the bucket!" We talked further. He commented, "Mom, it feels weird that I am going to heaven before you. Does it feel weird to you?"

"Yes," I agreed.

Eric continued verbalizing his thoughts, "You expect old people to go to heaven but not young. Does it feel weird that I am going to die first? Will I get to see you again?"

I reiterated that he and I would live together with Jesus for all eternity. I reminded him that the dead in Christ would rise first and be caught up with the Lord, and then those who were alive on earth would meet in the clouds (1 Thessalonians 4:16). I would see him again. He was a blessing beyond words, and his sweet, gentle, accepting ways brought tears to my eyes. I prayed that when he went to his Maker, I would be able to glorify God with my life just one fraction of the way Eric had. Eric's life couldn't be for nothing. Today, while I was feeling melancholy, I recalled my neighbour's grandson, who only had six months of life, and God had blessed me with twenty-one years with Eric. My anticipatory grief turned to gratitude.

I finished reading through Exodus 21 for Eric. He then asked me to read the Ten Commandments, and when I finished that chapter, he urged me, "Read on! Read on! My body is dying, but my Spirit is growing!" And so, I did!

His nightly prayers covered his family and ended with a request for a good sleep to awake refreshed. Every waking moment, he talked about heaven. "I will be leaving this world."

"Where are you going?" I asked nonchalantly.

"I am going to my Father," he replied in the same matter-of-fact fashion.

"What do you mean?" I asked as I always do.

"I am going to kick the bucket," he replied, laughing, and asked, "Did I make you laugh? I still have a great sense of humour." He continued to giggle. I told Eric how deeply I would miss his sense of humour. It didn't matter that he repeated the same joke. I laughed as if it were the first time I heard it. And so did he!

At his request, I read more chapters from Exodus, pausing in case he was bored by the details of the construction of the Ark of the Covenant. When I stopped, Eric would say, "Read on! Read on!" Finally, I finished and asked him what all these chapters were about. He comprehended accurately when he eagerly replied, "It's about building a house for God."

Later, I dashed back to his bed when I heard a crash. He had attempted to get out of bed. He said his head hurt, and there was a bruise on his thigh. I phoned our London doctor, who cleared her appointments to see him immediately. The doctor was kindly supportive and, after an extensive examination, concluded that the fall hadn't caused additional harm.

She asked Eric about dying, if he was scared, and he replied that he was not. She compassionately explored Eric's feelings. "When things get bad, do you want to die in the hospital or at home?"

"At home," Eric replied. She asked him if he wanted to be in London with his sister or in his hometown of Peterborough? He answered, "Both. I want to be in both Peterborough and London."

Eric's indecision seemed to favour London, so the doctor suggested he return to Peterborough to say goodbye to his friends and then finish his last days in

London. As the doctor spoke, tears sprung to her eyes as she recognized Eric was immersed in the peace of God. She told him that he had touched her life as he had touched many others.

Eric shared his recent experience at Tanya's church with her—the pastor called him to the front of the congregation to share his testimony and pray for the sick. Then he said solemnly, "I never thought I would die at age twenty-one."

The doctor wiped her eyes, "It's not fair, Eric. It's not fair." Eric empathetically attempted to comfort the doctor with the assurance of his eternal destiny.

When we returned home, Eric told me frequently, "Mom, God is preparing a place for me. God is preparing a place for me." As I helped him into bed, I told him again as I frequently did, "Eric, I love you."

"I think you are making that up." He teasingly giggled.

"Why do you think I am making that up?" I said as we savoured the fun.

However, there were also many serious moments throughout the day. Eric started to speak of himself in the third person. I attended to him and asked why he didn't refer to himself as *I* rather than as *Eric*.

"Eric is disappearing," he replied solemnly.

"I know," I spoke softly.

"My ability is disappearing," he uttered.

He seemed so aware, in the moment, so I asked, "Do you know how much ability?"

"Do you mean percent?" he asked.

"Yes." I nodded.

"No, Mom." His words were filled with the grace and peace of God.

"Maybe that's good," I concluded with deep sorrow. He didn't pursue it further.

On Thursday, Tanya's little flat was buzzing with preparation and great anticipation for the party she was hosting with her friends in Eric's honour. I sneezed, and Eric called out from his bed, "God bless you!"

"You are my greatest blessing," I returned to Eric.

"In what way?" he asked good-humouredly.

"Your gentleness, your loving attitude…" I started to list his attributes.

"My kindness?" he inserted.

We smiled in unison, and I agreed, "Yes, especially your kindness."

Later, Tanya's friends arrived and included Eric as they talked. He boldly stated to them, "I am going to heaven first."

Lightheartedly, they asked Eric to save a place in heaven for them, and he said he would. The conversation about heaven was natural and comfortable. Eric asked to share his favourite movie with the group, and they thought that would be fun. He'd memorized the character's lines, so he upstaged the characters, and Tanya's friends laughed and teased Eric affectionately. This was an evening to make memories and enjoy a comfortable, relaxed fellowship with Tanya's friends. They were kind, patient, and accommodating. Indeed, Tanya continued to be such a special sister to her brother. For years she had demonstrated her love by including him in her social life so that her friends were his friends also.

The following evening after her long day at work, Tanya helped Eric dress and took him out to one of his favourite fast-food restaurants to enjoy sibling time. When they returned, Tanya reiterated their conversation in the car. Eric had said to her, "This might be the last time you see me, Tanya." Realistically, no one knows what any day holds, so we should always live in the moment as if it were the last.

"Oh?" she replied.

"I am going to heaven," Eric continued, "I am going to get there before you."

"Save a seat for me," Tanya said, "You'll be able to talk to Moses and Lazarus. Tell Jesus and God how awesome they are."

"You are awesome," Eric replied. "You are my best sister. My only sister. I'm glad I am here." Tanya felt special to him. From the time he was a toddler, he had admired his sister. And when he was growing up with language and hearing impairment, memory challenges, and had been taunted and bullied, the brunt of jokes about being bald and short in stature, Tanya had been his defender, interpreter, and encourager. In return, Eric honoured and esteemed his sister. Oh, there were times when he was annoying; there were times when they quarrelled, but those times were few. She understood his limitations.

Eric was eager to delve into the scriptures and hear about David because David had a heart after God. He instructed me to underline the passage, *The Lord does not look at the things people look at. People look at the outward appearance, but the Lord looks at the heart"* (1 Samuel 16:7). I read for an hour from 1 Samuel, and whenever I tried to stop, Eric insisted, "Read on! Read on!" He never closed his eyes, and at midnight I had to tell him I was tired, but he insisted I read more. So, I did. To make sure he understood what was being read, I asked him questions which he answered correctly.

"Where did I leave off?" I queried, returning to the Bible.

"Saul was jealous. He was going to kill his son-in-law," Eric excitedly answered. I continued to read and again, when I complained I was tired, Eric urged me, "Read on! Don't give up." After chapter twenty-two, I did give up. He anticipated the next chapter. "Tomorrow, I want to read more about David. Didn't he sin, but God was still glorified because his heart was always after God?"

"Yes, that is true," I replied, agreeing, "and we will read about it tomorrow. It is 1:10 a.m." I fell asleep before my head hit the pillow.

Eric awoke the next day, trying to process his reality. "Do I only have one month to live?" I reminded him that was the doctor's prediction.

"God is in control. I will probably go to heaven from a dream. I remember most of my dreams, and when the time comes, I will have a good dream, and then Jesus will come in the middle of my dream and take me to heaven."

His bold declaration, sweet disposition, and anticipation of how God might bring him home to heaven were comforting.

When I finished reading 1Samuel, I wondered what book his next request would be. Suddenly, he sat up in bed unaided, got out, and started walking. It was as if the Spirit of God had energized him.

Back in bed, he spoke about going to heaven.

"Eric, I am going to miss you so much."

Eric's voice seemed tired, "You mean when I hit the bucket? I think Tanya will feel the same way. She has always been like an angel."

"The Lord knew you needed a special sister." Our dialogue continued.

"If it weren't for her, I wouldn't be here now," Eric reflected.

"What do you mean?" I asked.

"I have so much cancer. Tanya has been there all the time to give me a hand," he explained.

"That's true," I agreed.

"She has been more of an angel to me than a sister," he repeated twice.

Seconds later, he was asleep.

The next morning, during breakfast, he casually recalled a previous conversation. "Yesterday when Tanya was going out, I told her I was going to heaven, and she said, 'save a place for me.'" He said it so casually. Eric had asked her, "Tanya, do you worry about me?"

"No," she replied lovingly, "because I know you are inscribed on the palm of God's hand." She was quoting Isaiah 49:16. It was another verse Eric had memorized and treasured. I recalled when I had returned from Colombia with the little clay figure of a hand cuddling a child—he had asked where the verse was that we were inscribed in the palm of God's hand—he found it and had committed it to memory.

Eric asked her specifically, "Do you worry about me and my death?"

Tanya responded with the same loving tone, "No, because I know God is in control."

Her response had satisfied him.

Eric started to sway because of his poor sense of balance. I spoke a warning. "Eric, be careful you don't fall backwards."

"Is it because you don't want to see a dead body?" he asked comically. He saw it as an opening for more teasing.

I joined him in laughter, "Eric, is this your sense of humour?"

"It is *part* of my sense of humour." He enunciated each word, emphasizing one word.

On a more serious note, this afternoon, Tanya began a discussion to plan his memorial service. "What songs do you want us to sing?"

"When I die?" Eric asked. He listed worship songs by name and some by singing them. He started singing Acts 17:28 *"For in Him we live and move and have our being."* He paused. "Will you be my servant?" He was asking if we would do what he decided.

"Yes, Eric, I will be your servant," I replied.

Tanya playfully asked if it was a song called 'would you be my servant' and if so, she was not familiar with the lyrics.

They both laughed, and Eric continued, singing strongly from the Psalms, *"Praise the Lord, all you servants of the Lord who minister by night in the house of the Lord. Lift up your hands in the sanctuary and praise the Lord"* (Psalm 134:1–2). Then he quoted more scripture from the Psalms:

Who is this King of glory? The Lord strong and mighty, the Lord mighty in battle. Lift up your heads, O you gates; lift them up, you ancient doors, that the King of glory may come in. Who is he, this King of glory? The Lord Almighty—he is the King of glory. (Psalm 24:8–10)

He continued, jumping to another scripture:

Fear not, for I have redeemed you; I have called you by name; you are mine. When you pass through the waters, I will be with you; and when you pass through the rivers, they shall not overwhelm over you; when you walk through the fire, you shall not be burned... (Isaiah 43:1b–2b, ESV).

Eric jumped to Psalm 96:1–2 and boldly quoted, *"Sing to the Lord a new song; sing to the Lord, all the earth. Sing to the Lord, praise his name; proclaim his salvation day after day."* Then to Jeremiah 32:17, *"Ah, Sovereign, Lord, you have made the heavens and the earth by your great power and outstretched arm. Nothing is too hard for you,"* and then he jumped to Isaiah 43:19 *"See, I am doing a new thing! Now it springs up; do you not perceive it? I am making a way in the wilderness and streams in the wasteland."* The scriptures just rolled off his lips as his heart swelled with adoration and thanksgiving to Jesus.

Finally tucked into bed, he asked for Esther, our family dog, to snuggle with him. He reminisced about our day of fun at the park, Esther's leash attached to his wheelchair, pulling him on the path, our laughter, conversation and treasured indelible memories. "She gave me a great ride pushing my wheelchair," referring to his pet. Turning his attention to the Bible, he suddenly asked, "Didn't David sin?"

"Yes, Eric."

"Through it all, he had a heart after God," he quickly concluded. I read the scriptures to him as he fell asleep. A few hours later, he abruptly woke. "Jesus loves me more than you can imagine, and Jesus loves you more than you can imagine. He loves us equally." He felt moved to pray for the salvation of a woman close to his heart.

At church the following day, the pastor invited Eric and me to come forward to give an update. Eric shared that the peace of God was with us during this time. A woman came forward with a loud prophetic prayer that seemed more like her testimony than a prayer, admonishing us for our lack of faith to believe God for healing. Her words grieved me. She didn't know us, that God had been with us every step of the way and done many miracles. Later, when I asked Eric what he thought of the woman, he replied, "I think she needed a touch from the Lord. The Lord put me there to minister to her." Wow! Every experience to him was positive and purposeful!

Following the service, Tanya's friends came for lunch. Later, Tanya and I started a fierce water-balloon fight. Eric found our razzing and going after each other sopping wet immensely comical. He kept his water camera at the ready, so he could squirt us as we dashed by him, giggling and acting like kids. My dad filmed this animated action as we smashed our water balloons on bodily impact, I ran to escape Tanya's attacks, and she retreated from my pursuit, the bursting water soaking our hair and clothing. It was pure fun, entertaining for Eric, and a great release of pent-up energy for Tanya and me. We were thankful that their grandfather participated in the fun and was a significant part of our lives. It was the making of memories!

By the end of the day, Eric was exhausted. His voice was weak, but his words were firm as he talked about his end-time and going to heaven. He asked passionately, "Mom, am I worthy of going to heaven?"

"Yes, you are ready to go to heaven," I answered him, thinking he had asked if he was *ready*.

"No, Mom." He corrected me, "Am I *worthy* of going to heaven?" emphasizing the word worthy.

"Oh yes, Eric," I reassured him, "No one is more worthy than you because of Jesus's worthiness. His death, resurrection, and work on the Cross cover us so we can go to heaven. Your heart is right with God." He prepared himself for heaven with anticipation and questions. "God is calling me early to heaven." He emphasized what was most important, the soul, not the body, was more precious.

"My soul is in God's Hands. I don't care if they disassemble my body as long as my soul goes to the right place." Eric talked about sin, and he wondered if there was any sin in his heart. I reassured him that his heart was pure with his frequent prayerful repentance. In Ephesians 2:8–10, scripture teaches us that by grace we are saved. God's saving grace had prepared his heart.

God had given Eric some gifts during this season of dying. Eric wore a hearing aid, being deaf in one ear and severely impaired in the other. Still, now, even without the hearing aid, he could hear Tanya's whistling in the backyard while he was indoors in the front of the house with the dehumidifier humming. Only God could have done that for him.

Another night when Eric spoke about dying, again, my heart ached with grief, "I am going to miss you, Eric."

"Mom, the Holy Spirit will be with you. And I will be looking down at you like an angel." He tried to comfort me.

I felt the presence of God. "The Lord has given me an angel for a son. From the day you were born, you've been an angel. You have always been so good."

"How good is good?" Eric laughed. His question launched us into a playful discourse.

After preparing for bed, completing our scripture reading and prayer, Eric drifted off to sleep quickly. Dad had to return to Toronto but offered to drive us first to Peterborough.

Dad had been a quiet introvert, mostly observant and unobtrusive, but exceedingly helpful in many practical, silent ways. The children and I loved him dearly as he did them. Over the years, he was consistently available. His help and support had been a constant rock during our trials.

Tanya and I had been feeling cramped with four people in her tiny basement apartment. We talked about my inability to ease her stress and the guilt I felt for not being available or adequately supporting her. It had often been like that because whenever Eric was ill, I would pour all my energy into him, and she would get my emotional leftovers. I knew she understood, and she accepted my repentance, though it didn't change the emotional deprivation she felt. She was always so forgiving of my shortcomings.

Eric awoke ready to travel to Peterborough to house sit, visit friends, and say goodbye.

It was Tuesday, July 22, 1997, marking two months since my return from Colombia and Eric's surgery. Now we were back in Peterborough visiting friends and capturing video memories of Eric's final days. At a gathering of friends, someone tried to convince Eric that he should only confess healing and not discuss dying. Eric told him that he was ready to see Jesus and quoted Isaiah 49:15 and 16, explaining that God had him in the palm of His hand and was in control. People had difficulty understanding that Eric wasn't holding on to his physical life and was confident with his eternal life.

As we drove back, Eric spoke freely about the gentleman that admonished him spiritually, "I don't think he understands a brain tumour. Even Jesus's disciple, Stephen, was stoned to death, and he was young. Sometimes God takes people home early, like Stephen." Eric was inspired to read the scriptures about Stephen from the book of Acts, attentively absorbing every word.

When I read Acts 7:56, the stoning of Stephen, the scripture said, "'Look,' he said, 'I see heaven open and the Son of Man standing at the right hand of God.'"

Eric interrupted me, saying, "Mom, you need to underline that verse. I might be in that position right now." Immediately I did as he asked and highlighted the passage. Eric stressed over and over, "Mom, sometimes God takes people to heaven early, like Stephen." He connected it with the earlier discussion that a lack of healing resulted from a lack of faith. He reasoned that Stephen had faith, but God allowed Stephen's stoning to lead to death and that spoke about God as all-powerful. An all-powerful God who allowed death was a concept that challenged some people who tried to understand God with their mind instead of their heart.

The following day was filled with visiting friends and sleeping. At the end of the day, while preparing for bed, Eric perked up. "I want you to read the Bible.

Read the part where Abraham had a son, where he was going to take him to be on top of the... what was his child called?"

"Isaac," I replied.

Eric struggled with his thoughts to put the scenario together, "When they were going to kill him, then there was an animal God brought... he obeyed God." I explained to him that it was Abraham and Isaac, and turning to Genesis, I read chapter twenty-two. It satisfied his passionate heart to consider Isaac. Eric's endearing voice spoke in the dark, "I need to treat you out, Mom because you are so generous to me. You have always been so kind to me. You treat me like a baby. You have been more than a mother to me."

"What do you mean, Eric?" I tenderly asked.

"You took time out to be with me in the hospital... you hold me like a teddy bear."

"Maybe because you are so special," I added with admiration.

"In God's eyes," Eric replied.

"And in my eyes," I added.

He circled back to his original statement, "I just want to take you out to a place you want to go. Maybe a restaurant or something." I acknowledged his kind heart, and he shifted to another focus. "Tomorrow, read to me about the walls that came down."

"Eric, do you mean Joshua at Jericho?"

After his dreamy, "Yes," he was asleep.

At 11:30 a.m., Eric emerged from slumber, ready to face the day and embrace the scriptures. Before he set foot out of bed, he asked me to read Deuteronomy, and after chapter five with the ten commandments, he asked me to read about the walls of Jericho. I turned to Joshua and read chapter one to chapter six. It was well past lunchtime when Eric washed and was ready to dress. He put on worship music, ate egg salad sandwiches, and by mid-afternoon, we were picked up to visit his childhood friend, Dane. I was amazed at the improvement in his balance because, at times, he could walk unaided. The steroid drug was starting to have the desired effect of reducing some brain swelling, allowing him some mobility. At Dane's house, he played hymns on the organ with his right hand, then played computer games where they hooted and hollered as they raced animated virtual cars to victory. He cherished this time with his friend. We said our goodbyes, then went on to another friend's home for a visit. They had a daughter, Tora, who was very sensitive and kind and had always accommodated Eric's challenges.

Eric said, "Tora, do you know what I want to do before I hit the road to heaven? Play cards." He said that the last friend he played cards with was "*no competition*" because she was so easy to beat. We laughed. He played several card games with Tora, elated that he won two out of three. Tora knew that letting Eric win was a part of his thrill of playing. After cards, he announced, "They tell me I only have one month to live."

His sudden but simple disclosure startled the family. The question came back, "Do you believe them?"

"This is up to God," Eric replied confidently. He wasn't one to follow the social mores when addressing his feelings. He later said, "I feel that my life is falling apart, and I will be going to heaven soon." He was making an observation, not a complaint. He used language differently than most, and those who didn't know him well would not understand. Upon additional quizzing, they understood when he spoke fondly about his love and relationship with Father God.

His energy waned at the end of a busy day, but by the next morning, it had been renewed. While eating breakfast, he spilled food and laughed, "I am a messy eater. I am so glad my right hand is not passing away." He acknowledged his lifeless left hand, his fingers curled in a fist, dead on his lap. He laughed at the sight of spilled food as I joined in. At every opportunity, he tried to make me laugh.

My friend called and suggested I take Eric to Ottawa to a healing preacher ministering to the crowds. So, I prayed about it and approached Eric to let him decide about travelling six hours to receive prayer and healing.

Eric interpreted my proposal differently, "Maybe he wants me to join his ministry and pray for the sick." I explained to him that the healing was for him. He didn't respond right away but remained deep in thought. I dropped the matter. I went to the Lord with silent prayer. I didn't want to miss an apparent opportunity to receive God's healing.

We were on the road to visit another friend who lived out in the country when again, I broached the subject about driving to Ottawa to receive healing. Eric declared clearly and assuredly, "No, I'm supposed to stay between Peterborough and London. I don't care about my life. I have to die eventually. I only care about my soul. My soul is in God's hands. If I live, I live with Jesus, and if I die, I die to live with Jesus." He was paraphrasing Romans 14:8. I couldn't argue that!

He confidently restated, "God could heal me in Peterborough just as easily as in Ottawa if He wants to." It was final, forever settled in his heart. I was no longer anxious. I had given it to the Lord in prayer. Eric remained basking in the tangible peace of God (Philippians 4:6–7). And I was with him.

We visited Eric's piano teacher, Sue, and her daughter, that afternoon, took pictures, and again played cards. He had some trouble distinguishing between the club and spade cards but turned it into a joke using his error as a platform for humour.

Back at the house, Eric anticipated more visitors. My friends arrived and gave him a gift of two prints that one of them had painted, a painting of Jesus standing at a door knocking, taken from Revelation 3:20, and the other of Jesus carrying a lamb with two small sheep in the background, taken from John 10:11. Eric was thrilled that he identified with the lamb in Jesus's arm and reflected upon the Bible passages. We thanked them, and Eric expressed how he treasured their present.

Tanya drove from London to spend a few days with us and help her friend prepare for her wedding. When she arrived, Eric greeted her with the print of Jesus carrying the lamb, "Look Tanya, the two sheep in the corner are you and Mom because you are staying here, and I am the lamb in Jesus's arms because my name is inscribed on the palm of His hand." Tanya hugged him in agreement. Later, once again, Eric referred to himself as the lamb in Jesus's arms because he needed help.

My friends from Scottish Country Dancing arrived with a gift for Eric, a lapel pin of a miniature rainbow with a dove above it. He loved it, thanked them, and immediately attached it to his collar and announced, "Mom, there is a rainbow at end times." He was referring to Revelations 4:3 and burst into the rainbow song. I thanked God for reminding us of His presence, faithfulness, and promise depicted in a rainbow.

Not long after they left, another friend came by with a gift of a helium-filled rainbow balloon. Another reminder that rainbows were special to Eric. She stayed and witnessed his testimony that I videotaped, so I could listen to his voice in the future. A short excerpt from his testimony follows:

"... There's one thing we should all remember. When we have problems, we should trust in God all the way because God will make a way where there seems to be no way. He always works in ways that we can't see. Trust in Him. He will make the miracles.... Just to let you guys know. Nothing is too difficult for Thee. There's a scripture I'd like to tell you. Isaiah 49:15 to 16. "Can a mother forget the child she has birthed and have no care for it? Whatever the mother might forget, I won't, says the Lord. See, I have inscribed you on the palms of my hands...." In other words,

I have written your name on the palm of my hands. And you are always in God's hands. There are angels beside you so that you won't strike your foot against any stones.

When you are going through problems, never fear, …fear not, for I am with you, says the Lord. I have redeemed you. I've called you by name. Now you are mine. When you walk through the waters, I'll be there, and through the flames. Fear not! No way to return. Fear not! No way to be burned. For I am with you. Fear not, for I am with you. Fear not, fear not, fear not for I am with you, says the Lord. Always keep on trusting in God. Always go to the Throne every time you are in trouble. God will be with you all the time. He will never leave you nor forsake you.

How about Psalm 91? He who dwells in the secret place of the Most… will rest in the shelter of the Almighty, will rest in the shadow of the Almighty. Maybe, I should try it from the beginning. He who dwells in the secret place of the Most High will rest in the shadow of the Almighty. He is my shield and my refuge. In Him will I trust. Whatever happens to you, God will protect you—trust Me, I will protect you. I will send my arrows, my angels, to protect you, to protect your foot against a stone. An arrow will protect you from having anything hit your tent. A thousand may fall at your side, ten thousand at your right hand. You will only observe with your eyes and see the punishment of the wicked. I always forget some of the words I am going to say. "Jesus, Lord, I come to You right now. I pray for all the people who need to know You, Lord. I pray that You can soften Grandpa's heart. Lord, I pray that You open make a way to heal people that need to be healed. Do it in a special way. You're the One that knocks at doors. Lord, I pray that people learn to trust in You, especially in their suffering times. In Jesus's Name. Many people! In Jesus's Name, Amen."

I was surprised at how many scriptures he could quote from memory as he told his life story. It was astonishing that he had committed to memory a new scripture from Isaiah 49:15. Even as his brain was expanding with tumours, it was expanding more with the Word of God.

Tanya was absent for the entire day, visiting her friends, and when she returned, she asked Eric, "Who came to visit today?"

"I had two customers," Eric replied eagerly. Tanya laughed playfully at his choice of *customers,* and Eric joked further that he was "*charging*" people to come and see him.

Later, he insisted he wanted to take Tanya and me to his favourite restaurant because he wanted to be *generous* to us. So, I brought him to the banking machine and noted that he had difficulty sequencing the numbers on the pad. After several attempts, he allowed me to give minimal support without interfering with his independence. He was pleased to be making plans to treat the "*two ladies in his life*" to a meal after church the next day.

During the evening, a couple arrived, promising Eric their next visit would include their three young children. He answered their questions about his health and stayed on point through it all. At their request, he sang the scriptures from Isaiah 43:1–3 very clearly.

After the guests left, Tanya sat on Eric's bed for an hour while the two siblings spoke freely about heaven and their love for our Lord Jesus. Eric had this unshakable, solid peace that God was in charge.

Brain tumour cancers cause failure or decline in many parts of the body. But God had intervened! It was impossible that Eric had no pain except through divine intervention; impossible that he had no seizures, and it was impossible that he had no personality changes with a constantly growing frontal lobe tumour the size of two tennis balls. I knew without doubt that God was in control and not the cancer. I knew without doubt that God had already divinely intervened. The cancer would not take Eric, only God would take Eric to heaven, when everything He had ordained for his life on earth, had been accomplished.

The following day, Eric was eager to attend church, and while he prepared, he sang and recited scripture: "*To you, O Lord, I lift up my soul. O my God, in you I trust...*" (Psalm 25:1–2, ESV).

Compassionately, I asked if he wanted this scripture read at his service.

"You mean after I am dead?" he chirped back. Eric didn't hesitate to speak about dying, death, or any other topic.

Eric sang with all his strength, a marathon of worship choruses he loved, his voice reaching to the heavens. Then he paraphrased the scripture in Matthew 1:23, "Immanuel, Immanuel, His Name is called Immanuel, which means 'God with us.' God is with us Mom. He will never leave us." Eric commented that he used to play so many choruses on the organ and piano with two hands. We sang more worship songs. After he finished one song, he jumped into the next. It was based on Jeremiah 18:1–5 and one of his favourites. "Have Thine own way, Lord! Have Thine own way! Thou art the Potter; I am the clay. Mould me and make me after Thy will; while I am waiting, yielded and still."[12]

Conviction blended with gentleness, Eric spoke about his impending death, "I have something to tell you, Mom. I have total peace." His face, a landscape of

---

[12] Adelaide Pollard & music George C. Stebbins, "Have Thine Own Way Lord", *Northfield Hymnal with Alexander's Supplement,* 1907. Wikipedia: en.m.wikipedia.org/wiki/Have_Thine_Own_Way Public Domain.)

sweet tranquillity, was like a sparkling diamond ocean against the backdrop of a warm sunset. I caught a glimpse of the depth of his peace in Christ.

The day continued with more worship at church and our family outing for lunch. The afternoon was heightened with anticipation as he looked forward to the arrival of guests. "I can't wait until two o'clock."

I knew the reason but asked just the same. "What's happening?"

"I'm having company." Eric's half-smile broadened.

"Who is coming?" I asked, knowing the answer.

"Children!" he replied delightedly. He continued to speak about his previous babysitting experience, playing Legos with the children and how he had entertained them for hours.

As scheduled, the family arrived on time. The three children ranged from age five to nine. They brought Eric a brown, stuffed teddy bear with a red heart tucked inside a chest pocket, to remind him that he would always be close to their heart. I knew with Eric's profound hearing impairment, it would have been an arduous task for him to follow conversations with two people, so a family of five voices, chatting simultaneously, would be exceedingly challenging, but he responded correctly to every question, even without his hearing aid. That was phenomenal!

By the end of July, we prepared to return to London. Eric's piano teacher, Sue, offered us transportation, and we appreciatively accepted. We said our goodbyes to Peterborough, bundled our treasured memories in the cleft of our hearts, and set off on a five-hour drive to London with traffic jams and impatient drivers cutting in and out of lanes. During the entire long trip, Eric frequently confessed that he had so much energy and asked probing questions and made relevant observations.

When we arrived in London, he was exhilarated to receive an invitation to join the *boys* for a night out; his resilient vigour overflowed with expectancy. Eric had a very memorable time with the church guys, and a few days later one of Tanya's friends dropped off a lengthy five-page letter written by one of the chaps. The gist of the letter revolved around positive verbal confessions and a *name it and claim it* approach to healing. When I read the letter aloud, Eric was quite receptive to the lad's "*you're healed, confess it*" approach. He explained, "Mom, all things are possible. He has already started it. My balance has come back. This whole thing has to do with truth and trusting—I feel very positive about the letter Joe wrote, and I am willing to listen to anyone." Eric's confidence was firmly planted in God.

Later in the day, the palliative care nurse dropped by to assess Eric's needs. She was amazed that he hadn't experienced headaches with his dose of steroid and the size of the tumour growing in his head. He wasn't in any pain! While Eric was preparing for bed, he requested the story about Noah, so I read Genesis chapters five to nine.

The following day, I marvelled at how well Eric was looking and acting, walking so strongly, without even a limp, with an abundance of energy, so that it was hard for me to fathom that he was declining. The palliative care nurse made another visit, and I pointed out that the surgical scar on Eric's skull had become swollen. She explained that as the tumour expanded, unhealed soft spots on his skull from the surgery would expand due to brain swelling. The nurse's optimistic comment about his cognitive ability renewed my hope for healing and recovery. As I spoke to her, Eric was oblivious to our conversation as he located the channel for his favourite television show called Jeopardy; his second favourite was Wheel of Fortune. For many years, these had been Eric's viewing choices, attempting to reply to the questions before the contestants and cheering on his favourite.

As the evening came to a close, Eric felt tired but alert enough to focus on God. "Read the last book in the Bible," he suggested.

I read aloud from Revelations, and after chapter seven, we sang the scripture together that included the verse in 7:17, "and God will wipe away every tear from their eyes." I thought after we sang the song a few times that he would want to stop, but he urged me, "Read on! Read on, Mom!" At the end of chapter eight, I paused again. Eric jumped in, "Read on!" When I read chapter twenty-one, verse three, we stopped to sing the scripture: "Behold the tabernacle of God is with men, and he will dwell with them, and they shall be his people..." (Revelation 21:3, KJV). With Eric's insistence, I continued. When I reached the passage about the river of life in chapter twenty-two, Eric inserted, "That would be the best place to be!"

At the end of the book, I asked, "What did you think of this, Eric?"

"Wonderful," he replied, "like the place I want to be. That's what my heart desires," with a joyful, serene countenance, sighing deeply, inhaling the wonders of heaven.

"That's where we are going, honey." I smiled assuredly, and Eric nodded in agreement.

The following day, Eric requested Daniel's story about Shadrach, Meshach, Abednego, and King Nebuchadnezzar. After reading, Eric had many lessons to teach me—about God's faithfulness to us during our fiery trials, advising me to cling to Jesus, to remain steadfast in the love and power of God, praying without ceasing or fear, and fervently accessing His grace to stand firm in Him. He preached like an evangelist. Following his sermon, Eric was already thinking ahead. "Mom, do you know what book we should read next? Luke." I reassured him we would start Luke the next day, but it was past midnight, and I was tired.

NINE

Celebrating Life's Journey from Birth to Eternity

THE NEXT DAY, Eric was glowing with anticipation of the arrival in London of his aunt and two cousins from out of town. He stocked up with balloons for water play outdoors. Since his cousins were much younger, he assumed all children loved water balloons. However, it was my sister and me who were the first to dive into the fun, saturating each other with water balloon bombs, squealing with laughter like kids, with the children mirroring our pursuit of each other, filling the neighbourhood with explosive joy.

When Eric told me that he only wanted me to remember positive words, it reminded me of Ephesians 4:29. *"Do not let any unwholesome talk come out of your mouths, but only what is helpful for building others up according to their needs, that it may benefit those who listen."*

He said thank you for every little thing that his sister or I offered to do for him and often complemented us. "You're the greatest mother I ever had. I'm never going to forget about you."

While eating lunch, Eric capriciously sang and quoted the scriptures, *"But you, O Lord, are a shield about me, my glory, and the lifter of my head. I cried aloud to the Lord, and he answered me from his holy hill"* (Psalm 3:3–4, ESV). He sang and spoke it again, then joyfully declared, "I am rich because I have Jesus in my heart, and His Spirit is in me, and nothing is too difficult!" Eric overflowed with joy, finding so much to be thankful for in Jesus and pointing me to the Lord.

It was the Word of God found in Colossians 3:16 that resonated with me. *"Let the Word of Christ dwell in you richly, teaching and admonishing one another in all wisdom, singing psalms, hymns and spiritual songs, with thankfulness in your hearts to God."* Eric applied that Word, literally!

Before bed, I read aloud Luke followed by our nightly discussion of the scriptures, reflections of Jesus's presence in our lives, and concluded with sincere prayers. Eric woke several times during the night to use the commode, and when I helped him back to bed, he said, "I think you are the best nurse. Thank you."

My dedication to him emerged through my sleepiness, "You are the best."

"I think God has blessed you." Eric continued our dialogue.

"Yes, He gave me you, Eric," I approved.

Eric asserted compassionately, "As long as I live, I'm going to bless you with kind words. Thank you for this…" (pointing to the commode). "You serve me like a king. I have to give you something back for your kindness. Thank you for the movie and those Dorito chips. You make me feel as good as I do. You're my best nurse. She's my best sister." (Referring to Tanya). "She makes me feel like I'm on a ride at Canada's Wonderland." (Referring to Tanya pushing him in the wheelchair at the park). He drifted off to sleep.

The next day, he was swamped with phone calls and visits. The pastor came and chatted with Eric, asked him if he had any idea when God would be taking him home to heaven, and Eric replied, "No one knows the day or the hour, only God." What an apt response, as the Bible tells us to be prepared to answer everyone (Colossians 4:6). The pastor immediately asked him if he feared death, and with typical Eric faith in Jesus, replied, "No. My life is in God's hands." He was the third person who had asked Eric if he was scared to die—the family doctor in her office, then the physician who made the house call, and now the pastor. What was this fear about death? The Bible told us that there was no sting in death because of victory in Christ (1 Corinthians 15:55–56).

Later, Eric treated us to take-out lunch, so we sat by the river at the park to enjoy our time together. He asked Tanya what she would like for her birthday the following week. "Only you, Eric," she replied with a sparkle in her eye and a smile on her lips.

He then offered to take her to their favourite restaurant, her alone. Tanya laughed and said, "Including the family would be nice." They both laughed, and he agreed.

Soon it was time to prepare for sleep. Eric recalled the exact place we left off in the Bible. I was perfectly healthy and couldn't remember! We read Luke and finished the book. He was already prepared to read the next Bible book. It seemed like he absorbed every scriptural word as his lifeline that would transition into eternity.

During the night, Eric awoke, and we talked about heaven and how he would know when it was time to go. Insightfully, he answered, "My Spirit will know. I was listening carefully as you read the Bible in Luke. I've been listening *very* carefully."

Indeed, he heeded every spoken word both from the Bible and in conversations. I was impressed with how his memory had improved. Earlier this evening, we watched a movie, and during his chatty moments, I had forgotten the title, and he recalled it. It was a mystery how his short-term memory was able to maintain trivial information even as it speedily deteriorated. Again, he remembered the exact place from the previous day's Bible reading. How was it possible he had such a specific recall? God's grace never ceased to amaze me. I was thankful for God's intervention. The next two books Eric yearned to read were Ruth and Isaiah.

A research scientist from Sick Children's Hospital, Cherri, who had monitored my son's progress and medical setbacks since his brain tumour at age four, called to see how Eric was managing. He was a living anomaly, and I remembered when he was growing up, I would receive questionnaires from John Hopkins University in Baltimore, Maryland, and for years, researchers followed the quality of his life. His case study had been published in many scientific journals and discussed in the scientific community as *the most unusual case.* The researcher disclosed that everywhere she had travelled, from Japan to far-reaching countries worldwide, when scientists convened, to discuss childhood cancers with genetic mutations, Eric's name and case study had been mentioned. She said that his unusual stomach ache symptoms, at age four were discussed to prevent the medical community from becoming *complacent* about labelling any brain tumour condition with fixed symptoms. Again, like at age four, Eric's massive brain tumour had no headaches, and at this time no symptoms, not even a stomach ache. That was a miracle from God. She talked about the hope of continuing their scientific investigations after Eric's death and referred to organ donation. I asked Eric if he was okay with this, and he asked, "Mom, will it help people?" I told him it would, and so he consented to participate to help others.

Later in the afternoon, we made a wheelchair trip to the grocery store for ingredients for homemade pizza, his sister's favourite. Eric wanted to please Tanya, knowing she was working two jobs and would arrive home late. She was indeed thankful for his thoughtfulness and enjoyed his culinary skills. Eric endeavoured to lavish on us only good memories. "I'll only be here for certain days before I disappear."

"What do you mean, Eric?" I asked.

"I don't know how many days before I die," he explained.

"Nobody knows the day, Eric," I agreed.

"It won't be long," Eric said.

Just before sleep, Eric was next to my cheek, and he whispered, "I love you so much, Mom, I can't explain it." I shared mutual affection. He had such love for everyone. He passionately prayed every night and many times during the day for friends, his grandfather's salvation, his sister at work, and for God to be glorified. He listened to gospel music all day, particularly one song by Michael W. Smith called "I'll Lead You Home."[13] Eric memorized the lyrics and sang them at the top of his lungs. It talked about God calling us, and I was reminded of God calling the boy Samuel in 1 Samuel 3 and another story of Isaiah's obedient response to his calling in Isaiah 6:8b *"...Here I am. Send me."* That was the essence of Eric's heart, to hear God calling and obey.

When we attended church, Eric asked, "Do you ever worry what the future will bring to me?"

I nodded, "Yes, sometimes. Do you?"

"No, because God is in control. He holds the future and knows what will come ahead." Eric responded in his poised tone.

So true! So true!

Eric sang the scriptures while preparing for bed. I was so blessed that Jesus was constantly on his mind, in wakefulness and preparation for sleep.

The following afternoon, I was crushed and weeping, deep in sorrow. I went to the cemetery, and my tears fell. Eric said that he wanted to see where he would be buried, so I decided to first go by myself to the cemetery, and there I beseeched the Lord with ardent prayers for healing. There, among grave markers, the reality of Eric's death gripped me, and I collapsed with heaving sobs. On my knees, I poured out my heart to God to heal Eric without medications or any intervention. Like Abraham with Isaac on the alter, maybe in the last hour, God would reverse this whole dying process. I wrestled with God until I submitted to Him solely.

Before sleep, Eric was eager to read Isaiah, and at the end of chapter six, he quizzed me, "Mom, do you understand what is going on?"

I was a little surprised by his authority and turned the question back to him, "Do you?"

Eric replied quickly, "Yes, it will come to an end if they don't ask for forgiveness! My Spirit understands! Woe to them who will not repent!" Eric said firmly with his eyes closed.

---

[13] Michael W. Smith, "I'll Lead You Home," *I'll Lead You Home*, Reunion Records, 1995.

His mind was crystal clear. I told him that I was amazed that he had this level of comprehension and ability to engage in meaningful conversations all day. Eric reflected his ability to the source and told me it was the Spirit of God, alive and active in him, that equipped him to communicate so well. He articulated spiritual matters clearly. He spoke about his life and his impending death freely.

The doctor made a house call early in the morning, administered medication, and was intrigued with Eric's stories about his trip to Hawaii after the Wish Foundation granted him a dying wish. Eric's body was declining in strength, but his mind and memories were strong and active.

Tanya arrived home from work feverish. She had been burning the candle at both ends with two jobs, trying to save for her course expenses. How I wished I could relieve her of all these responsibilities. I anticipated her upcoming birthday and was disappointed that she had to work on her special day. I prayed for my children constantly, asked God to hold them both close to His heart and never to let pain, suffering or disappointments cause them to turn away from Christ.

August 12th was Tanya's birthday, to be celebrated after a long day of two workplace commitments. When she was a teenager, whether her job was volunteering at high school, the community at the Sports Injury Clinic, the Handicapped Children's Centre, or babysitting the neighbour's children, Tanya had consistently been a person who was reliable and dependable. Even in university, working in the lab and volunteering at the Cancer Regional Centre helping with breast cancer research, or working her part-time job in a department store, she had been loyal, trustworthy, and accountable. She was the most wonderful blessing in all my life, and to think she was turning twenty-four years old. How was it conceivable that the time had passed so quickly?

When she returned from work, she was greeted enthusiastically by both Eric and me, with happy birthday balloons, hugs, kisses, gifts, video clips, and best wishes, to engrave the memory of her special day on our hearts. The video shots were teeming with humour and just silly fun. After her special meal, fatigued as she was, she lay down and invited the pranks and comic exchanges between us. I urged Tanya to cut her special birthday lemon-meringue pie while it was still hot, and the lemon slid out of the crust while the white meringue followed closely behind. We laughed as I videotaped the episode, catching Tanya's *I'm not impressed* comical expression. Later, we watched a movie, and Eric reflected on it, recalling details. As a family, we created sweet memories to mark Tanya's special day.

Eric woke up several times during the night, frequently speaking about going to heaven and wondering if he had a clean heart. He examined himself to ensure he was right with God; he talked about heaven with serenity and eagerness, his life permeated with God's joy. He told me that he'd had a good life, and he didn't mind having to die young. His sensitivity to spiritual things was an excellent example for me. His mind was sharp and his responses to discussions pertinent. Another time during the night when he awoke, he was quoting from Isaiah. Then he said, "Who was it that said that I am a man of unclean lips?" I told him it was Isaiah and promised to read aloud in the morning.

Later in the day, when I was pushing him in the wheelchair to purchase groceries, we talked again about dying so young. Eric spoke in a matter-of-fact tone, "We are all different. Some people in Africa have no food all their life. Mom, some people die young. Some children in poor countries have no food. Those children have no control over their food, and I have no control over dying at age twenty-one. I don't mind dying young." Such an awe-inspiring faith.

When Tanya arrived home from work, we drove to the cemetery, and with Eric in the wheelchair, we viewed the entire area. Eric said he wanted to be buried where there would be sunshine, then when he noticed all the towering pine trees that swayed gently in the breeze, he remarked that he liked the shade as well, recanting his preferences with, "Actually, any place will do." We spent time taking in the day's sunshine, the growing flowers at the headstones, and the cool gusts of wind that refreshed our perspiring brows.

On the way home, during a lull in the conversation, Eric told us, "Thank you for taking me to see where I will be buried." He said he liked the cemetery with the lofty trees and garden flowers. Throughout the evening, he referenced the cemetery and thanked me again for taking him to "see where he would be buried." Chatting on the phone with his grandfather, he referred to the cemetery as a "really nice place." When I talked about death with Eric, it sometimes felt like it was a nebulous, far-off possibility, with the quiet, inner hope that God would still raise him to complete health and recovery. After all, as Eric confessed frequently, "Nothing is too difficult for Him."

Every night before bed, Tanya and Eric had a little ritual. Eric was childlike, and Tanya was sensitive to her brother's needs. Eric hugged his sister and said, "Good night, big sister." Tanya returned affectionate hugs with, "Good night, little brother." Tanya was extremely helpful when she was not working. She spent most of her evening relieving me and would often help feed her brother. I would use that free time to walk the dog and pray alone. Eric's disposition was so gentle, tender, and sweet, and he welcomed his sister's help and support with appreciation.

He was excited for our Bible time, and I ended at Isaiah chapter twenty-two. However, when I read chapter thirteen, Eric stopped me and said, "My Spirit understands everything." His passionate voice lifted heavenward, "I pray that Mom will get some sleep, and Lord, I pray that You make a way for Mom to get a job. I pray for Grandpa and also my cousins to know You. I pray that You bless Tanya for being such a nice sister and all the nice things she has done for me. In Jesus's Name, Amen." Then Eric said, "Good night, sweety-pie."

"Goodnight, sweety pie," I echoed, and he was asleep.

Eric woke up during the night and spoke further parting counsel about spiritual things. Every word hinged on the omnipotent, omnipresent power of God. "Mom, trust God. He is the only one you can depend upon."

I snuggled him more and told him repeatedly how much I loved him. He returned affectionately, "I want to hold on to you until I hit the grave." I, too, told him that I wanted to hold on to him and never let go and how much I would miss him. He started to speak words of encouragement to me. With my heart aching, I implored, "Eric, who will encourage me when you are gone?"

"Mom, the One in your heart. God will be with you. God will always be with you, and He will never leave you." His words were directive, purposeful and consoling and left an indelible God imprint on me. "Mom, when you feel sad, remember my Bullfrogs and Butterfly song. If you feel sad, keep those corners up." He was referring to a smile. "If you choose to feel defeated and to feel that you've been cheated, then you are forgetting one important fact—God loves you and cares about you, and he will never be far from you. Mom, you can choose to take the steps for being healed."[14] His advice reflected the theme in the album. He continued to speak inspiring words even as I jotted them down.

Another research doctor from Toronto, intending to write a scientific paper on Eric's recent diagnosis and surgery, had sent me a copy of Eric's current medical report to correct any misinformation. To follow up, he called to see if the report regarding Eric's diagnosis was accurate. I told him that I had found a few errors in the medical report. In May, the onset of symptoms was severe headache, which was not true for Eric. He'd had a grand mal seizure, interpreted as a stroke with loss of his left arm function, without headache. I casually mentioned to the doctor that I had written a homage to Eric, a synopsis of his life, strengths, character, determination, accomplishments, and most importantly, his love for God and people. The doctor, moved with grateful compassion, requested that I include my written tribute to Eric with the report, so that researchers would be

[14] Mike Deasy and Barry McGuire, "Bullfrogs and Butterflies," *Bullfrogs and Butterflies*, Music Group Candle, Alpha Omega Publication, 1978. Album.

able to appreciate Eric's impact on science—foremost, as a person who relied on God—who lived, loved, and contributed to society in more meaningful ways than just facilitating research.

Tanya worked till 9:30 p.m., and when she arrived home, Eric asked her to play cards. Tanya downplayed her skill so he could enjoy victory. She mentioned her concern to me about the noticeable rattle in his lungs, with increasingly laboured breathing. Eric had spoken often that day of being "so very tired." I suggested that morphine tended to make people sleep, and it was important that people using painkillers like morphine not drive vehicles. Tanya told me that he had related to her verbatim my explanation for the careful use of morphine.

Before Eric's Bible time, he offered a lengthy prayer for his sister, grandfather, friends, and relatives, and generally, blessings on everyone. Then I read aloud from Isaiah up to chapter twenty-eight. I thought he was asleep, but when I stopped reading, he said he wanted me to continue, and I did until his loud snoring was a signal to end.

The following day, Eric slept with brief periods of wakefulness. He whispered, "I am so tired. I feel drained." Yesterday, I attributed his extreme fatigue to the morphine. He barely had the strength to sit upright. Struggling with his balance, he spoke sincerely, "I still have one thing in my prayers that I would like to have. I would like to have some of my left movement back."

Softly, listening to his heart's cry, I asked, "Do you think you will get it?"

"If I trust in God, God can make a way. Can we pray?" Eric replied. I gently held his hand, and he prayed timidly, "Dear Lord. Can I have some of my left-hand movements before it's too late?" I, too, prayed that God would make a way where there seemed to be no way. Eric added, "I want to be able to raise my hand."

Eric's gospel music filled every corner of the room with melodies of devotion to God. He and I spoke further about spiritual matters, and he wisely instructed me, "Mom, if you read your Bible, you will grow. If you don't read your Bible and pray, you won't grow." Attentive to the song lyrics about how delightful it was to know God, Eric asked, "What does delighted mean?"

"Very happy," I replied.

His voice filled with peace and gratitude, "I am very happy for what God has done for me. He gave me friends. He made me unparalyzed when I should have been paralyzed when I had my first brain tumour. He made a way so I could have hair." Eric always appreciated his wigs. I recalled how delighted he was when we raised sufficient funds to buy his first wig around age eleven. He was so happy to have hair and always thanked God for it. His attitude continually overflowed with thankfulness even as his body declined. He was mindful of the goodness of others, and earlier, when we watched a show with a rescue team, he interrupted my attention and asked, "Mom, do you understand this? They risk their lives to save others." He was so moved by altruistic people, not recognizing that he was also such a person.

When Eric awoke from his sleep, he repeatedly lamented, "I'm so drained. I have no energy. My legs are tired. My head is tired." Exhausted, he listened to worship music. I tried to comfort him with the assurance that it wouldn't be long until he went home. He replied, "Mom, there's a whole lot of people going home. This earth is not my home, and there's a whole lot of people going home."

Eric asked to pray. His words were filled with love and life. He prayed that I would find a job, for his sister and all her needs, and then, "Thank you, Lord, for showing me where I would be buried. Please keep it nice." Then he remembered I had injured my wrist earlier and added an extra prayer, "Lord, please heal Mom's wrist and let her have a good sleep and have strength for tomorrow."

Though drained from her heavy work schedule, Tanya would always make time to spend with her brother in their nightly ritual of exchanging hugs and affectionate words before retiring for the night. He told his sister that he was taking her out for dinner the following evening. He had been eagerly holding on for days until he could give us this gesture of his love.

The following morning, he repeatedly declared, "I want to go to Red Lobster one more time before I die." Eric knew the time was near, and so did I. His decrease in energy and failing ability from day to day were alarming. Hundreds of times during the day, I told Eric how much I loved him.

He responded with gentleness, "I love you, too. My love for you will never change. You are more than a mother." Eric's affectionate appreciation and his vulnerable heart warmed my heart as I sensed the presence of Jesus with us.

Eric sang continuously, "Hear me calling, hear me calling. Just leave it to me, I'll bring you home."[15]

Throughout his waking moments, he would quote scripture or lyrics from encouraging Christian music. Often, when I would crouch by his bedside to see if he needed anything, he would say, "Thank you, Mom. Thank you for helping me, for cleaning me, for being so kind to me." When I explained how much I loved him, and he didn't need to thank me, he would say, "I only want you to hear and remember positive words."

---

[15] Michael W Smith Wayne Kirkpatrick, "I'll Lead You Home," Track 7 from *I'll Lead You Home*, Capital CMG Publishing, Union Records, 1995, CD.

I recalled the scripture, *"Finally, brothers, whatever is true, whatever is noble, whatever is right, whatever is pure, whatever is lovely, whatever is admirable—if anything is excellent or praiseworthy—think about such things"* (Philippians 4:8). Eric lived that scripture daily.

That was just like him. He only spoke positive words, so that positive words would be my memory. He was leaving this world, and he was still conscious of what he could do to help. That was all he ever wanted to do with his life, help people. He had accomplished that with all the kind words he had sprinkled on me and everyone he met.

Finally, it was time to go to Red Lobster. It was the highlight of our week as a family. He enjoyed his usual baked potato and popcorn shrimp. Tanya, Eric, and I laughed as we took silly, funny videos, and while Tanya and I wrestled over the possession of the video camera, Eric was oblivious to our commotion. He asked, "Do you think they will give me a baked potato refill?" We laughed more.

"No, because they only give drink refills," Tanya explained. But she said it wouldn't hurt to ask, and indeed Eric did ask, satisfied though his request was denied. We had to get home for 2:00 p.m. so Tanya would be on time for her second job. Exhausted upon arrival home, Eric slept.

When he woke, I lifted him, and with his arm wrapped around my neck, Eric laughed and said, "I love you so much I don't want to let go of you." I reassured him that he didn't have to let go. I was talking about hugging my neck as I carried him. He said, "Mom, I have to let go."

"Why do you have to let go?" I asked playfully.

Eric wasn't talking about the hug, "I'm going to die someday," he said solemnly.

Still hugging, I added, "Yes, Eric, and then you'll have to let go."

He changed it around. "No! *You*, Mom, will have to let go." How true. His words pierced my heart. Spiritual astuteness flourished when Eric spoke.

That night, I read from Isaiah, and after prayer, we snuggled and talked further about life and death. He said his time was soon. Eric had said yesterday in the car coming home from Red Lobster, "This is the last time I will take you to Red Lobster before I die."

He was awake, "I was thinking about a song, it's called One Day at a Time." I asked him if he wanted to sing it, and together with his feeble voice, we sang. We talked about the lyrics—about living in the moment and looking to God for his provisions. Eric quoted Matthew 6:34 *"Therefore, do not worry about tomorrow for tomorrow will worry about itself. Each day has enough trouble of its own."* He told me that God only gave us one day to live every day, so we should live in the present, making the most of that day by praying to God for His will and direction.

Eric looked pensive. "What are you thinking?" I asked.

He was sure, "Yes, there is a rainbow at end times, and Jesus is standing waiting for you. He is waiting for me. Maybe he is waiting for me in the shed of light."

I didn't understand his use of 'shed' and asked for clarification. "In heaven," he replied, quoting from Revelations 4:3 that talked about a rainbow around the throne at the end of time.

During the middle of the night, Eric frequently spoke about spiritual matters and sang spiritual songs, and I joined in. He commented, "Soon we are going to see the Lord." Then he prayed, "God, we pray for wisdom. She doesn't want me to suffer. I'd rather be in God's presence than on the earth to suffer." He was referring to me.

His reliance on God was notable, "My soul is in God's Hands. Have you ever thought how you want me to die, in my sleep or naturally?"

"What do you want?"

"I'd rather die in my sleep. I'd rather see heaven like Stephen," Eric continued, "He was stoned to death. He was stoned, but heaven was open for him."

"Do you want heaven open for you?"

"Yea," he nodded in agreement, "that would be a nice picture. That would be a nice thing to tell you, Mom. That would be nice to tell you of my death instead of going the long route."

I agreed, "I hope you don't go the long route."

"I'll take the route God gives me." Eric was resolute.

"Eric, do you want to die in your sleep?" I inquired.

"Yea, I'd rather die in my sleep," he answered, "What do you think? No more suffering. No more pain."

"Are you in pain?" I probed.

"No," he asserted, "I wouldn't be in pain if I died in my sleep. Then you can rejoice with me."

"What do you mean?" I asked.

"Because you don't like me in pain."

"That's true," I replied.

Eric concluded, "Then there would be no more suffering." He and I dialogued in the dark as he drifted off to sleep, reminding me again, "I love you.

Just remember there is a rainbow at end times." He was asleep, but I promised I would never forget his words of a rainbow at end times. I didn't know then how significant rainbows would be to me at the end of Eric's time on earth.

The next morning, Monday, August 18th, Eric spoke more about heaven. He said, "I am ready to go home. I am waiting for God to call me. I want one more Wendy's hamburger before I die." I promised him I'd swing by the fast-food drive-through.

He changed the subject, "I would like to read the book of Esther before I die." So, I sat down and read aloud the book of Esther. He stayed awake and contributed and commented appropriately as I read. Eric articulated, "All the evil things Haman tried to put on the Jews and Mordecai happened to him instead." What an astute observation!

We played Christian music all day, repeating his favourite songs. We read scripture, and he reminded me again of rainbows in the book of Revelation. "There's a rainbow at end times. Mom, trust God. He will bring me home to heaven." Tonight, when Eric prayed, he covered his sister, family, and friends with prayers to *trust God*.

After Eric went to sleep, Tanya and I had a meaningful conversation about God, our relationship, and Eric. She worked such hard, long hours; I had utterly neglected her, and I needed to confess my failure to support her in ways that she needed.

Then next morning, Eric awoke ready to hear his Christian music. "Mom, will you put on the CD with God Can Make a Way?[16] God will make a way for you to get a job, Mom." He started to sing the lyrics that talked about how God would make a way when things seemed impossible and that God works in mysterious ways.

"Thank you, Eric." I was encouraged.

He started to sing another hymn and said, "Mom, it is well with my soul." His voice sounded angelic as he sang with conviction, "When peace like a river attendeth my way, when sorrows like sea billows roll. Whatever my lot, Thou hast taught me to say. It is well, it is well with my soul."[17]

After singing, he paused, "Mom, I used to be able to play that song with both hands on the organ at Dane's house. Would you play it at my service?" My heart was breaking when I said I would.

---

[16] Don Moen, "God Will Make A Way" *Songs of Hope*, Integrity Music, 1987, Cassette. Hosanna! Music www.donmoen.com Wikipedia en.m.widipedia.org/wiki/Don-Moen)

[17] Horatio Spafford, composed by Philip Bliss, "It Is Well With My Soul," 1873, Public Domain

Later in the afternoon, we read from Isaiah to chapter forty-nine. When I read 40:11, *"He tends his flock like a shepherd: He gathers his lambs in his arms and carries them close to his heart,"* I had barely spoken the scripture when he identified with God's words and said, "Like me!" When I read 40:25–26, he commented, "The Lord! The eyes of the Lord. It's I the Lord." Isaiah 41:10, *"So do not fear, for I am with you;"* spurred him to repeat, "Fear not for I am with you" and he started singing the scripture song from Isaiah 43:1–3. Another passage, Isaiah 44: 15–17, prompted him to pipe up, "This scripture is a song on my favourite album." And Isaiah 45:6, *"so that from the rising of the sun to the place of its setting people may know there is none beside me."* Then he burst into song, singing the scripture he had quoted. Isaiah 46:11–13 states, *"...What I have said, that will I bring about; what I have planned that will I do. Listen to me, you stubborn-hearted, you who are far from righteousness, I am bringing my righteousness near; it is not far away...."* Eric added, "I come from the east to the west. People who do not listen to my words will be put on shame." When I read Isaiah 49:15–16, he interrupted me eagerly, "That's Isaiah forty-nine!" and he proceeded to quote it from memory. I stopped to listen to him. "Can a mother forget the baby at her breast and have no compassion on the child she has borne? Though she may forget, I will not forget you! See, I have inscribed you on the palms of my hands," Eric spoke with confidence.

God had given my precious son the most beautiful gift, the ability to hide His Word in his heart, for today, tomorrow, and all eternity. When I returned from Bucaramanga, Colombia, with the carved hand holding the little child cradled in the palm, Eric had asked for the scripture reference in Isaiah and immediately committed it to memory. How do you have a brain tumour the size of two tennis balls and still memorize new scriptures, remembering them months later even as your body is shutting down? I would always treasure this miracle from God.

Little things gave him great pleasure. Eric had requested Kentucky Fried Chicken, and as he sat in his wheelchair eating his meal, I was shooting a home video, and he said clearly to Tanya, "This will be the last time I have Kentucky Fried Chicken before I die." And it was.

Again, Eric was thankful, "Mom, I'm happy! I got a chance to go to Red Lobster twice. I got a chance for Kentucky Fried Chicken, a chance to go to sleep, and so far, today I haven't suffered any pain.... I slept, ate the meals I like, all that I wanted, and tomorrow I'll have more meals I want, like my Beatles." I chuckled over his nickname for his favourite taco chips. Simple things made him happy and content.

Eric had a distinctive gargle in his throat. He fell asleep, and I awoke many times fixated on his shallow breathing.

When he awoke in the morning, he wasn't hungry but heard Tanya getting ready for work. He called to her, "I love you, big sister. I love you, Tanya." Tanya affectionately doted on her brother before she rushed off to work. I told him again how much Tanya loved him, and he said, "Mom, I want to get Tanya a thank you card to thank her for being such a nice sister and to tell her how much I love her." Throughout the day, he spoke more about getting Tanya a card. He also added his words of devotion to me, "Mom, I love you so much. I don't want you to walk away from me."

Not sure what he was communicating, I asked plainly, "What do you mean?"

"I want to live with you forever," Eric explained.

"We will. We will live forever with Jesus," I assured him.

He paused, then added, "He won't go away until He sees you through. That's a word for me. He won't go away until He sees me through. That's a good word for a person in stress." Eric paused, then added, "I like that song that says God is a good God." I agreed with him on every point. Then he said, "You like looking at the past, don't you? You like looking at the positive side. Mom, He will never give up on you. He will never give up on you. You are going to get a job. He never gave up on *me*." Eric emphasized the word, *me*. Funny enough, we hadn't been talking about a job, but Eric often spontaneously encouraged me about getting a job when God's timing was right.

Showering him with affection, I said, "Eric, you are so special."

"Mom, where does it say in the Bible that love never fails?"

Fetching the Bible, I located the passage, "Corinthians, would you like me to read it to you?"

He said he would, so I turned to 2 Corinthians 13 and read aloud the chapter. He repeated emphatically, "Love never fails. Love never fails." Later, when I was feeding him, it popped into his mind, "There's a rainbow at end times. Love never fails. There's a rainbow at end times" (Revelations 10:1). He was looking forward to the rainbow around the heavenly throne of God's love. I asked Eric if he would like me to play his Christian cassette tape, and enthusiasm spurted from his fragile frame. "Oh, yes!" Praise and worship songs ignited his spirit with a burst of energy. I played the tape, and he drifted off to sleep, basking in the words of praise music. When he awoke, he asked for Isaiah, so I read aloud up to chapter sixty. His weak body slipped back into a deep slumber.

I was profoundly aware that Eric's time was short and that God could take him home even while he slept. I prayed that no matter what happened, Tanya and I would know Him, love Him, serve Him, and walk and talk with Him all the days of our lives, no matter what the cost.

Our family dog, Esther, had been very sensitive to Eric. She jumped up on the bed and refused to jump off when I commanded her, even resisting my tug at her collar. She rested her head on Eric's leg as if she knew the time was near, and Eric needed her comfort. Later in the afternoon, I wouldn't let her back on his bed when she came indoors with muddy paws; she spontaneously jumped into the tub and would not leave until Tanya returned home and bathed her. Immediately after her bath, she jumped back on his bed, her head resting on his leg. Esther had been with the children for twelve years and was very sensitive to their struggles with health.

When Eric awoke twice during the night, he moaned that his legs and the front of his head both hurt. There was some relief with morphine. He had no appetite and repeatedly voiced that he was feeling tired. In his ailing voice, he sang over and over, "Hear me calling. Hear me calling. Leave it to me; I'll bring you home." Eric was paraphrasing Michael W. Smith's song "I'll Lead You Home."

He was so ready to meet his Maker. He talked about when young Samuel thought Eli was calling him when it was really the Lord. I asked Eric if he would know when God was calling him, and he confidently answered in the affirmative. He entreated me to read the story about the calling of Samuel, so I read aloud 1 Samuel chapter three. Eric drifted off and slept until noon, and when I suggested a sponge bath, he assertively declined and explained his legs were in great pain. He asked me specifically to read Psalm 91, his favourite Psalm, that he could still recite from memory. When I asked if we should also finish the book of Isaiah since we only had six more chapters, he agreed. As I read, he remained attentive with relevant responses to my questions, although very weak.

Later in the afternoon, he felt nauseous. In the evening, after Eric prayed for his grandfather's salvation, his sister, and all his friends and relatives, he wanted to talk more about heaven. "Are you ready to let me go?" he asked me.

"Yes," I replied, "Are you ready to meet Jesus?"

"Oh, yes!" he declared. I asked Eric if he'd been ready for a long time and was waiting for me to be ready to let him go, and he said yes. He lay clutching the teddy bear that Peterborough friends had given him. He explained that he named the stuffed bear Charlie Brown because he was a clown, and it would remind me after he died that he had a good sense of humour. My heart was silently shattering moment by moment as I watched Eric's life softly slip away.

Tanya's friends, a couple from church, dropped by while she was at work and chatted with Eric, teasing him about his love for Dorito chips and that he was weird. He picked up on the playfulness, and his sense of humour followed, "Lots of people think I'm weird for lots of different reasons, and it's the only thing I do very, very well," he whispered with a grin. He spoke to Dan about his favourite songs and spontaneously sang the lyrics. "We are children of God," Eric whispered. And he fell asleep.

Tanya arrived home from work tired, having worked her second job till 10:00 p.m., and helped me tend to Eric. She gently humoured Eric while brushing his teeth and spending quality time snuggling and chatting about heaven. We prayed together and sang in unison, *"Give ear to my words O, Lord, consider my groaning. Give attention to the sound of my cry, my King and my God, for to you do I pray. O Lord, in the morning you hear my voice; in the morning I prepare a sacrifice for you and watch"* (Psalm 5:1–3, ESV). Eric and Tanya remained closely linked to each other through the common bond of their love for Jesus.

As previously mentioned, Eric's decline continued until the end of his story when he went from dreaming about Jesus to being in His presence in heaven, worshipping his Lord.

Tanya, 2, Eric, 3 months, Mom, 22, December 28, 1975

Tanya, 3, Eric, 1 year, 10 months, Mom 24, July 1977

Eric 4 yr 7 mo (last picture with his natural hair before brain surgery), April 1980

Tanya, 9, Eric, 7, Grandpa, 59, Summer 1982

Eric, almost 8, baptized CFNI, August 7, 1983

CFNI Grad Week, Dallas Texas , Tanya 11 Eric 9 and Mom 31, May 1985

Tanya, 16, Eric, 14, Esther (dog) age 4, Summer 1989

Eric, age 14, 1989

Family: Eric, 14, Tanya, 16, Mom 36, 1989

Playing piano at home: Eric, 15, 1990

Eric, 16, receiving the Award for Volunteer of the Year for Ontario, 1991

PETERBOROUGH EXAMINER   MONDAY, OCTOBER 5, 1992—

Left to right, Tanya, Janet and Eric Williamson, Peterborough's Family of the Year.

Susan Clairmont, Examiner

Family of the Year named

By SUSAN CLAIRMONT
Examiner Staff Writer

The Williamsons are more than just family — they're friends.

And, as of today, they are also Peterborough's Family of the Year as selected by a city committee.

Janet Williamson, her son Eric, 17, and 19-year-old daughter Tanya, were nominated for the award by some friends Janet knows from her involvement with Scottish country dancing.

Choosing a single-parent family to be

able, even though he's got his own handicaps. He's sensitive to anybody who has any kind of struggles."

Eric, who is in Grade 10 at Adam Scott, has been volunteering at Marycrest for three years and also volunteers at Anson House.

Tanya is also busy with volunteer work, including volunteering at the sports injury clinic at Sir Sanford Flemming College. During the summer she worked at Five Counties Children's Centre. Currently in Gr. 13 at Adam Scott, Tanya wants to be a physio therapist.

The amount of energy the Williamson's put into their community is phenomenal. And the

"We've gone out west in a Lada," she says, "we've been to Texas, Florida, Kansas, New Brunswick, Missouri, the Bahamas and Cuba."

"We travel a lot together," says Janet. "I couldn't give my kids a lot of things but I gave them trips. Consequently my kids love to travel. It's a great experience for them."

And a strong faith in God is what ties all of the other family elements together for the Williamsons.

"We have a real strong faith and belief in God as a strength and support in our life," explains Janet. "For 10 consecutive years we were at the hospital every year for one

Family of the Year Peterborough Examiner, October 5, 1992

122

Peterborough Examiner photo: Family of the Year, 1992

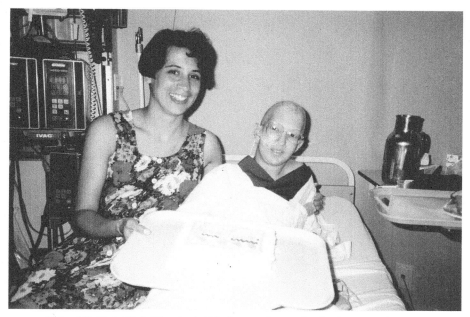

Eric, 17, Sick Kids Hospital, IV chemo, 6 months discharge, July 1993

The Wish Foundation, Snorkling Day, Maui, Hawaii, August 1993

Eric, 19, September 1994

Thanksgiving: Tanya, 22, Eric 20, Grandpa, 72, October 1995

Grandpa, 73, Tanya, 23, Eric, 21, Mom, 43, January 1997

University of Western Ontario Graduation with Grandpa, June 11, 1998

Tanya, Bachelor of Science Honours, Genetics, June 1998

PART THREE

Tanya's Journey Continued

THIS PART OF our story is told in Mom's voice, starting with where we left off after Eric's death and writing in italics flashbacks to stories before the onset of Tanya's illness. It is a victorious story, triumph over cancer, but it is also told with raw vulnerability, the mistakes that I made that needed my repentance and God's forgiveness. God is gentle to bring us closer to Him so that our expectations do not exceed our reality.

TEN

Renewing Our Vows

ONLY FOUR MONTHS after her brother's death, Tanya poured herself into her walk with God, church participation, and her honour's year thesis. She dedicated herself to her university studies and volunteered at the Cancer Regional Centre, while financially supporting herself with her part-time job.

That Christmas, Tanya and I decided to forgo our family Christmas tree traditions and instead buy and adorn a Norfolk pine with red bows to honour Eric's memory, which consoled us. He would grow in our hearts like the plant, just as he now existed with Jesus in heaven.

I had moved back to Peterborough, and my first teaching position was assigned for the new year and would last until June. However, my thoughts and energy were divided. I desired to teach well, but I also wished to commit myself to Jesus and fulfill a legacy of devotion that Eric had lived. My son's unconditional love for God and scripture had inspired me to become all I was created to be in Christ. After all, he had led the way with his example!

During a visit to see Tanya, I was drawn to the cemetery where Eric was buried, and while I sat under the shady tree next to his grave, I wept a flood of tears as I talked with my Saviour. Sobbing inconsolably for my only son, my lacerated heart melted into prayers. I talked to God about the numerous times Eric had declared, "Mummy, I love God first and you second." It brought me great joy that God had come first, a consistent thread woven through the tapestry of his life.

I prayed for God's grace so I could live to glorify Him as Eric had. He had loved the scriptures, so I read the Book of James aloud, just as I had done before he died and on previous occasions at the cemetery. Eric had spontaneously worshipped God, so I lifted my voice to sing the songs he loved most in his memory. Worship was the one thing I could still do with him, for he now lived in heaven to worship God forever.

While visiting Tanya, I also made a stop at her physician's office. The doctor greeted me with a sympathetic expression and a gentle hug, stirring indelible memories of Eric the day he died. She recalled an earlier conversation we'd had about a torrential thunderstorm with flashing streaks of lightning, which she assumed had happened at the very moment Eric had been welcomed to heaven.

The doctor's office was permeated with a mysterious stillness. We embraced the comfortable silence between us. She said that she had been moved by Eric's final words, "I am going to ask God to turn me into a rainbow, and every time you see a rainbow, you will think of me. The job of a rainbow is to help people, and Mummy, you are one of them." Of course, you can't have a rainbow without rain. Stories like this one brought me comfort.

God had comforted me in many special ways, especially through unexpected rainbows. In recent days, the sky had erupted with generous rain. I had accidentally left all my windows open, so I dashed from room to room to shut them. Then magically, the sky changed, and I was drawn to the front door. My breath was swept away by the most gorgeous sight: a magnificent double rainbow stretching across the eastern sky, a brilliant display filling the heavens with the glory of God. I crumbled to my knees with tears of joy, gazing at the astonishing beauty of it all. Spellbound, praise and worship flowed from my lips.

I saw Eric in this incredible display of colour, and his sweet melodious words echoed again in my ear. I knew God had helped me through Eric's dying words and shown compassion for my aching heart. His absence seemed insufferable… I missed him dearly!

Back in Peterborough, my thoughts were interrupted when the telephone rang. Tanya was excited that her professor had been impressed with her progress and predicted that she was destined to make a major contribution to genetic history!

I suggested we take the professor's words to God. This professor had asked Tanya what her plans might be after graduation, and Tanya had replied that she was waiting for God to reveal the next steps. She had a viable option since a leader in breast cancer research had invited her into his master's program. That same term, Tanya volunteered at the London Regional Cancer Centre researching breast cancer, so she strongly considered this possibility. It seemed like the goodness of God had opened these doors and made provision for her.

In previous conversations, Tanya had casually mentioned having felt excruciating pain behind her eyes; the doctor reasoned that this was caused by stress and the demands of her university schedule and personal life. Her brother's death had left her grief-stricken, and now she had full-time studies at the university, in her honour's year, a thesis to write, a volunteer commitment, and part-time work. She was also active in church ministry and maintained a social life. It was amazing how she was able to juggle so many activities! It was nothing short of a gift from God. Tanya seldom complained, which led me also to believe that the headaches were stress-related. We prayed together for God's grace and strength to carry her.

Shortly after this phone call, she defended her thesis on the Molecular Pathway of Colorectal Cancer. She had dedicated her work to the memory of her brother. Her future lay before her when, on June 11, 1998, she joyfully glided across the stage of the University of Western Ontario and received her Biology Degree with Honours in Genetics. The sunny skies that day paled in comparison with Tanya's radiant smile. This was a euphoric moment! I shared her joy, thankful to God that I had witnessed the first steps of her dream and had been able to celebrate her achievement along with her grandpa, other relatives, and friends present—what a remarkable day forever etched in my memory!

For now, university was over, and we anticipated the next chapter of her life while wondering where God would lead her to complete a master's degree. The interim time allowed her to relax and regroup at home over the summer. She came home where she tilled up the back yard, and then she planted a vegetable garden with dirt under her nails. Her expansive heart expressed her love for me when she designed and built a fishpond as a belated Mother's Day gift and early birthday present. She accomplished this monumental task in record time. The hole she dug was transformed into a beautiful pond with a sparkling fountain surrounded by rocks and critter ornaments, filled with water plants and darting fish. It resembled fine art, a picture postcard that I would treasure forever. Yet, something about this troubled me: why had she been in such a hurry to get this project completed in forty-eight hours? Why had she been so intense about a self-imposed deadline? Was it habit ingrained from meeting the stressful demands of university deadlines? Time would tell.

So much had transpired in a short time that it was mind-boggling! After the pond was completed, Tanya hosted a surprise party to celebrate my 45th birthday on July 16th. Without Eric, I had anticipated a dismal day until she surrounded me with a chorus of "Surprise, Happy Birthday!" that ascended heavenward.

My heart soared with delight; it was breathtaking. Over thirty friends wished me birthday blessings. The last time many of these friends had come together was ten months earlier to express sorrow and condolences at Eric's funeral. This celebration was a balm for the heart, filled with joy and good wishes.

The next day, Tanya was diagnosed with shingles, but she kept her promise to go horseback riding with our house guest. Even with medication, the pain grew worse, and her head throbbed. By the third day, the pain spiralled throughout her body. She had an intense headache, stiff neck, dizziness, nausea and vomiting. Our doctor examined her and noted that she might be experiencing a reaction to the shingles medication. That explanation sounded logical and treatable. The doctor admitted her to the hospital to have her intravenously hydrated with fluids and ordered a CT scan because of the severe headaches.

Before her shingles diagnosis, Tanya had called a geneticist, a friend at Mount Sinai Hospital in Toronto, to investigate her strange headaches. At times, she had described it as feeling like her brain was swishing back and forth, hitting against her skull. The diagnosis then had been stress. The new diagnosis from the CT scan sent a shockwave through us. The doctor solemnly delivered the news, "I have bad news. Tanya, you have a brain tumour."

My world imploded! I disintegrated into inconsolable sobs. Tanya was speechless, stoic. I should have focused on her, but I couldn't stop weeping to see her need. My already broken mother's heart was drained from the loss of Eric less than ten months before.

Devastated, I cried. How could God ask this of me again? Wasn't I in enough agony with the death of my only son? Must I suffer more? What about Tanya? She had just finished five years of university studies, her biology degree, honours in genetics, with a promising future ahead of her. What about her dreams?

I then recovered enough to realize that Tanya was in shock, numb, withdrawn, and silent, as my weeping shut her out. She was practical and couldn't believe that God would allow her to plunge into debt to earn a university degree—only to leave her an invalid or cognitively impaired should she have brain surgery. She was anxious to get on with any necessary procedure while simultaneously hoping there had been a mistake with the CT scan. We clung to each other, blinded with tears. I validated all her emotions as she opened up about them.

Returning home, I packed clothes and phoned prayer warriors to intercede for Tanya. I wondered—if I had had more people to blanket Eric with prayer, might he still be alive today? Then it occurred to me that God's power was sovereign. After I hung up, spontaneous praises turned my focus to the epitome of all truth, Jesus and the certainty of God's control returned.

The plan of action was finally decided. The best neurosurgeon would take her case, and we were immediately transported by ambulance to Toronto. At the hospital, we felt anxious awaiting the MRI results to decide if surgery was inevitable. The attending physician described the tumour as aggressive, large, and irregular, the size of a golf ball, in a difficult position on the brain's right temporal lobe. Removal would cause post-surgical limitations in hearing, vision, paralysis, and memory. The doctor was blunt, devoid of emotion, rational and swiftly delivered the verdict with a scientific tone. He was surprised that Tanya hadn't had seizures. "Tumour reoccurrence will be something Tanya will have to deal with again and again," he flatly stated.

If they removed the entire tumour, there would be maximum damage and the most limitations, but a lesser likelihood for reoccurrence. If they removed enough to make her comfortable, she would have less damage but also more tumour reoccurrences. What a quandary! Since the doctor determined it to be aggressive, Tanya and I were distraught about how to proceed. Remove all and risk massive brain damage, or remove some and risk frequent tumour reoccurrences? What horrible choices!

We agonized over her uncertain future. Amid her collapsing dreams, Tanya expressed her inability to move forward with the Lord unless she saw evidence of His guiding presence and power! I prayed with her. My heart implored our Father to reveal Himself to Tanya in a way that she would understand. I, too, needed a fresh revelation of the Lord's presence, for how would I be able to support Tanya to hold on to the Lord if she felt rejected, downcast, and confused? I, too, was struggling with uncertainty and weakness. My strength was depleted! I knew I was in the right position for God's strength to emerge. The Apostle Paul taught that weakness triggered God's strength (2 Corinthians 12:10). She and I sobbed, hugged, prayed, but still felt weak, despondent, and isolated.

Tanya struggled to understand. Again, Proverbs 3:5–6 reminded us to trust God, not our understanding. She continued to search for meaning, "Mom, it's as if God had put a cookie jar within my sight, and after working hard to earn the cookie, He pulled the jar away. Why would God let me finish all those years of university, a biology degree and honours in genetics, and submerge myself in enormous university debt, and give me the desire to serve Him in genetic research, if my intellectual functioning is going to be deficient after surgery?" I agreed. Would she be able to apply to a master's program if she was cognitively impaired? As we embraced each other, our tears mingled in prayer. She pleaded with God to reveal Himself. Then she transitioned to an adamant stance, that

God *must* tangibly reveal Himself if He was to remain real to her. Her prayer sounded like an ultimatum, and I didn't know what would happen to her faith. Through heart-wrenching sobs, I prayed in agreement with her.

From the age of six, when she had been 'born again,' Tanya had loved God with all her heart. She never wavered from her faith in God. She had already endured childhood cancers and multiple surgeries, with grave, life-threatening complications. God had seen her through adolescence, university demands, and her brother's illness. She even told her university professor that she was waiting on God for the next steps post-graduation. I couldn't suffer the thought of her rejecting God! That would be more than I could bear! Throughout Tanya and Eric's lifetime, my consistent prayer had been, "Lord, please do not allow my children's suffering to cause them to turn away from You. That would be more than I could bear." Again, that became my passionate prayer.

Tanya was logical, intellectual, and pragmatic, and I appealed to her strengths. I beseeched her, "Tanya, where would we go if we don't walk with Lord? Who else has the Words of eternal life? Don't you see the strategy of the enemy? Satan would like us to turn away from God, but we must pray for His grace to keep our eyes on Him. Promise me that we will always remain united together in our love for Jesus and our love for each other no matter what happens. You are all I have in the whole world, and you must not give up, but only surrender to God's love and power."

She agreed. We recommitted our lives to Jesus afresh, vowing in prayer and in our hearts to love Jesus, worship, serve, and walk and talk with Him all the days of our lives, no matter what the cost.

After our tearful prayers, Tanya was wheeled to her hospital room and was introduced to the patient beside her, Marie, a Christian. Marie spoke words of encouragement to Tanya about trusting God, and Tanya instantly recognized her words were words from the Lord. What were the chances of being placed in a hospital room with a Christian who would speak boldly about trusting in Jesus? It must have been God!

My father was gravely concerned for his granddaughter and offered his home, a meal and a bed to support me. The following morning, I hurried back to the hospital. Elated, Tanya declared, "Mummy, last night I was half asleep and half awake, and I had a visitation from Jesus." Savouring every word, I listened intently. "A man dressed in white came toward me. There was something in His hand, a lamb. He hugged me and extended His hand as we walked through the door. It was dark on the other side." Tanya wasn't afraid. She had pledged her allegiance to Jesus, and her reliance on God was grounded. I speculated that the darkness on the other side of the door might represent upcoming battles she would overcome while holding on to Jesus. Her downcast spirit had been encouraged with renewed hope. She had heard from God!

With confidence, she announced that she would take her chances with God preserving her intellect and authorized the neurosurgeon to remove *all* of the tumour. She said that Jesus had revealed to her that her analogy of the cookie jar gone wasn't accurate, the jar was out of sight. However, the promise of cookies was still hers, referring to her intellectual ability after brain surgery. That would become the evidence in her future that God was active in her life.

Tanya's friend, a geneticist at a neighbouring Toronto hospital, dropped in and reassured Tanya that she would speak with the neurosurgeon to influence his decision to perform surgery promptly once he understood the details surrounding her brother's genetic history and death. She acknowledged to Tanya that Eric's life and abilities were indeed a miracle, recognized as such in the medical community. Tanya was grateful for her friend's intervention. She basked in God's peace that guarded her heart and mind in Christ Jesus, certain that God was in control (Philippians 4:7).

My heart vacillated through waves of hopefulness and hopelessness. I was troubled by the reality that right-brain damage would hinder Tanya's sense of awareness. Only I would know the extent of the damage. I dismissed my anxious thoughts and replaced them with uplifting ones when our pastor from Peterborough arrived. I was still in shock as we chatted over lunch, reviewing all that had transpired. When I shared that Tanya's professor had said that she was destined to impact genetic history, he persuaded me to hang on to those positive words. I told him that Tanya had applied to a university to do her Masters in Genetics. The present felt enigmatic, like a perplexing hallucination. The last few days seemed surreal, slow-motion mingled with speed; too much had happened too fast as I reflected in conversation that only one week before, on July 16, she had hosted my surprise birthday party. How could all this be happening less than a week later?

Tanya's vivaciousness was evident as she spoke to friends, both on the phone and later with a crowd of visitors. Unscathed by the unknown, she expressed unwavering cheerfulness, "This is a new challenge, and God wouldn't have given me a challenge if He hadn't prepared me. He always prepared His disciples for everything." Tanya was exuberantly optimistic!

The surgical team, the anaesthesiologist, and later the neurosurgeon arrived and informed Tanya that surgery was scheduled immediately. The neurosurgeon had advised her that it would be two or three months before she could return to school. He suggested whole brain radiation, 5,000 rads. When I asked him about the long-term effects of massive doses of radiation, he suggested we wait for the pathology reports after the operation. He explained that the degree of malignancy would determine post-surgical treatment. I prayed for a miracle!

Tanya spent time on her hospital phone, speaking with her friends and grandfather, her jubilant personality blessing all. She asked me to sleep at the hospital, read the Bible out loud, and pray with her. For hours we talked about our hope and faith in a miracle-working God. She articulated well that God had prepared her for this new challenge and that the lessons God had been teaching her over the school term were to steel her for this gigantic hurdle. She repeated her analogy that the cookie jar was still there, only out of sight.

On Friday, July 24, 1998, I prayed with her in the surgical waiting room as nurses prepped her for surgery. I prayed for God's guidance with the neurosurgical team. I prayed that Tanya's mind would be fixed on God's Words as the last words remembered before sedation and the first words remembered when she awoke in the ICU. Tanya was jovial as they mapped her for surgery with donut-shaped stickers across her face and forehead numbered 1 to 10. She cracked jokes that she resembled one of those accident test dummies seen on TV car crash commercials. She was her natural, animated, bright self. When the nurses gave us a private moment, Tanya decided to recite all of Psalm 91 that she had committed to memory when she was a child. I bent over to kiss her and whispered in her ear my love for her and God's love for her. I watched from the doorway as the anaesthesiologist rolled her stretcher into the adjacent operating room. I was thankful to Jesus that the neurosurgeon had permitted me to stay with her.

After five hours of surgery, the neurosurgeon reported that the surgery had been successful, and it would take several days for the pathology report. I burst into praise and thanked God for bringing her safely through the operation, and I thanked the neurosurgeon for his gifted expertise, which he received humbly. I was no sooner in the ICU when Tanya stirred, squinted through swollen eyes, her head wrapped with a white, turban bandage. The oxygen machine and IV equipment hummed as she spoke coherently. She repeated twice, "Jesus is hugging me right now. I'm having a vision that Jesus is hugging me." Tanya beseeched me, "Mom, can you see Him?" I looked in her direction and all around me. "Mom, it is Jesus. Can't you see Him? He is standing at the door. He is stretching out His hand to me. He is giving me His love. He is hugging me. Can't you see Him?" She whispered with inexpressible joy.

I sensed the presence of God in a palpable way, but I couldn't see what Tanya could with her spiritual eyes. We prayed, giving thanks and glory to the Lord for His presence and protection. Then Tanya whispered that it was like the scripture we read the previous evening when the women were at the tomb and saw Jesus after He arose, but those around couldn't. I thanked Jesus that Tanya's mind was steadfast on Him. She requested I read specific scripture passages: Psalm 27, Psalm 23, Psalm 91 and Hebrews 11, 12, and 13 were among them. She said that as she was falling asleep in preparation for surgery, she had recited Psalm 91 but didn't get through the entire Psalm. I reread it, prayerfully.

In the days following brain surgery, she tested her physical and cognitive skills and found no deficits. She hadn't lost any university information and concluded that the surgery hadn't damaged her intellectually or physically. Again, we thanked our Lord Jesus for healing, and her faith in God strengthened and increased significantly. Her heart's desire to pursue a master's degree was possible! She believed these major events were merely a hiccup in God's plans, grounded firmly in the belief that God wanted her to continue her education.

Tanya and I consulted with the neurosurgical oncologist. I asked him plainly if he had any survivors ten years post-surgery, and he replied flatly, "No."

"What was the survival timeline?" I asked bluntly.

"Two years," he replied. Another dagger of despair penetrated me. Tanya was taking everything in stride. She had accepted that post-graduation studies would be postponed but remained optimistic for her future.

"Mom, I am waiting on God for direction and purpose," she said. Her tenacious, steadfast confidence in God should have grounded me, but I silently wavered. What could God's purpose be? Why was I feeling uncertainty? I was her mom, and I had lost my only son less than a year before, so when the doctor told me treatment might give her two years, I felt discouraged. However, I was encouraged and thankful that there were no changes in her personality, cognitive or physical abilities post-surgery. The neurooncologist painted a bleak picture; the radiation would cause short-term memory and hearing loss. He told Tanya to expect a year in treatment because he wanted to finish the year with chemotherapy after radiation. A year of treatment to live two years. Tanya needed another miracle of healing. I needed a miracle of grace!

Tanya felt close to the Lord with her thoughts, words, and prayers. We prayed and read scripture daily. After we finished James and the Gospel of John, we dug into the book of Acts. My unwavering prayers and hopes for her future were that her relationship with God would grow, and He would inspire her to pursue her genetic studies and bring glory to His Name.

The neurosurgeon informed Tanya that he would be comparing her malignant tissue with her brother's. Tanya asked him if he'd read the published journal articles regarding her case, and he replied he had been following her for years. He also stated he would write and publish a new and more recent updated journal article about her current condition. Tanya was pleased as they chatted like colleagues about her genetic condition. She mentioned that the intestinal pictures in a specific scientific journal, which were familiar to him, were her colon. She and the surgeon engaged in scientific dialogue. A lifetime career in genetics was Tanya's passion, and I prayed that God would fulfill her desires. *"Delight yourself in the Lord, and he will give you the desires of your heart"* (Psalm 37:4).

She was discharged five days post-surgery on Wednesday, July 29, 1998, and when we arrived home in Peterborough, we were surrounded by God's support and love through phone calls, cards, and visits. We vowed that we would always seek God's Face and not His hands and walk with Him all the days of our lives no matter what the cost. For years, Tanya had been coaching me, "Mum, seek God's Face and not His hands. The Face of God is the presence of God, and the hand of God is the blessings He gives us. Seek His presence, not blessings." Now her words were our spiritual sustenance. God was our only hope, and we clung to Him for life. We pledged to seek His Face constantly.

On August 12, I joined Tanya and her friends to celebrate her twenty-fifth birthday at a restaurant. Animated, Tanya laughed, conversed, and giggled, and I thanked God for her joyful energy. She blended in inconspicuously with her peer group as she basked in her birthday limelight. What a memorable celebration!

ELEVEN

Memories and Rainbows to Encourage the Autumn Journey

AUGUST FADED INTO September, though it seemed that time had stood still for the entire year since Eric's death. When September 6, 1998, arrived, memories of him flooded my heart. This date fell on Sunday, so the pastor compassionately acknowledged this sad anniversary as he prayed and warmly recalled Eric's life at church. I felt caught in a time warp. I'd barely begun to grieve for Eric when this new crisis with Tanya's life and death diagnosis pulled my energy and emotional resources. As on the day her brother had died, loud peels of thunder rang out while magnificent flashes of lightning illuminated the bleak sky, followed by more thunder that resounded, as it had the year before. It was as if the heavens opened and flooded the earth with my bottled tears. Tanya and I were deeply moved that God had replicated the pelting rain like on the day Eric died.

His departing words echoed anew in my heart, "I am going to ask God to turn me into a rainbow."

My heart sighed, "You can't have a rainbow without the rain."

My previous teaching assignment ended in June, and in a summer filled with crisis, I gave no thought about work until God's grace opened a door for me to accept my first permanent contract, teaching grade four. During the weeks of radiation treatments, Tanya was incredibly supportive, and after treatment, she volunteered in my class to tutor many special needs students. Her natural inclination toward students with learning challenges had been developed years before when she had tutored her brother. Again, her skills were invaluable. The students loved her and worked hard to please her.

It was one year and two days after Eric's death, and it had been a long day that lasted after school and into the evening, so the trek home was exceptionally exhausting. A sudden downpour slowed traffic. Clouds grew black and dark when patches of light and blue sky exploded through the darkness as the rain cascaded over the windshield. Then, emerging before my eyes and stretched across the highway, was a brilliant, full rainbow, a splendid arch of colour, its glory fading in minutes as the spectacular display melted back into the sky.

"Eric, Eric, Eric!" I cried, hot tears stinging my cheeks and obscuring my vision. I recalled his rainbow words that he wanted to help people, and indeed I was one of them. I prayed out loud, "It helped me, Lord, to see this beautiful rainbow and remember my cherished Eric."

God continued to bless me with more rainbows. A week later, while driving home from work in the evening, a torrential downpour forced me to reduce speed. The rain continued when the most dazzling ray of sunlight streamed boldly through the tear-drenched clouds. Like an enchanting mystery, arching across the sky, was another gorgeous rainbow in soft, effervescent colours. I praised God, awestruck, as I drove toward the rainbow that vanished and then magically reappeared in my rear-view mirror. For a moment, I glimpsed the essence of God, who was still with me when viewed through the rear-view mirror of life. I was reminded of Eric's words that you couldn't have a rainbow without the rain.

I was driving to work as the sun rose early the next morning to welcome the day like a rich, red melon glowing in the sky—the brightest, most penetrating sunrise I had ever seen. And then it happened! Suddenly, the rain that had flowed as if in a fountain tapered off to a drizzle, while in the eastern sky a morning rainbow coloured the vault of heaven. I had never seen such wonder, but God used it to comfort me with hope and assurance that I would be reunited in heaven with Christ and Eric. It felt that Father God's tangible love and presence had embraced me with special memories of Eric just because He loved me and knew how significant this special sign was to me.

Tanya and I had promised God that we would be careful to give Him all the glory for shielding her from the ill effects of brain surgery and radiation. To fulfill our commitment to honour God, we shared our testimony at church to inspire others to rely on God's love and faithfulness. A friend was moved by our testimony, which led to her church leaders inviting us to share with their congregation a few months later. We accepted the invitation. We believed that sickness was behind us, and Tanya and I were thrilled for opportunities to move forward praising God.

We were still basking in the prospects to witness God's faithfulness when another challenge hit us. Tanya received a call for an emergency MRI that had been scheduled for the next morning. We were mystified. The appointment was unexpected. What could it mean? Why had the oncologist put her on the urgent list for another MRI when she had recently received affirming MRI results after radiation? Tanya and I prayed and anticipated another opportunity to glorify God.

The following day, Tanya drove herself to Toronto for the MRI. It was late evening when a colleague dropped me off at home after work. Because Tanya hadn't returned, I assumed her MRI results must have been negative, and she was out celebrating with friends, so I went out. When I returned home later, Tanya was there sobbing on the telephone with a friend. The MRI results were discouraging. The neurooncologist had referred to the tumour as *stable* and hoped that the next MRI would show signs of *regression*. Tanya was baffled as to why the MRI results after radiation, three weeks prior, had been received with the neurooncologist's approval. We felt confused!

This ambiguous MRI report didn't prevent Tanya from volunteering in my classroom to tutor individual students and small groups for remedial English and mathematics. One morning when I woke her to accompany me to work, she declined due to a sleepless night and severe discomfort in her back and head. She said she felt depleted of energy as if a transport truck had run over her. I suggested she rest. When I arrived home late from work that day, she was still in pain but greeted me with a warm hug. Her specialty lemon chicken simmered on the stove, the table was set with candles and the good dinner plates, and she had a newsletter she had written to encourage the body of Christ. She'd entitled it, *Back in Business*.

She wrote:

"Back in the Saddle again because God is Awesome."

Hypothetically speaking. Mother, I promise that I will not horseback ride for at least…. A couple of months!!! God is good, and His mercy endures forever…. All glory, praise, honour goes up to the one who extends the hand of mercy to all mankind. "One thing have I asked of the Lord, that will I seek after: that I may dwell in the House of the Lord all the days of my life, to gaze upon the beauty of the Lord and to inquire in His temple" (Psalm 27:4, ESV).

Seek The Face of Our Lord and His Hand Will Follow:

Do not be so busy doing or wanting to do God's will that you forget to do what God asked you to do presently.

Jump for Joy to Proclaim the Faithfulness of Our Abba Father, *"Be Exalted, O God Above the Heavens! Let Your Glory Be Over All the Earth!"* (Psalm 57:5, ESV)

Well, as always, when the going gets tough, the tough get going, but only when the physician says it is okay. God has been faithful, and His mercy is extended in all situations. People may wonder what got me through all these challenges. Nothing other than God's mercy and grace can sustain us through trials and tribulations. Finding an anchor in Christ is also quite helpful. The main thing or action that sustains us is the art of prayer. What an unlimited amount of strength can be found there. (Strength in God, how?) *Rely on Him daily and pray without ceasing. Prayer support is the greatest source of strength. God is a gracious Father who allows His children to come to Him even with expectations! Mine have been to remain in the will of my Father and give Him the glory that is due Him. Lastly, the expectation for healing is that I know that he is faithful and gives us only what we can bear. (1 Corinthians 10:13)*

The Big Message:

It isn't so much what happens to you in life that really matters, but rather what you do with what happens to you that is significant. In a quick summary, what comes out of you in the tough times reveals what was there to begin with. Remember that the devil would like you (us) to be upset and angry with God or even bitter because of the challenges given to us. The challenges are for the glory we give to God as it says in Romans, "…we rejoice in our sufferings, knowing that suffering produces endurance, and endurance produces character, and character produces hope" (Romans 5:3–4, ESV). When we give God glory, even when we have to make a conscious choice to do so, we are literally stepping on the face of the evil one, thus defeating his assignment against us. Therefore, persevere in your struggles, and remember the story of when Jesus and his disciples were in the boat crossing the Lake of Galilee. A terrible storm arose, and Jesus was sleeping peacefully in the bow of the boat. An important note to this analogy is that the disciples were seaworthy men and had been through their share of storms. However, this storm scared them. Their only fault was that they put their confidence in themselves and their abilities to man a boat. They forgot the most important thing—Jesus told them that they would make it to the other side even before they got into the boat, and of course, before the storm!

Another Important Insight:

Jesus came walking on water, and Peter wanted to walk out to Him. The action of stepping out onto the water was Peter's choice. But, the surroundings, the environment, swayed his focus from Jesus to the storm. Hence, he began to sink.

Likewise, in times of entering new territory, we need to keep our focus on Jesus and take the step of faith out of the boat onto the water. Taking such a step of faith and trust is essential. I know that I do not want to miss out on God's plan because I decided that I would prefer to stay in the comfort of the boat. By keeping my eyes fixed on Jesus, not looking to the left or the right, and not worrying about the surroundings, God can then fully accomplish His ultimate will for my life. Then on judgment day, I hope that as I approach His throne, my Lord will be pleased and call me His faithful servant. Leave all circumstances and storms in God's capable Hands!!! Anchor yourself to God—you are supposed to anchor your boat and yourself to something that is fixed—so that there is maintenance of position. Remember, Jesus said that you would make it to the other side, so don't throw in the tea towel before you have experienced the maturation of your faith and trust.

Receive mercy; Give mercy:

The act of giving mercy to others because you are a recipient of mercy is the same format that we should use when we forgive. Make the choice to forgive, knowing that our Father has forgiven us and even sacrificed Himself so that we could be heirs with Him for eternity. Being a Christian is the constant act of dying to self."

Tanya not only believed the words that she had written while in pain—she lived them. Indeed, *'being a Christian was the constant act of dying to self.'*

Two weeks later, on November 13, 1998, God unexpectedly revealed his love to me in a way that I understood. At school, after the recess bell rang, a stampede of children filed into line. The sixth graders were disruptive. I permitted the quieter grades to enter the school first. The chatty older students had their necks craned skyward and urged me to look up. Like an umbrella directly above my head, there was a glorious circular rainbow. I gasped in wonder and amazement. Making only a feeble attempt to settle the children, I gazed heavenward, spellbound, my mouth agape, fixated on this stunning, spectacular rainbow of soft hues hovering over my head like an angelic halo, a drop ceiling of colour borrowed from heaven.

I thought of Eric, "I'm going to ask God to turn me into a rainbow... The job of a rainbow is to help people." The thought of his words comforted me as I prayed aloud, "Thank you, Jesus, for Eric. Thank you for this circular rainbow, a sign of hope that has helped me." With my concerns for Tanya and the demands of student report cards looming, the rainbow and memory of Eric's positive assurance defused my stress. Since Eric's death, I had seen rainbows in the evening, in the early morning driving to work, and now after morning recess. God's heavenly colours were displayed directly above my head, drawing me anew closer to Jesus. My constant prayer was that Tanya and I would love God and walk with Jesus always, and the rainbows inspired me. I wanted to serve God always. Tanya often told me that when she meets the Lord, she would love to hear, "Well, done, good and faithful servant!" (Matthew 25:21). Me, too!

Tanya started having fluctuating high fevers in the fall, fighting a virus. When she felt well enough, she volunteered in my class again and kept her commitment to her high school science supervisor to design and teach a genetic unit.

Even though she wasn't feeling well, Tanya coordinated and led a worship service that combined the college adults and high school students singing together. As one of the soloists, she realized that she had difficulty hearing the music and reaching some notes. After the service, the headaches behind her eyes became so piercing she went for tests. There were still no answers to explain the pain. The year had ended with pain, and the new had begun with pain.

TWELVE

Keeping the Faith Through Winter's Journey

AS THE NEW year began, Tanya returned to the hospital for more investigation. The MRI results devastated us. I felt bewildered, despondent—perhaps I was praying amiss. Shocked, I gasped in disbelief. A seismic wave of grief threatened to swallow me. The neurosurgeon's words reverberated through the recesses of my being, and my eyes pooled with tears. He explained that Tanya had four brain tumours in four different locations. Four brain tumours! Dazed, I repeated it over and over, "I just don't understand. I just don't understand." Proverbs 3:5–6 washed over my mind as I searched for answers, reminded by the scriptures to trust Him when I couldn't understand.

I prayed silently, "Lord, You tell me to trust You with all my heart, but all of my heart is shattered and aching for Tanya. Jesus, we need your grace and strength." Alone with the diagnosis, we prayed, imploring God for understanding, wisdom, and healing. Tanya remained coolly detached from the new diagnosis, emotionally paralyzed. This extended nightmare seemed surreal. The throbbing pain of more cancer exploded into deep grief.

The day after her new diagnosis, Tanya attended her interview at the Board Office for work at a local high school as a supply science teacher. She also had a commitment at her former high school. She had submitted her course outline with plans to teach a genetic unit to the students. She prepared quizzes and was determined to teach the unit and report the student grades to her supervisor as planned. She was adamant that brain cancers would not interfere with her obligations. There was no evidence of cognitive or physical limitations from the surgery, radiation, or four brain tumours, so we simply believed they weren't obstacles for God. She continued her volunteer work. I never ceased praying for healing.

When Tanya and I prayed together before bed, I pleaded with God, "My Father, if it is possible, may this cup be taken from me."

She inserted her prayer and finished my sentence, "Yet, Lord, not mine but Thine will be done."

I was silently disturbed by her prayer. How could she pray that so freely? I wanted God's will to be healing for Tanya. Was that selfish? We asked God for divine intervention. Was that wrong? Tanya had prayed the psalms of hope for a future and long life while simultaneously surrendering the outcome to Him. I felt bemused. Shouldn't she be focused solely on healing? Back in July, I believed that Tanya had been healed and defeated cancer. I clung to God with that belief.

On Sunday, January 10, after the morning service, Tanya and I knelt at the altar. We committed ourselves to Jesus anew, that no matter what happened, we would always love God, worship, glorify, walk, and talk with Him all the days of our life. Satan came to kill, steal, and destroy (John 10:10). We recognized that Satan would attack our minds to divert our attention from Jesus to the existing challenge of four brain tumours. We had determined to trust God and put our hope in His faithfulness regardless of the cost. *"Though He slay me, yet will I hope in Him"* (Job 13:15).

On the days when Tanya wasn't teaching the high school students or working at the second job tutoring, she volunteered in my grade-four classroom, coaching students in math and language. We were studying Medieval Times, and to demonstrate our theme Tanya drew a life-size knight and noble lady, displayed it on my classroom walls, and subsequently it was admired by students and staff. Although she was active and engaged in living her life, I contacted the school Human Resource Representative if I needed a sudden leave of absence. He suggested that with the cumulating stress I ask my principal to exempt me from the scheduled teacher evaluation. My principal lacked compassion, and she refused. "Lord, I need more grace," was my constant prayer.

During the times that Tanya taught at the high school, she recognized her love for teaching science. She decided to apply to Teacher's College at York University in Toronto. Immediately, they emailed a reply that the cut-off date for Teacher's College applications was December 1st, 1998, but they would be willing to accept her late application. It was well into January. This had to be the hand of God orchestrating her future! God had allowed her to be accepted to university for the coming fall even as she was inflicted with four brain tumours. I saw this as evidence that she would be healed!

By the middle of January, Tanya's left leg was extremely painful. Her neck was stiff and shoulders sore, so the oncologist booked another MRI for a baseline entry to the clinical trial, SU101. She also emailed the neurosurgeon and hoped that the tumours were operable. They were not.

With so much to process, we compartmentalized all the recent challenges and put suffering on hold. We decided that fun activities would divert our attention. Tanya and I went to our favourite restaurant for shrimp and crab legs and ruminated about our last family meal at this restaurant shortly before Eric died. We talked non-stop on many non-medical topics, light, airy conversations. Tanya's treasured, detailed childhood memories were full of fun and humour. We talked about her ability to be methodical. Her organization skills were a strength that I admired and sorely lacked. We talked about when I had travelled to Europe for a month when she was a teenager, and I had called her at intervals to see how she was managing. She had been delighted to report the house stayed neat, the dog was happy, her job was going well, and she was thriving in my absence. She juggled many activities with her superb time-management skills. At the restaurant, she recalled numerous stories about Eric and their escapades together that entertained me for hours. I tried to etch her delightful memories into my mental journal.

Another mental compartment was reality. Upon returning home, I talked to a trusted friend about my entangled feelings as I tried desperately to comprehend what God was doing. I felt like I was wading through muddy waters that were rising with every step. I told my friend that I cried out to God and heard only silence. Why couldn't I hear from Him? I exposed myself to her, but she lacked understanding. Instead, she instructed me to surrender all and reminded me that the rich, young ruler who wouldn't surrender all lost all.

I listened to her spiritual admonishment and felt disconnected; she hadn't understood. I asked her if it was unreasonable that I wanted Tanya to live and to grow old? I was her mom and had already watched my only son die. Children were born to outlive their parents. I knew what could lie ahead, and I wanted my only daughter, my only surviving child, to live. Was that selfish? I had prayed that God would have mercy upon Tanya and spare me "sorrow upon sorrow" (Philippians 2:27).

(I have shared this story, leaving my friend nameless, so that believers in the midst of a crisis or struggle who have made themselves vulnerable might also consider that the one listening is also on a journey. They may say things that don't resonate. We must keep our eyes and heart focused on Him. If words of admonishment don't resonate, the expression, "don't throw out the baby with the bathwater," applies. We should be sensitive that believers may sincerely be trying to help in their counsel, while also noting that this counsel is coming from their current place of spiritual maturity and insight.)

A few days later, when we attended church, Tanya's pain had escalated to excruciatingly sharp jabs in her legs, catapulting the pain to her arms and back. She suffered in silence. I felt so alone in the absolute stillness of the crowded church service. A fellow parishioner asked me about Tanya's university plans for the fall. She didn't know that the pain Tanya had been battling had become our focus, and university in the fall was becoming a wistful, fading dream. The words choked out when I disclosed that Tanya now had four brain tumours.

I was feeling desperate for prayer. I telephoned Mama and Papa Blessing in the United States. They had adopted us as their spiritual children when we had attended Christ for the Nations in Dallas, Texas, from 1983 to 1985. When I broke down in a desperate plea for prayer, they passionately prayed for miraculous healing. I sensed God's presence as their focus directed us to Jesus. I realized that sometimes all we needed was someone to pray with us.

Tanya's neurooncologist had suggested an experimental clinical trial, a phase 3 study called SU101, a drug with risks not approved for public use. However, the subject selection was randomized and not guaranteed to her. We decided to explore this unconventional means of healing. We asked the neurooncologist more about the promising SU101 clinal trial. Tanya had researched the drug, and the doctor used terms Tanya understood to explain it. The loading dose consisted of six hours of SU101 IV infusion for four consecutive days. Then she would receive a weekly maintenance dose for six hours. He added that the tumours wouldn't shrink but only cease to grow. I was optimistic that God could make them shrink, even disappear. I pondered the words of Tanya's professor that she was destined to impact genetic science, and the disappearance of tumours would be a genetic anomaly that would definitely impact science. Tanya lived her life to glorify God, and what a marvellous way to do it through the scientific community!

SU101 started on January 26, and the six hours of IV infusion went smoothly. Even though it had been a long day, Tanya's immeasurable tranquillity oozed from her sunny disposition.

Many of my prayers were spoken, many unspoken, but all were emotionally draining. I believed God's love would buoy us up in His grace and strength.

I believed Tanya and I would be available in years to come to offer speaking engagements and write a book to glorify God, as we had often talked about. I believed Tanya would be healed!

We investigated the constant pain in her ribs and discovered that they were broken. In addition, she had intolerable pain under a previous surgical incision scar and pain in her back, shoulders, neck, and legs. Apart from these, there wasn't a hint of repercussions from the multiple brain tumours, no cognitive or personality changes. This astounded the neurooncologist.

With the IV pole as her attached appendage, Tanya hobbled over to the adjacent hospital to speak with her gastrointestinal surgeon about the horrendous pain under her abdominal scar. The surgeon examined her and reassured her with no concerns about abdominal complications.

This triggered our memories of past surgeries and her ability to push through discomfort toward new adventures and a full life. Reminiscing was an escape to past recollections that encouraged us in the present.

On her fourteenth birthday, when she had her large intestines removed due to malignant polyps, she endured a year of post-surgical complications followed by a period of wellness. Immediately after, Tanya reengaged in living life to the fullest. She was a self-advocate, confident to ask questions and seek answers. She asked me if she could take horseback riding lessons, and I had replied with an unequivocal no! With the removal of her large intestines, I imagined an empty cavity in her abdomen that, when jostled by the movement of a horse, would cause her internal organs to shift. I thought my response was logical but unconvincing. "Mom, if I ask my surgeon, Dr. F, who is also Chief of Surgery at the Children's Hospital, and he says it is okay, will you permit me to take horseback riding lessons?"

Surely, I couldn't argue my case with someone with that calibre of expertise, so I agreed. Tanya contacted the surgeon, and after she offered a synopsis of her case and he agreed with her, she handed the phone to me. The surgeon affirmed her desires and confirmed that horseback riding would be beneficial and not jeopardize her health.

She found an instructor and started lessons immediately. The lessons were lengthy, so I stayed and watched her progress as she gained skill and confidence on the horse. To my horror, during one of her lessons, the horse bucked her off, and she sat stunned on the dirt. Her instructor sternly ordered her back on the horse and later explained that it was imperative that the rider not feel intimidated by a horse—getting immediately back into the saddle regains control and confidence. That applied to our life lessons past and future. When you fall off with life's disappointments, you get back into the saddle of life. Horseback riding was the highlight of Tanya's week. She became a skilled rider, and a few years later, she volunteered at a Christian ranch for children as the Horseback Rider Trail Leader; she cleaned the stables and groomed the horses as part of her volunteer service.

Her love for horses and people was evident when she promised our adolescent house guest that she would take her horseback riding last summer; even with a shingles diagnosis, she kept her word. That was Tanya! She was my example to follow!

Childhood memories sustained us, and we called on them frequently. We encountered a scientist, researcher, and friend at the hospital, Cherri, who had followed our family's genetic story for decades; we appreciated her interest in our personal lives. She was another part of God's signature of ongoing support.

Tanya wasn't anxious. She was quietly resting on the promises of God for a long life and a hopeful future. *"With long life will I satisfy him and show him my salvation"* (Psalm 91:16). I, too, sought God's peace and promises. Sometimes when the threat of death loomed, I reached deep into the Word of God planted within and quoted scripture that restored my peace. We spent many opportunities reminiscing. I listened as Tanya described many childhood memories with clarity and detail as we waited for appointments and procedures. It was comforting to hear her speak as an adult with contentment and joy about her childhood experiences.

The oncologist said that Tanya's only hope was the SU101, but he was incorrect; her only hope was in Jesus Christ. Tanya filled out a Quality-of-Life questionnaire for the clinical trial data. She wrote this comment in response to a question about her quality of life during this trial, "My life quality is dependent on my relationship with God, and everything else is a blessing." Wow! What a confession of faith!

Despite painful, sleepless nights, we attended church when we were home again. When Tanya was invited to watch the Super Bowl with the Adult College Group after service, she accepted with joy. I, too, was grateful that she could compartmentalize her affliction and enjoy the company of her Christian peers.

Tanya pushed past her pain and anticipated good things. She accepted, with me, an invitation to speak at a church in March, and she decided that prayer would be the topic for the message. We determined that no matter what adversity would come, we would keep this commitment to glorify God.

Another conundrum was the subtle changes she observed in her performance. She sang a Christian song and corrected herself when she sang off-key. I tried to convince her that the air quality in the house was the culprit, but she brought to my attention other subtle changes she had observed when she typed emails.

She made errors when using her left hand, so she compensated by reducing her typing speed. Tanya and I had wondered if the SU101 interfered with the quick automatic response necessary in typing. It sounded rational. She planned to discuss this at her upcoming appointment with the neurosurgeon.

The next day, on a rainy, fog-laden freeway as trucks sped past, obscuring our visibility, we drove to the Toronto hospital. Inspired through scriptures, Tanya spent most of our journey brainstorming and making notes as she prepared an uplifting sermon on prayer that we planned to deliver as guest speakers in March. Her theme and ideas resonated with me.

At the hospital, I was disturbed by the neurosurgeon's findings, but Tanya took it in stride. Before he disclosed his MRI report of her spine, Tanya told him the sixth lumbar vertebrae felt most abnormal when she had pressed her fingers to her spine. That was precisely the area that was atypical on the MRI. The neurosurgeon was impressed with her knowledge and respectful of her familiarity with her genetic history. They conversed like professionals. He believed a cancer cell travelled through the cerebral spinal fluid down the spine and lodged in the lower lumbar. He suggested she take a more aggressive approach and use both systemic treatment, the SU101, and radiation to the spine. When we addressed the possibility of further surgery, he said that Tanya was asymptomatic, cognitively astute, and surgery wasn't warranted. Her calm demeanour, an aura of peace, prevailed as she quietly contemplated this new development. I was feeling confused and disorientated!

Cancer in her spine!

Four brain tumours!

Cancer suspected in her bone marrow!

The seriousness of her condition became more apparent with every test result. She needed a miracle! Tanya had peace that passed understanding, a gentle spirit, and an inquiring mind. I felt troubled, constantly praying in my heart, "Dear Father God, we need You! We need You! Have mercy on Tanya! Have mercy on me!"

After our appointment, we drove to my father's flat in Toronto. Even with the disturbing report of cancer in her spine, she wanted to bless her grandfather and prepared her lemon chicken dish. We enjoyed her culinary skills, and as I started to clean up, I could hear the squeaky apartment floors and the bathroom door echo as it shut. Suddenly I fled toward her cries, "Mummy, Mummy, come here!" Cramped in the confined tiny bathroom, Tanya's body convulsed into a grand mal seizure. Alarmed, I prayed in tongues, beseeching the Lord's intervention.

The paramedic arrived within minutes of Dad dialling 911. The seizure subsided, but Tanya's left arm lay limp, as if lifeless and detached from her body, as the ambulance sped to the hospital.

At the Hospital Emergency, the physician was astounded at Tanya's low hemoglobin and cautioned her to receive a blood transfusion before her SU101 infusion the next day. Equally alarmed, he reported that Tanya's anti-convulsive medication levels were significantly lower than the therapeutic range and immediately administered a daily dose. As strength returned to her arm, the muscles remained exhausted. At Grandpa's apartment, our evening prayer time was most important before we snuggled in bed for the night. It was a sleepless night. Her back ached with excruciating pain even as I massaged it, and she was apprehensive when I escorted her to and from the bathroom.

The next day, we reported the events to the nurse: the MRI results, the neurosurgeon's warning to be aggressive with the treatment, the seizure, and the low haemoglobin. Another bone marrow test was conducted. Tanya said that extracting the bone marrow, though painful, wasn't as agonizing as the seizure. The neurooncologist explained that radiation to the spine, as the neurosurgeon had suggested, wasn't viable since the bone marrow tumours were throughout her body, and one can't radiate every bone. He thought the sudden drop in haemoglobin was due to the bone cancer since haemoglobin is produced in bone marrow. He suggested a blood transfusion to boost her level, followed by the SU101 treatment. Although this complex trauma was challenging, Tanya remained steadfast. She accepted the logic that frequent blood transfusions would be necessary to continue in the trial.

We prayed over the blood that God would purify it so that only the blood of Jesus would flow through her veins. They scheduled another blood transfusion for the next day, followed by six hours of SU101 treatment.

Even in her suffering, Tanya was concerned about me. Before they hooked her up for the blood transfusion, she called my friend Deanna, who worked in Christian Television Ministry and who supported and prayed with me. Imagine, my dear Tanya was enduring horrendous suffering, and she called my friend for my support. How great was God's love being expressed through Tanya!

I shared with my friend the recent events and complications. I felt numb, spiritually drained from the setbacks. I needed to unload. My friend's prayer confirmed Jesus's presence. I knew God was with me, and He would never leave me nor forsake me (Hebrews 13:5). God had placed so many wonderfully supportive godly people in my life that directed my focus back to Him. I recognized the miracle that Tanya hadn't lost cognitive functions through all this trauma, and her memory of the past and present remained untouched. Her personality hadn't changed with the pain. I interpreted this as God's endorsement that she would be healed and fully recover.

Travelling down memory lane was an escape to the past, to embrace God's faithfulness. One of Tanya's strengths was that she was a person of her word. I taught the children that this was the most significant thing they could give me and others. Do what you say and say what you do with no excuses—no hurtful words, only words to encourage and support one another. If you couldn't keep your word, it was your responsibility to go to the person and say what you had intended to do and the reasons why you changed your words. Therefore, I could count on her word, and she could count on mine.

When we negotiated an agreement, I would relax knowing that whatever Tanya had agreed to was a done deal. I recalled when our words hadn't been clear. Garbage day was a comical drama of racing against time to get the bins outside before the truck's screeching wheels halted at our door. We made a mad dash from room to room to empty trash and sprinted to the curb just in time to relay the garbage can to the worker's hands. It was an exhausting ordeal, so I sat with Tanya to discuss the problem. She insightfully observed that I nagged her to put the garbage out, and she disagreed that it was solely her job. We redefined her job description and classified it as her weekly responsibility. She asked me to refrain from nagging, and she agreed that I could remind her with one prompt. If the trash wasn't out by 11:00 p.m. the night before, I had permission to wake her up, and she would willfully comply. I kept my end of the bargain, and for weeks everything went smoothly until there was a glitch. A late evening, more homework than anticipated, an unscheduled commitment, whatever it was, Tanya was tired and asleep by 10:00 p.m., and the trash was still in the house. As per our agreement, I waited until one minute past eleven o'clock and crouched by the side of her bed, my lips to her ears, softly chanting, "Tanya, don't forget the garbage. It's 11:01. Garbage, remember, garbage."

She stirred, groggy with sleep, "Mom, can I do it in the morning?"

I continued to whisper my reply, "I trusted your words, and you gave me permission to wake you up after 11:00 p.m., and you agreed you would put it out. Well, it's after 11:00. Garbage time." I whispered in a gentle, matter-of-fact tone.

She couldn't sleep. "Okay, I will." She slid out of bed, marched the garbage to the curb without complaint, and returned to the comfort of her restful sleep. She never forgot again. Keeping your word continued to be the crux of our family unity.

During her blood transfusion, she delighted me with detailed accounts of her childhood memories, and she shared the scriptures dear to her. I recorded them. *"I delight in your decrees; I will not neglect your word"* (Psalm 119:16). *"This is the confidence we have in approaching God: that if we ask anything according to his will, he hears us"* (1 John 5:14). *"For nothing is impossible with God"* (Luke 1:37, ESV). *"One thing I ask of the Lord, this only do I seek: that I may dwell in the house of the Lord all the days of my life, to gaze upon the beauty of the Lord and to seek him in his temple"* (Psalm 27:4). *"But my eyes are fixed on you, O Sovereign Lord; in you I take refuge—do not give me over to death"* (Psalm 141:8). *"I am still confident of this: I will see the goodness of the Lord in the land of the living"* (Psalm 27:13). *"You may ask me for anything in my name, and I will do it"* (John 14:13). Tanya had received these scriptures during the summer as reassurance when she had had her first battle with this horrific disease, and reviewing them renewed her faith.

The following two days found her tied to an IV pole for twelve hours—six hours for blood transfusions and another six for treatment. To pass the time, we planted ourselves in front of a comedy movie and laughed nonstop until our sides ached. It was a snapshot in time when nothing in the world existed except for slap-stick comedy and silly humour. Truly, laughter was the best medicine!

THIRTEEN

Words Impact Us on Our Journey

AFTER THREE GRUELLING days, we were en route home to Peterborough. Many supportive people had left messages on the answering machine, including church friends Barbara, Dennis, Winola, Nick, and the pastor. I returned Barbara's call and thanked her for her prayers and expressed how her message cheered us.

Later I received an unexpected call from a Christian woman with whom I'd had a previous disturbing conversation, in which she had claimed that I had "used her" at Eric's time of passing. I had called her for prayer frequently, without thinking I was *using* her. Her comment that she had felt *"used"* made me question if it was possible to feel *used* when praying for another. I had often prayed, *God, use me.* What did that really mean? Tanya scribbled a note that urged me to tell the woman to pray about the conversation, and to apply forgiveness. After the discussion, Tanya and I prayed for her and forgave her.

Words were important. They could wound, or they could heal.

God had *used* many people to support us. As Tanya entertained two church friends who prayed with her, another woman we knew from church called and prayed, followed by yet another who held up our weary arms with prayer. Our church family rallied around us in prayer, and I prayed that God would return immeasurably more to these supportive Christians than they had given to us and that God would *use me* to help others when they needed prayer and love.

That Sunday, dog tired, I emailed our pastor explaining we wouldn't attend service because of seizures that necessitated a 4:00 a.m. hospital visit. The minister read my prayer request to the congregation. As a result, many believers phoned to encourage and pray with us. A friend of Tanya's called to find out if she was well enough for company and a movie, and on Tanya's behalf, I invited her over. However, shortly after this call, Tanya awoke, plagued with more seizures.

She interrupted the seizure's progression up her arm by focusing on Jesus by singing praise and worship songs. Tanya reasoned that the seizure on one side of her body indicated that neurons were firing erratically in the opposite side of her brain. So, by activating the part of the brain not involved in the seizure by singing, she could reduce or interrupt its intensity. That's what we did as I sped to the hospital with her that morning. We sang worship songs to redirect her thoughts from the seizure to God. Seizure activity occurred every twenty minutes throughout the day, so we sang every waking moment. I asked Tanya if she would like us to record our worship time together, and she agreed. She woke many times during the night requesting me to sing worship songs with her to intercept pending seizures.

The pain in her bones grew increasingly unbearable, along with the pain in her joints, lower back, and hip. Her eyes wouldn't focus, she was unsteady on her feet, her gait was unbalanced, and her left arm flopped limply in pain from the on-going seizures. God comforted us as we recited scriptures. My good friend, Karin, dropped by with a timely word of encouragement, a fervent prayer, and a meal. Karin and I attended the same church and her friendship, generous heart, sensitive understanding of our suffering, and faithful prayers, encouraged me to find solace in my faith. Later, Tanya's two church friends, Elle and Selena, visited. God sent so many supportive people who offered kindness in spiritual and practical ways.

After her guests left, the phone rang, and Tanya answered it. She barely spoke; she only acknowledged the conversation with grunts. She hung up, seemingly detached. The caller had been the clinical trial nurse with disheartening information. In a voice void of emotion, Tanya shared, "Mom, they will continue to do blood transfusions so that I can stay on SU101. The official bone marrow results showed the same cancer that is in my brain. Mom, the cancer cells' growth rate is escalating, which explains the increased pain level that I am feeling." Tanya spoke frankly in a placid tone that reflected her exhaustion.

The aggressive cancers in her brain, spine, and bone marrow were advancing. She was weak and weary, yet such a warrior. We prayed, pleading for her life and healing. I focused only on healing. In an instant, God could reverse these cancerous effects, eradicate every malignant cell, and heal Tanya completely. Why wouldn't God heal her? How far would He let her go in pain and the metastatic spread of the disease? Why did she have to journey on this road of illness? How did this glorify God? I searched my heart for answers, but the only answer I heard was Proverbs, 3:5–6. I was to trust God, lean not to my understanding, and follow His directions. Tanya had prayed the scriptures of hope that she believed God had given to her, clinging to the knowledge of God's love, and focused on the Truth of all truths, Jesus Christ. I knew God was faithful, and He would not let her hopes be dashed. Yet oddly, I felt fleeting moments of abandonment and aloneness in my solitary darkness. When these negative thoughts resonated too long, I knew I needed prayer.

I phoned my spiritual parents, Mama and Papa Blessing. They had alerted the CFNI student body in Dallas, plus two American television ministries, to include her on their prayer chain. It stirred hope when they invited us to share our testimony when Tanya's healing was manifested. We accepted their invitation with anticipation of glorifying God. We shared with them that we had also accepted a speaking engagement at a local Baptist Church in March, steadfast in faith that God would heal Tanya for this occasion, so we might exalt Him and encourage believers to focus on God with prayer.

Reverend David Mainse at 100 Huntley Street, a television ministry in Toronto, returned Tanya's phone call, prayed, and encouraged her to stay in touch.[18] Tanya felt God's presence, and she was grateful that Reverend Mainse had used his time on the weekend to phone and pray for her. God was allowing so many people to be available to pray for Tanya. Surely that meant she was going to be healed.

At her SU101 treatment, I privately asked the neurooncologist for *aggressive treatment* strategies as the neurosurgeon had recommended. The neurooncologist explained that there were no aggressive treatments apart from SU101—it was systemic, and it wasn't feasible to radiate every bone in her body due to cancer in the bone marrow. Every cell of her body, every organ, every place where blood travelled would have cancer. He said the cancer cell travelled to the bone marrow by blood in the first place. It was quite rare that a cell from the brain would cross the blood barrier and metastasize from the brain to other organs. He repeated that Tanya's case was so rare he didn't know what to do. He said, "*It's basically guesswork.*"

I collapsed into a heap of tears, but after the doctor left, my tears merged into prayers. I couldn't go back to the treatment room where Tanya was undergoing her SU101 when I was so broken and distraught. I was totally lost as to why Tanya had to suffer so much.

I phoned the neurosurgeon to define aggressive treatment. He was evasive, and he confessed Tanya's case was unprecedented. A second opinion would be

---

[18] Reverend David Mainse Founder of 100 Huntley Street, (1977), Toronto Ontario; used by written permission.

Dr. C in London, known to Tanya through her volunteer work at the Cancer Regional Centre and a brief involvement with Eric. Tanya had also contacted him several months earlier when she had been investigating a novel treatment in Texas. His response had been discouraging. What was God showing me? What was God teaching me? I searched for His direction on this path of uncertainty. "... *This is the way, walk in it*" (Isaiah 30:21). I prayed, "Show us your way, O Lord."

While Tanya remained in the hospital, her friends from church, Selina and Elle, visited for over two and a half hours leaving her strengthened and validated, reinforcing her belief for healing. While the girls were talking, the hospital bedside phone rang. It was my dear friend Sharon, with whom I had shared how God had given Tanya grace to refocus her thoughts away from the seizure activity by singing worship songs to Jesus. Sharon reminded me how blessed I was to have a child who would intentionally focus on Jesus through inexorable suffering. Indeed, I was blessed! During our evening prayer time, Tanya spoke confidently about the promises of God for a long life, and that her hopes would not be dashed. I joined her in belief.

While still hooked up to the SU101 for treatment, Tanya's lethargy became worse, and it worried both of us. She asked me to call the neurooncologist in London and suggested I use her friend's phone, a Genetic Counsellor at the adjacent hospital. Her friend accommodated my request and offered me privacy by visiting Tanya while I was on the phone. She was the one who had inspired Tanya to pursue her honours in genetics at Western University, and later, to pursue a master's in genetic counselling.

The next day, treatment was over, and Tanya attended art therapy. On route to the class, Cherri, the researcher involved with our family for many years, greeted us at the elevator with a pillow and a hug; that kind gesture emphasized God's provisions. During her art session, Tanya shared her faith and belief in God with other patients. Her approach was humble and inviting.

Meanwhile, I had phoned the neurooncologist, Dr. C, in London. I was searching for a second opinion lest we learn in six weeks that Tanya should have combined another drug with the SU101. The doctor stated that there were no other drugs to work with SU101, and with Tanya's genetic history, chemotherapy had already proven to be ineffective. He suggested she continue with the SU101 and only introduce other drugs like thalidomide, thermoxacyde, P.C.U., CCNU, procarbazine, and vincristine if SU101 became ineffective, noting these drugs would be inferior. His soft-spoken response resonated with compassion. He admitted several times that he didn't have the answers and didn't know enough about Tanya's condition. I related my conversation to Tanya, and she remained steadfast in her position that God would heal her for His glory.

Tanya had never demonstrated a hint of anger, distress, or fear. No matter what words of doom and gloom were spoken, she stood firmly planted in Christ, peacefully clinging to the promises of God she adopted from scripture. I confessed to God that if there were any hidden sins, rebellion, or anything that grieved the Lord in my life, or that would interfere with God's pathway of power and healing to Tanya, that by His grace He would tell me specifics so that I could confess my sin, repent, and turn from my ways. I sought truth. I realized that I was vulnerable to deception, so I tried to keep my eyes, heart, mind, and spirit tuned in to Jesus. I knew experientially that God loved us, and Tanya wasn't concerned about a point in time when God would heal her. She was confident He would! My doubt, based on my experience with Eric, did not diminish my knowledge that God had the power to heal him, but for some reason, He had chosen not to. I knew I must not extrapolate from Eric's experiences the same outcome for Tanya.

The following day, Friday, February 12, 1999, we planned to visit a friend, Deanna, who lived a far distance from our city of Peterborough. However, I wondered if the visit was rational with approaching inclement weather until Tanya convinced me with a story from her memories.

It was a time when blustery weather didn't deter us from pursuing an impromptu vacation. Eric and I had chatted about travel memories, so for fun, I spontaneously called a phone line that offered last-minute travel deals. The operator said she had an all-inclusive, airfare, four-star hotel, and all you could eat meals for a week for a ridiculously low price if we could leave early the next morning. I immediately called my principal, and he excused me from work. Tanya arrived home around 10:00 p.m., weary from a full day at school and her evening babysitting obligation. Eric greeted her with vivacious delight, "Pack your bags. We are going to Cuba, now!" Tanya wasn't amused by his late-night humour and proceeded to her room to undress for bed. I echoed his words. Then, when the reality gripped her, she animatedly joined in our exuberance. We packed and drove through the night, crawling through a blinding blizzard. The children were wrapped in blankets to stay warm because the car heater wasn't working, and our windows had to be rolled down so we could scrape freezing rain and ice pellets from the windshield so we could see. We laughed wholeheartedly, sang worship songs, and prayed, thanking Jesus for the opportunity. We would soon be on a beach basking in the sun. Hours later, we arrived at the airport, our flight delayed due to the adverse weather. Our plane was the last to leave the tarmac before all flights were cancelled.

Through our heavenly Father's provisions, the weather didn't prevent us from experiencing an amazing adventure in warm, sunny Cuba. It was on this holiday that Tanya had met a biology student from the University of Western Ontario who would later invite her to his campus for a full-guided tour, thus inspiring her to do a biology degree at UWO. So, to persevere through tempestuous weather could be a blessing in disguise.

As we drove to Deanna's home, freezing rain crusted our windshield, which then transitioned to thick snowflakes as the bleak sky was softly painted white. The stress of the intensely slow drive was soon forgotten when Deanna greeted us with open arms, wrapping us in warm hugs and delicious stew to fill our famished tummies. More satisfying than dessert and more nourishing than a meal was our worship time together, honouring our Father, thanking Him for His faithfulness and Jesus's redemptive work on the Cross. God ordained this spiritual nourishment.

Once we were safely back home, we anticipated the following evening. Tanya dressed elegantly for a fund-raising event that she had helped organize for the mission team: a Valentine spaghetti dinner at the church. She had contacted the youth and organized entertainment at the dinner, called an *undesirable orchestra*. The musicians would intentionally play their instruments dreadfully out of tune and squeaky until the guests donated money to get them to stop. It was a hilarious way to stimulate the guests to empty their pocket change for the mission trip. It was a huge success!

Karin dropped by later in the evening for a chat and surprised us with food and dessert. We had a pleasant visit and shared faith-building stories. Tanya sat by the fireplace and joined us for most of the conversation until our friend left. She was tired from the church event and in significant discomfort. She showed me her old surgical scar on her stomach, lamenting that a painful knot under the scar had plagued her all day. I anointed her with oil and prayed for healing to remove the pain, as well as pain from the multiple malignancies, seizures, unrelenting pain in her back, ribs and legs and the numerous other medical concerns. Tanya bravely suffered while concomitantly living her life to the fullest.

The next morning, we prepared for Sunday church. After an episode of vomiting, her stomach remained queasy, but she yearned to worship God, so we left for the service. As the pastor preached, I couldn't pay attention because my focus was on praying for Tanya as she leaned heavily on me to ward off a seizure.

After church, three friends dropped by with a video. Tanya could lay on the couch and still be aware of the video, the group conversation, and the pleasure of having friends visit.

The day came to a close with our daily scripture reading and prayer, and I anointed her with oil in obedience to the scriptures in James 5:14 to call the elder and anoint the sick. As the elder in this home, God appointed me to pray the prayer of healing, a nightly routine that bound us to Jesus and to each other. We reminisced about the time when she had accepted Jesus and her spiritual growth over the years.

From age six, when Tanya had accepted Jesus, she had kept her faith even through suffering, cancer, surgical complications, and several near-death crises; she adhered to Jesus like glue. There was a time in adolescence when she became disillusioned about the organized church. Her Christian peers behaved differently at school than at church, and their incongruity led her to skepticism. She decided to maintain a relationship with God but not attend church. I prayed for wisdom, for we weren't in unity as a family. I couldn't leave my daughter at home alone on Sunday. I felt led of the Lord to support her.

"Okay, Tanya, if you won't go to church, Eric and I won't go to church. Let's have church at home."

She agreed, so the three of us sang worship songs, read scripture passages, talked about the application, and prayed earnestly. We followed this pattern for what seemed like weeks until I felt increasingly spiritually malnourished as I missed the church fellowship and message from the pulpit. I asked Tanya to pray about where we should worship as a family. It hadn't mattered to me where, just that we were together and received spiritual sustenance from the pastor's Sunday message.

She and her brother checked into several different youth groups. One particular youth group leader called and expressed his concern that she was absent from a session. Tanya was impressed. "Mom, with such a crowd of kids attending, how would he remember all the kids that were absent?" This was a sign to her that God wanted our family to attend that church. She learned the spiritual benefits of receiving God's Word from a pastor. It carried her forward so that when she moved to her university city she immediately committed to a church.

Tanya spoke of a new development: a feeling of extreme pressure in her head along with all the other body parts that remained painfully tender; her calf on both legs radiated excruciating pain, and one leg was severely bruised. She made observations rather than complaints. She spoke about her pain as a fact of life and only in answer to my probing questions. Her pain drew us closer in fervent prayer, Bible reading, and discussion. To divert her attention from the pain, we went to her favourite restaurant for supper, then visited the jeweller who replaced her watch battery. This was followed by a visit from a loyal church friend who arrived and offered her an inspiring get-well card. Tanya felt significant to God, truly surrounded with His tangible care expressed through her friends.

We took in stride the weekly six-hour treatment with SU101 in Toronto. She rested while I read aloud from the humour section in various magazines. It gave us opportunities to giggle and laugh. It was late evening when the treatment was finished, so Tanya's grandpa brought us to his apartment, and she went to bed with a pounding headache on the tumour side.

Early the following day, we were back to the hospital for Tanya's art therapy, where the clinical trial nurses questioned me about Tanya's night, to which I replied that she hadn't slept well. She had had a severe headache before bed that persisted throughout the night, despite morphine. As well, she felt nausea. Her lower back hurt, and I had tried to massage it during the night but without relief. Neither Tanya nor I had slept. Not even Esther, her dog, had slept.

She was exhausted. The clinical trial nurse wanted to rule out drug toxicity, so she arranged blood work after art therapy. I expressed my anxiety with the nurse—would it be too late to try another treatment if the SU101 was ineffective or too toxic? She didn't respond.

While Tanya was in her art class, I shared with the nurses some of her unique attributes. They recognized her wide range of intellectual and social strengths. Her cognitive ability had remained intact. She never asked *why* but rather *what's next*? Or she would pray, "Lord, what are you trying to teach me? What can I learn from this?"

She tackled suffering as manageable challenges. I explained to the clinical nurses that we were praying for a miracle, not from the SU101 which was limited, but for a miracle of healing from God. They listened. I shared with them Tanya's faith in God which they were aware of, and her array of strengths. In addition to academic aptitude, her other abilities included surprising me with a hefty refund after she completed my income tax, and in forty-eight hours she installed a beautiful fishpond complete with liner, pump, fish, and décor. She amazed me when she repaired broken door jambs, installed new door handles with a new lock and key set, and when she assembled the new barbeque using logic and common sense while her grandfather and I were still reading the manual. Tanya juggled many commitments simultaneously. The nurses were intrigued and urged me to tell more.

On the drive back to Peterborough after art therapy, my brakes failed, so I gauged my stopping distance by removing my foot from the gas and shifting to a lower gear slowed the vehicle. Not at all safe! I prayed to God for protection and wisdom to drive slowly and carefully on the highway.

Feeling anxious about the failed brakes, I called the mechanic the next day, and he advised me to service the car immediately. The mechanic discovered I had no brake pads. He was baffled and couldn't explain why the brake pads had worn so thin since he had recently performed the brake job. I was grateful that God had protected us on the highway!

Meanwhile, Dennis, Tanya's church friend, took her for a country drive and an ice-cream treat. They returned later in the evening. The outing had lifted Tanya's spirits, as evidenced by her happy chatter. A welcome little oasis of joy in her desert time of suffering. Again, God had provided.

In the middle of the night, she had a grand mal seizure. Conscious, she asked me to sing a slow worship chorus. Our voices joined when she was able. I sang, "We are standing on Holy ground. And there are angels all around. Let us praise Jesus now..."[19] Suddenly, her whole body convulsed violently, and I was alarmed when her eyes protruded from their sockets. Singing was difficult, but she persevered, then prayed out loud begging God to help her, "Jesus, I need You! Jesus, I need You! Jesus, I need You!" she cried over and over. She intermittently sang, "Jesus, Jesus, risen and anointed One... I love You; I love You...."[20]

Tanya sang the words sporadically between prayers for help. I remained composed, mindful she needed a steady, calm presence and prayed silently in my heart, distraught by her unrelenting suffering. At times she couldn't sing when the convulsion was too intense. I started singing in the Spirit. When the seizure subsided, and she was at rest and peace, we sang together, "Majesty, worship, Your majesty. Unto Jesus, be all glory honour and praise...."[21]

I felt helpless. I felt sad. I couldn't understand why she had to suffer without relief. She hadn't even complained. She accessed the power of God to stop the seizure and worshipped Him humbly. She moaned that her head hurt, her vision was blurred, and her aching eyes remained protruding from the sockets. I held her close and prayed sincerely, telling her how much I loved her, and that God loved her, intermingled with prayer for healing. This cycle of pain and seizures

---

[19] Geron Davis, "Holy Ground." Meadowgreen Music Co. Capital CMG, 1983.

[20] John Barnett, "Holy And Anointed One." *Wow Worship* Mercy Vineyard Publishing, Admin. by Vineyard Music USA, 1988.

[21] Jack Hayford, "Majesty, Worship His Majesty." Hayford Ministries, Wikipedia en.m.wikipedia. org/wiki/Jack _W._Hayford, 1986).

wouldn't be relieved apart from the intervention of God. "Father God, we are desperate for You," I prayed.

The following morning, Tanya prayed, a mere whisper, "Please, Abba Father, let the miracle of healing be soon. I am getting very weak." She had no relief from head pain. Also, if she moved her leg, her arm hurt, or if she shifted weight, her side would hurt, sending shooting pain to her arms, neck, shoulder blade, stomach, back, side and legs. Every part of her body exploded with pain. Overnight, her strength had deteriorated so that she was unable to sit up without assistance. She needed to be propped up like an infant. Unable to bear any weight on her legs, I had to carry her! The morphine was ineffective for the pain.

We read aloud from the Gospel of Matthew and prayed for healing. The scriptures helped us to keep focused on Jesus. Tanya agreed I should call Mama and Papa Blessings. My spiritual parents prayed powerfully to boost her faith for healing and complete restoration. Tanya told them that she needed the prayer they delivered, a prayer of authority that revered God and affirmed His persistent activity in her life. They fortified her faith.

We couldn't attend Sunday service, so I phoned the young adult pastor and invited anyone from church to come over after service to anoint Tanya with oil and join us in united prayer for healing. Eight young adults and others arrived, and one suggested a twenty-four-hour prayer vigil to commence immediately to determine if it was God's will for healing. I felt disheartened at the suggestion of prayer to determine if Tanya should live or die. I wanted my only living child to live. The young adult pastor supported the idea of a prayer chain to ask God for healing. One person dove into a theological discussion about sickness resulting from fallen humanity and man's independence from God. I felt weary and reminded her that Tanya was very dependent on God. Her intellectual deliberations weren't helpful. Sometimes there was nothing that needed to be said, and just prayer and being with us in the moment was most supportive.

Jesse, Tanya's friend and a pharmacist, phoned twice, and both times prayed with her and offered to research anti-seizure medications, concerned that she wasn't receiving the right cocktail of drugs. Tanya was receptive and appreciative of her investigation. Her friend offered to visit later in the week and bring the printout of the information. That encouraged Tanya to advocate for herself any possible alternatives to her current treatment. All day, she was afflicted with a severe headache behind her forehead, temples, and eyes. Also, the distention of her eyeballs out of their sockets seemed to be worse.

Later, she was too weak to pray much other than to whisper, "Lord, I am still believing You for a miracle." I, too, echoed her prayer, and I continued to petition the Throne of Grace on behalf of my child. We knew the power of God could halt this disease at any time. My prayer was always the same: a desperate cry for mercy, for healing.

In the following days, Tanya continued to suffer with this severe, unrelenting, incapacitating headache. Her left side, legs, hips, arms, neck, and shoulder joints were all in excruciating pain. She couldn't walk, balance, or sit up from a horizontal position without help. The clinical trial nurse phoned, and I explained Tanya's increasing physical limitations since Saturday's seizures. She arranged for the mobile lab to make a house call for blood work to check her anticonvulsive levels. The neurooncologist instructed Tanya to double her decadron dose to 64mg. Tanya slept much of the day even while her two faithful church friends, Dennis and Selena visited. Her school chum, Portia, dropped by. The girls had a time of giggles and chatter before Portia left. Tanya appreciated her visit.

Another of Tanya's friends came over with her relative. The relative had learned about the prayer chain that had been organized for Tanya's healing, but she believed the healing had been accomplished on Calvary and it should be a prayer chain for praising God for the healing Tanya had *already* received. God knew my deep anguish and how my heart ached for my daughter's health to be restored. I wasn't sure about the implication that I might be missing a miracle by voicing a prayer incorrectly. After all, God looks at the heart, and I wasn't fearful, but rested in God's perfect love that casts out fear (1 John 4:18).

After they left, I was thankful that Tanya was grounded in her faith and the scriptures, and the discussion hadn't shaken her confidence in God. There were many spiritually uplifting visits and friends. Those with troubling views grounded us deeper in our faith. We are all at different places spiritually, and God knows and understands the good intention of each heart.

Every night was a sleepless night of suffering intolerable pain. I prayed passionately next to her in bed, massaging her aching body. She took sips of water and vomited repeatedly. Through her unbearable pain, her spirit was as gentle as her body was weak. "Lord, please show us the manifestation of your healing soon." She whispered this prayer frequently.

My mind drifted to events years ago when intolerable suffering had followed post-surgical complications. The gastrointestinal surgeon performed a novel procedure and removed all of Tanya's large intestine. He fashioned an internal pouch as a reservoir for her stools using the ilium, which was the remaining small intestine, hoping that it would work as a substitute for the missing bowel. On her fourteenth birthday, she was barely conscious, recovering from the sedation of an eight-hour operation, a massive incision, one tube in her nose and another in her neck, several IV needles in her veins, a tube in her abdominal cavity, and an ileostomy apparatus attached to her side. She was in agony, paralyzed with pain. The surgeon had warned that although the surgery had been successful, pneumonia was a threat. She needed to get up and walk as soon as possible, but her resistance resulted in the dreaded pneumonia. Now the pain of the surgery was compounded with the pain to breathe with compromised lungs. It was now a matter of life and death to move.

As she shuffled, she whimpered in anguish, "You don't love me, Mummy. It hurts so much to move. You don't love me to make me walk."

She couldn't understand my deep love for her. I had to cause her more pain in walking to begin her healing for her to live. Sometimes I thought my walk with God was like Tanya's story. In my suffering and pain, I was forced to walk with God to be healed in Him. And when I couldn't see that He loved me because of the pain, it was then that He loved me most.

Tanya eventually recovered from pneumonia but suffered a host of subsequent complications. She spent weeks in hospital and was discharged just in time to start her grade eight year. But complications continued with internal bleeding. Her surgical pouch became infected and intestinal blockages were painful. She was hospitalized two weeks in September, October, and again in November. In December, she had surgery to close her ileostomy and was discharged four days before Christmas. She still endured chronic abdominal pain in January. She said she was sick and tired of feeling 'sick and tired,' so she invested her energy in volleyball practice and qualified for the team, a new commitment she took seriously. Her team won the school championship and moved to higher competitions with other schools in the district. Nearing the end of the season with only a few games until finals, Tanya looked poorly, and though she wouldn't admit it, I knew her pain was severe.

After the team's final victory, she whispered, "Mom, take me to the hospital." She was diagnosed with another internal infection, and her pouch was bleeding again. She didn't thrive back home, and whether she ate or fasted, the intolerable pain persisted with intestinal kinks and blockages. She was back in the hospital with complications on Good Friday and again in the following months with infections. The doctor prepared her that she would likely miss her grade eight graduation. Tanya had accomplished all the requirements for her grade with excellent marks, despite dealing with one health crisis after another. She'd been adamant that even if she had to discharge herself from the hospital, she wouldn't miss graduation. As she had determined, she graduated and celebrated her prom with her peers. In the face of pain, she had created a joyful memory to end her elementary school days and launch herself into high school.

With the summer holiday upon us, the surgeon surmised that the operation the year before had been unsuccessful since the pouch wasn't functioning as designed. He urged her to undergo more surgery to remove the pouch and equip her with a permanent ileostomy. Tanya strongly disagreed with the plan and was unyieldingly resistant, declaring that she would not have a bag for the rest of her life. Doggedly, she determined that the internal pouch would eventually function. She had become a mere skeleton, five feet six inches and eighty pounds. Due to her severe weight loss, she was diagnosed with anorexia. Unlike true nervosa, she wanted to eat, but she couldn't because of the intensity of the pain and the intestinal blockages. Curled up in a fetal position and whimpering in pain on her bed, she had spent her days begging God to let her die. I constantly prayed, feeling we were trapped in a descending spiral of discouraging pain. I wanted to support Tanya's decision but wanted her to have the suggested surgery to stop this downward cycle.

After much prayer, I suggested we drive to Dallas to be with friends and get a new perspective on things. She agreed that she could suffer in the car just as readily as on her bed, so we embarked on this journey to visit our beloved Bible College friends in Kansas and Texas. Our friend's husband, who had medical knowledge, understood Tanya's small intestines weren't functioning correctly and changed her diet to liquids. He created a concoction of nutrients and calories in a drink. Tanya's small bowel settled, absorbed the nutrients, and she gained weight. In fact, during the month we were on pilgrimage, Tanya gained over twenty-five pounds, and when we returned, her transformation surprised the surgeon and nutritionist. She continued to gain weight, and with the gradual introduction of solid food, her small intestine transitioned from liquid to solid with no ill effects. She went from 80 pounds to 105 pounds and felt pain-free and healthy. She felt so healthy she resumed her sports activities and even gained another ten pounds. Her story, to me, was a reminder that God never exempted us from pain, but he did give us the grace and strength to walk through it victoriously. He never promised that our lives would be easy as Christians, but He promised He would never leave us or forsake us (Hebrews 13:5).

As my mind came back to the present reality, we were still at home. Tanya's grandpa arrived unexpectedly and offered his help; delighted to see him, we sent him on an errand and thanked him appreciatively for his faithful support. My father's activity and practical assistance in our lives brought me comfort.

Jesse, Tanya's friend, who was a pharmacist, arrived at the same time as Dad and surprised Tanya with several bags of groceries. Tanya cherished Jesse's friendship and the work she had done researching information about anti-convulsive medications. They conversed over tea, and Tanya was exceedingly thankful to learn from her.

After she left, another friend arrived. Portia offered Tanya a yellow rose as a symbol of their years of friendship through school, which lifted Tanya's spirits as she felt the closeness of a dear friend. In sequence, Selena came over and brought a mustard seed that symbolized that great things came from small faith. More encouragement. Her grandfather, Jesse, Portia, Selena, and those who demonstrated God's love were gratefully received.

Early the following day, February 24, the Cancer Society driver drove us to Toronto for SU101. It was no longer safe for me to drive while so sleep-deprived and with Tanya in such a dire condition. She hadn't been sleeping well due to severe back pain and a blasting headache. Immediately upon arrival to the hospital, it took six long, tiresome hours to complete the blood transfusion, followed by six more hours of SU101 infusion. During those twelve hours, Tanya's unrelenting suffering increased even after the morphine limits. I continued throughout the evening to rub her back, legs, calf, thigh, and knee cap. I restlessly slept on a chair beside her bed. Just after midnight, the nurse removed the SU101 bag and hooked Tanya up to a saline solution, explaining that the doctor wanted her on IV all night; I was relieved—dehydration was a concern with the incessant vomiting of the past few days.

The following day, the hospital social worker coordinated homecare supports, a nurse, and physiotherapy. Tanya's piercing head and back pain never ceased. We planned to return home with the Cancer Society transportation, but as the day progressed, Tanya's health deteriorated. The nurse arranged for Tanya to remain on a stretcher and be transported home by ambulance bus. The first patient on the bus was dropped off in the community where I had taught grade four. It felt like decades since I had seen my students and conducted my class when, in reality, only one month had passed. As Tanya slept, her head slowly sagged to the left on the stretcher; I repositioned it, and it would sag again. I ran my fingers through her silky, soft hair, silently praying. She awoke and whispered that stroking her hair felt comforting. She reached up, grasped my hand, and brought it to her lips and gently kissed my hand repeatedly. What a strong bond I felt with my daughter.

We guarded our bond as a gift. I remember when she had asked for two identical rings for her 22nd birthday. I curiously inquired why two rings. She replied that she wanted me to wear one, and she would wear the other as a lasting covenant, a promise between us—never in our past had we broken our relationship and never would we do so in our future. We remained true to that pledge.

We had to work out some growing adjustments in adolescence. When Tanya was a perky teenager, she picked up some of the carefree lingo of her peers, specifically the term, 'whatever.' Immediately, the response 'whatever' felt like indifference to me. Tanya and I were respectfully open and honest throughout her childhood. I explained that it was okay not to have a strong opinion, but her response, 'whatever' felt like she didn't care, and caring was important to me. I explained why it was crucial for me to have an unbroken communication with her since my relationship with my mother had been severed at a young age and never restored. I wanted to protect our relationship so that we would never become distant. I could listen to anything she had to say, I could agree to disagree, but it would be unbearable if she should shut me out. She agreed to guard our relationship and practiced new responses. After years of adolescence and into adulthood, we had never gone to bed angry, nor had we broken our communication.

Our strong spiritual and emotional ties continued to carry us forward. At the end of February, we were provided with a hospital bed. It would be an adjustment to have Tanya sleep in the adjacent room and not with me in my room. The nurse assigned to home care visits arrived, took detailed notes, and charted her future daily visits. She seemed so caring and empathetic. Simultaneously, Patti, a friend from church who offered prayer, illimitable support and an empathetic ear, dropped by, arms bulging with groceries, followed by Tanya's faithful friend, Portia. The girls chatted like old chums, and she reassured Tanya of another visit before returning to university. I phoned many people to thank them for the food and generous, supportive, kind words and cards left at our door while in Toronto.

The phone rang again. It was the Toronto nurse calling to explain a new complication. What more could happen? Tanya's blood work came back with abnormal liver levels, so they booked an ultrasound. We were numb as ongoing complications heaped even more suffering upon her. I prayed without ceasing, "Oh, dear God, our need for a miracle gets bigger and bigger."

Vivianna, Tanya's out-of-town friend, also a cancer survivor, phoned. Tanya's voice was merely a murmur, and she fell asleep while talking. Vivianna and her mom arranged to visit soon.

A representative from the Baptist church phoned and confirmed the date to share our testimony in March. Our commitment meant that we trusted God's miraculous healing would enable Tanya to stand erect to glorify Him.

I pleaded with God for that healing. Tanya's headaches increased to the point of nausea, and with the bucket in position to catch vomit, a seizure erupted. I rubbed her back, prayed slowly in the Spirit, for I knew not how to pray, and begged God to interrupt the seizure. It seemed like an eternity before it subsided. We shared our daily prayer, scripture, and Christian music time before bed. Every day seemed to be more of the same or worse than the day before.

The next day, when Tanya spoke on the phone to her friend, I noticed her voice was clearer, and she responded and participated in conversation—unlike the day before when she had fallen asleep on the phone. Surprisingly, the day was free from seizures, a dose of hope. I was deeply thankful to God!

We started making the tape recording for our March 21st message to glorify God at the Baptist Church as guest speakers. After Tanya and I discussed that prayer was the direction God wanted us to take with our testimony, we had our own evening prayer time. Our sanctuary was Jesus, and from Him, we drew His peace that filtered into Tanya's gentle spirit and quiet disposition. Talking was energy-draining, so she whispered her positive, insightful, and uplifting words in prayer.

In the midst of her weakness, she appreciated the congregational prayers, and when the pastor called, I shared that we needed the body of Christ. He responded that the body of Christ needed us to teach the church about prayer. Our prayers were our lifeline. Our strength and peace were in Him. We wanted to glorify God with our lives—we believed God would give healing to us as a testimony.

Sunday, February 28, 1999, started well. The pain appeared under control. Mama and Papa Blessing called, prayed a mighty, inspiring prayer that lifted us both. They were truly conduits of Father God's love and compassion. Papa Blessing again extended the invitation to share our testimony at the Bible college after the healing. We agreed, excited that one day we would return to Dallas to acclaim God at CFNI.

Sunday was, most importantly, the Lord's Day. Since Tanya was too infirmed to attend church, we sent an invitation to the body of Christ to join us in prayer at home. We were delighted that eight believers arrived to pray for an hour. The friends remained for a short visit after prayer, and then she had another seizure.

Tanya was exhausted and needed sleep. It was later in the evening when her church friend Cori arrived. Tanya started another focal seizure, and while Cori coached her with deep breathing, I turned up the Christian music to direct her focus to Christ while praying in the Spirit. I gently stroked her hair, distracting her attention from the seizure. The entire length of her left calf had black and blue bruising. After every seizure, the discolouration in her skin was noticeably bigger, and the muscles more tender. Tanya had endured so much, and I was baffled why nothing relieved her torment. Another church friend, Sonya, phoned and encouraged Tanya with plans to visit the following Saturday. Her friend Elle also checked in to inquire if Tanya was feeling better. Also, my friend, Eric's elementary school teacher, Linda, offered to visit the next day. There were so many caring, supportive, loyal, faithful friends that God had placed in our lives that reminded us that His everlasting love endures forever.

FOURTEEN
Hope and Hopelessness in Our Journey with God

ON MONDAY, MARCH 1, 1999, Tanya again awoke in insufferable pain, particularly behind her right eye and temple. She implored me to massage her temple and top of her head, but to no avail. The pain roared on, so in addition to her regular morphine dose, I gave her more. Fifteen minutes later, the pain was still intense, so I phoned the nurse, and she said to give her more morphine, and if the pain persisted more than fifteen minutes to give another dose. I did that. The nurse phoned back to let me know that our family doctor would be making a house call. The doctor came and doubled the time-release morphine and increased her liquid morphine, then arranged for home oxygen.

Tanya whispered several times, "Mummy, it feels as if I have a watermelon in my head. It hurts so badly; it feels like I have a watermelon in my head," she bemoaned. The added dose of morphine caused drowsiness, yet when she awoke, the pressure in her head, severe pain, and nausea were even worse.

The clinical trial nurse in Toronto phoned to tell us that the neurooncologist wanted to see Tanya after she had blood results, but the earliest outpatient appointment was in nine days. Since the drug was synthesized in the liver, he wanted to determine from the liver results if the elevated enzyme levels would allow her to continue the SU101 treatment. I doubted that Tanya would survive that long, and with no immediate treatment plan, I asked about a plan B. The nurse said if the liver malfunctioned, there was no plan B. Any treatment would be ineffective since all her drugs were metabolized in the liver. Perhaps that was why morphine was ineffective. The diseased liver wasn't able to metabolize it and send the medication to her body. The increased decadron dose was far higher than the therapeutic ceiling, and it too seemed ineffective. The plan was to admit Tanya for pain control, an ultrasound, and an MRI.

Moment by moment, Tanya was declining. Oxygen equipment was installed, and the mobile lab service made a house call for blood work, followed by a visit from the home care nurse. Sandwiched into her activities, she made room for her friend Dennis when he arrived with a comedy movie that they watched together.

Selena stopped by earlier in the afternoon with a great rice casserole made by her mom and stayed the remainder of the day. She stood by Tanya's side almost daily. Later in the evening, Selena was still present when Patti arrived with her guitar, and as we sang praise and worship songs, two more friends arrived, Cori and Linda. Patti knew what we yearned for—strumming her guitar, our voices lifted heavenward in worship, grounding us deeply in our purpose for living—to worship our Lord Jesus and be mindful of His saving grace and forgiveness through the Cross.

Sharon, my longtime friend, called and prayed with me, as did Dennis's mother. Their prayers reminded me that God hadn't forgotten us and was in control. She said she had been burdened to pray for Tanya's complete healing. I received a letter from Carolyn in the USA, a loyal friend from CFNI, so I called and thanked her, and we prayed together. God had sent encouragement through many strong believers. I thanked the Lord that Tanya had one more day free of seizures. Every tiny relief from suffering gave me hope for healing. I believed by faith that seizures would end, and she would begin to manifest evidence of a regression of this painful illness and leap forward to display God's grandeur in complete recovery. My only hope and optimism were in Jesus.

Tanya spoke to me many times about the story in Mark 4:35–41 when before He fell asleep in the boat and before the storm, Jesus told the disciples that they would go to the other side. The storm was part of the process from the beginning. She compared that Bible story to her current circumstances and explained that she was in the storm, but Jesus had spoken that even though He was asleep, she could rest assured that she would arrive safely on the other side. I shared this with Carolyn, and she said it raised her faith to believe in miracles. That was part of our purpose, to encourage one another to trust God.

Although weary, Tanya remained awake for our scripture reading, and we had an extraordinary time of prayer. We had previously watched two videos on the book of Matthew, so on this night, we watched the third Matthew video.[22]

---

[22] Shepard Design, director, "Matthew, The Visual Bible NIV," Dallas, TX: Visual International and Visual Entertainment, Inc. 1997 Four Volumes, VCR.

It inspired us as we saw the scriptures unfold on screen and hear verbatim the scripture passages that corresponded with the action.

Later, we watched a Christian television broadcast called 100 Huntley Street, and the testimony was about a pastor's child whom God had healed from deadly meningitis. That inspired Tanya to trust God deeply for healing, so we called the prayer chain, and Tanya prayed with a counsellor. It reassured her to feel God's presence through this television ministry.

I also read aloud a book on prayer to her. At the part about casting all your cares upon Him, she reminded me that she had done that with no expectations, except for Christ to live in her heart. No expectations, except Christ! That reminded me of the lesson Tanya had taught me while she was in university. She would say, "Mom, to be content in Jesus, do not let your expectations exceed your reality." She expected to know Christ more, which wasn't beyond her reality, so she remained content. She was very weak, but God gave her the strength to trust and focus on Him alone. Only God could do what we were too weak to do in our flesh (2 Corinthians 12:10). The Apostle Paul wrote that when we felt weak, we could access the strength in Jesus. He was strong in us.

Our doctor made a home visit and studied the pictures of my children on the mantle. As she gazed at Tanya's photograph, I spoke softly that she needed a miracle, and she agreed. When we discussed the upcoming ultrasound for Tanya's liver, she matter-of-factly informed us that the oncologist would be looking to see if the cancer had metastasized to her liver. The ineffectiveness of all oral-pain medication indicated the liver wasn't metabolizing the drugs due to the advancing cancer.

Several times during the day, the scripture in Mark 4:35 came to mind, *"We will get to the other side."* Surely the other side was healing! I wouldn't give up hope!

I repeated it to Tanya in conversation and prayer, and she mumbled almost imperceptibly, "I know." I had a strong belief we would get to the other side despite the storm; if Jesus was sleeping in the stern, how much more should we rest? This confirmed what I read aloud today in 1 Peter, *"Cast all your anxiety on him because he cares for you"* (1 Peter 5:7).

A timely phone call came from Dr. C., the neurooncologist in London, brilliant in his specialty. He confirmed it was time for an MRI to see if the SU101 protocol was working and recommended the drug thalidomide if it was discontinued. I had hoped this promising treatment SU101 would have been the method God used to restore her health.

After his phone call, we welcomed several visitors. Vivianna, Tanya's friend who trained with her as a camp counsellor for kids with cancer, and her mother. They exchanged stories of times they had spent together. The nurse and her supervisor, along with the case manager, arrived and offered helpful support. Everyone who appeared in our lives that day was evidence that God was lovingly supporting us.

Alone again, Tanya's sense of humour was precious. Although her voice was weak, her quick responses with witty, humorous comments emitted rays of sunshine into an otherwise gloomy day. She enjoyed teasing me in fun—I received and returned it. When I fussed over her and wanted to serve her in any way, she whispered, "Mum, just relax. Quit fluffing me. I'm okay. You do so much for me. Just relax." We giggled; we told each other frequently that we loved each other. We were compatible, and even in this most painful time in our lives, we enjoyed one another's company. I strongly felt Tanya's love. I knew she felt mine, too. Another trip down memory lane and a time to unwrap past treasures.

Everyone feels the specialness of their children, but my feelings seemed exceptional! When I was turning forty, Tanya contacted my friends from various circles of my life, church, neighbours, work, and my Scottish Country dancing friends. She and Eric planned and sprung a surprise birthday party with over forty guests. Eric had taken a cake decorating course, and he made and decorated the most beautiful cake to honour me. I was flabbergasted and delighted, astonished at the outpouring of love. I received many gifts, but the most moving gift that I would deeply cherish forever was when the children presented 'a daughter and son's pride ring,' a gold band with three sparkling stones mounted on the top, Tanya's, Eric's, and my birthstones. When I slipped the stunning ring on my finger, Tanya footnoted with deeply felt love and gratitude, "Mom, we could have bought the ring with just cut glass, but we decided to pay the extra cost for authentic genuine stones, because you are worth it." Tanya and Eric esteemed me so highly! Joy flooded my being at their loving thoughtfulness, and for years to come, their affectionate words echoed in my heart, "Mom, you are worth it." They had demonstrated love!

I showed the home care nurse my photo album of Eric. It started with a comment that Tanya and I could pass for sisters, so I pulled out the album to show them the lookalike pictures Eric had snapped of Tanya and me in 1997. They were captivated by our lookalike stories and Eric's photography.

Tanya and I, as look-a-likes, had a history of fun. One Saturday, when Tanya was a teenager, while we were window shopping, she tried on a new outfit and excitedly asked, "Mummy, what do you think about this dress?" As I commented, a stranger in the store burst into our conversation. "Mummy? Did she call you Mummy? I thought you were fraternal twins." We both laughed, the same laugh—we had similar voices as well.

On another occasion, I was a teacher assistant at Tanya's high school, and in the staff room, her teacher approached me. "Tanya, students are not allowed in the staff room." I chuckled as I explained to his embarrassment that I was Tanya's mother.

We did look alike, the same complexion, hair length and colour, and the same weight, but she was slightly taller. She admonished me when I impersonated her on the phone when her friends would call. But she had fun doing the same with my friends.

Later, her dependable friend Dennis arrived and handed her a card from his mother, filled with kindness and affection. We were humbled by the ongoing outpouring of love and support through Dennis and many faithful friends. Our thankful response was to praise the Lord continually, filling our house daily with music as we lifted our voices in devotion to God. Twice that day, I anointed Tanya with oil and prayed earnestly for healing. She was seizure-free again, and that was at the top of my thanksgiving list. We wondered if the equipment that provided her with pure oxygen made the difference.

A few days later, when the ambulance to Toronto was scheduled to pick us up at 9:30 a.m., it was delayed until 4:30 p.m. due to a blinding blizzard. Bill, a paramedic and long-time friend, happened to be in the neighbourhood, so he popped in, anointed Tanya with oil, prayed over her, and gently kissed her forehead. It was as if an emblem of love from heaven had been bestowed upon her. Tanya said it felt like Father God had kissed her lovingly. Bill may never fully know how much his benevolent gesture meant to Tanya. She spoke of it many times throughout the day and evening. It seemed that God had strategically placed this kind gentleman in our lives to help Tanya experience God tangibly. It lessened her suffering when she felt God's love and presence through His people.

It was 7:30 p.m. when we finally arrived at the hospital. I stayed overnight at my father's flat, and when I checked in on Tanya the next morning, she looked even frailer, and her pain level was still alarming. She could barely swallow her medication, and her eyes were glassy and bulging. I gasped at how much she had declined from the previous day.

"Phone your Mama and Papa Blessings," Tanya whispered urgently. I called my spiritual parents as Tanya requested, and they prayed with her, encouraging her to remain steadfast in her belief for healing. They also prayed with me and quoted the scriptures to cling to Jesus. God ordained this moment to strengthen our feeble knees and, having done all, to stand strong (Ephesians 6:13).

After the phone conversation, I repeated to Tanya, "Fight! We will get to the other side. Don't give up. You have a job to do! Fight!" She weakly nodded. That morning I read the scriptures in Mark 4 again, and when I got to verse thirty-five, I felt compelled to reread it and was reminded that we would get to the other side. Jesus said it. "That day when evening came, He said to his disciples, "Let us go over to the other side…" (Mark 4:35–41). We were in the storm—but the wind and the waves of cancer would obey Him. In the midst of this storm called cancer, Jesus was asleep at the stern. The disciples were terrified, but Jesus calmed the storm, and they arrived safely on the other side. I reassured myself with this scripture over and over. Tanya agreed to fight and keep her faith in Jesus.

While we were there in Toronto, she had been in unrelenting pain for a full week. The neurooncologist ordered blood work, an MRI, and an ultrasound of her liver. The clinical trial nurse delivered the MRI results while Dr. Q was assessing Tanya's pain control. When I asked if the SU101 had helped, she flatly replied, "No." She proceeded to tell me about another tumour at the base of her skull when Dr. Q, the pain control specialist, interrupted her saying that only doctors were qualified to give MRI results. She then returned with the neurooncologist, and he explained that the SU101 hadn't worked and nothing would work. He repeated his dismal assessment and said it wouldn't matter what he tried—nothing would work. He said that Eric's oncologist at Sick Children's Hospital had called and suggested implementing Eric's protocol that she had used for his lymphoma. He didn't believe it would work on brain tumours. He had no further treatment to offer.

I pleaded with him, "You can't just give up! There must be another treatment! What about thalidomide that Dr. C had suggested over the phone?" I was desperate for him to try anything.

The neurooncologist found words that ended all hope. "It would take two weeks to get it from Ottawa." When I suggested I drive to Ottawa to get it, he said it originated in New Jersey. I crumpled into tears. He had given up on my daughter, my only child. The nurse led me away, inconsolable. When I regained my composure, she and the doctor brought me into his office and highlighted the MRI scan of January 20th and contrasted it with the scan of March 4th. He pointed out that the tumours were five times larger, and now there were eight tumours. Her brain was bursting with tumours. I couldn't grasp the magnitude of what I had seen. Eight brain tumours! We desperately trusted God to intervene in Tanya's life with four tumours, and now there were eight! This challenged my faith further!

He discontinued SU101 and decided to try an untested high dose of experimental chemotherapy treatment for colon cancer, CPT11. Tanya was like a lab rat, and he was grasping at hollow straws in an empty box. The doctor was lost as he fumbled in the dark for a solution. I asked the neurooncologist what the most aggressive treatment would be. He said that at the current rate of cell division, the brain wouldn't accommodate eight tumours rapidly increasing in size. He said that Tanya would die within two weeks, and she would be in a coma for one of those. He explained that it would take chemo a month to work, and there wasn't enough time to see if the CPT11 would be effective. I was distraught and felt sick at the dismal prognosis but doggedly clung to my faith for healing. It was March 4, 1999, when the neurooncologist gave up on Tanya.

Tanya was bereft of emotions when she received the news of eight brain tumours and two weeks to live. She seemed peaceful and undisturbed. She was too weak, too frail, drained of energy, to respond. I don't think any new developments would have alarmed her at that point. She was confidently trusting God to intervene. There were many times when I reassured her that we would get to the other side; she agreed and whispered, "I know, the other side is heaven." After an exhausting hospital ordeal, we arrived home to find a church friend left a phone message that we should hang on to our faith. God knew the precise timing that I needed that message.

I continually recalled Jesus's words, *"Let us go over to the other side."* From Mark 4:35. The news from the neurooncologist the previous day had been traumatic, juxtaposed with my hope in Christ that the other side was a miracle of healing. I felt compelled to grasp for life. Tanya's recent prayer resonated with me. "Enlighten me with the understanding of your Word. Lord, I still believe You will heal me. Forgive me if I have said or done anything not in accordance with your Word." What a gift of God's grace that secured her position in God, submissively searching her heart for sin. She wasn't in a coma as long as she was nestled in the palm of God's Hands. Our Father in heaven focused us solely on Jesus.

Later in the week, the pastor whom I had seen on television returned my call. My faith in Jesus grew when he assured me that a young girl in his church would stand as a proxy for Tanya's healing. He inspired me to be decisive, firmly planted in God. When I shared the scripture from Mark 4:35 onward, that we would get to the other side and receive healing, he reminded me that there were two reports; the report of the doctor, based on the medical evidence, and the report of our Lord Jesus based on God's Word. We were to believe in healing. He said Christians needed to be fervent in prayer and too often gave up just before the manifestation of the healing. The pastor's words reinforced the urgency I felt for our church family to tenaciously stand with us in prayer until the evidence of Tanya's healing was revealed. I was reminded of James 5:16 that instructed us to repent and to pray fervently. *"Therefore, confess your sins to each other and pray for each other so that you may be healed. The prayer of a righteous person is powerful and effective."* Daily, Tanya and I searched our hearts for unrepented sin. To add to my confirmation of God working in our lives, Papa and Mama Blessing called, inspiring us to persist further in prayer, believing God for miraculous healing. I perceived that these inexhaustible contacts with believers pointing us to God had been prompted by God.

I reflected on the oncologist's prediction of a coma while I observed Tanya's amazing attention span. She focused on telephone conversations for over four hours with two high school friends, Velody and Lorraine. Then five church friends dropped by, and for another hour, she conversed with them. Even though Tanya was cognitively astute, she disciplined her frail body, overwhelmed as it was with exhaustion, to be attentive to her peers. They had planned a party. Indubitably, the anticipation of a fun-filled gathering was more evidence that Tanya would be completely healed.

Later in the week, we travelled to the Toronto hospital for treatment and arrived home late in the afternoon. I left Tanya unattended and dashed to the kitchen momentarily. Suddenly, I heard a heart-wrenching crash followed by agonizing moans. Tears blinded my eyes as I scooped her up and carried her to bed, repenting and imploring her to forgive me. I felt so badly for leaving her without support.

With comforting kindness, Tanya reassured me repeatedly, "Mom, I'm okay. Don't beat yourself up." However, I was certain that my neglect had caused her more suffering, and I was distraught. I couldn't move forward even with Tanya's forgiveness and assurances.

Unexpectedly, the home care nurse phoned and through tears, I begged her to come over and examine Tanya. Within minutes she arrived, took Tanya's vital signs, and reassured me that she hadn't suffered additional harm. Tanya invited me to cuddle with her in bed and comforted me that she was okay. Every time I repented, she gently reminded me that I shouldn't beat myself up.

Later, my church friend Karin surprised us with a visit. When I confessed that my failures may have caused Tanya additional pain, she empathized with my sorrow. Her compassion, coupled with a generous supply of groceries, helped me to refocus. I appreciated this special friend God had prompted to support us in such lovingly, generous ways.

The following day, Tanya dozed all morning. My friend Sharon came by with lunch, and Tanya joined our discussion, alert in her wheelchair. She was able to attend to the stories from events in my friend's life. I felt truly blessed and grateful for Sharon's loyal, genuine friendship that transcended many decades. Another gift of God's love for which I was thankful.

Later in the day, the pastor arrived, and when his prayer seemed generic and brief, it concerned me. I asked him if he was having difficulty with Tanya's illness, and he acknowledged it was so. It was heart-wrenching to watch her have no reprieve from suffering. His prayer and honesty ministered his authentic love for us as our pastor. The stream of visitors continued.

The physiotherapist that came to assess Tanya's range of movement suggested that the bathroom door be removed to negotiate the wheelchair to the tub. When I struggled to remove the lower door hinge, Tanya proposed using a nail and hammer to pry up the hinge pin. Tanya's idea worked! Even in her weakened condition, she had phenomenal awareness. Her logic was sound, and her memory was sharp. When I wanted to clean the area rug but couldn't locate the rug shampoo, I was about to give up when I nonchalantly asked Tanya. Without hesitation, she whispered, "The rug cleaner is on the shelf between the furnace and the basement-bathroom wall. You left it there when you cleaned a stain on the downstairs rug two years ago." Sure enough, the cleaning product was exactly where she said it would be. How she recalled such detail from so long ago remained a mystery. With soft laughter, she joked about her exceptional memory. We were both amused. I welcomed Tanya's humour. I was witnessing the grace of God that operated in her life moment by moment. If she weren't so physically fragile and depleted, I would almost think that she had been misdiagnosed. Her short and long-term memory had been preserved despite this horrific, debilitating disease.

A few days later, we had an eventful morning! Tanya directed my attention to an eye seizure, visible twitching on her eyelids and eyeballs. She observed that her vision flipped like the vertical control of an old-fashion tube television. Thinking her brain was lacking oxygen, she boosted the levels, and eventually, the twitching subsided. Our doctor made a house call, examined Tanya, and explained the eye seizures indicated the brain tumours had increased in size. Silently, we deepened our belief, hoping in God for miraculous healing. We had nothing to grasp apart from our hope in Jesus.

FIFTEEN
Experiencing God in Many Ways

JEAN, FROM CHURCH, surprised us later in the day with a delicious cheese-cauliflower soup and fresh bread. We talked about how we experienced God differently. I shared that the Holy Spirit would lead me into a deeper experience with God as I seek His Face. I suggested that, for me, there were many prerequisites to experiencing God—repentance, forgiveness, obedience, praise, worship, reading the scriptures, and listening to His still, small voice with the Holy Spirit's guidance. I was thankful for the numerous believers who had helped me experience God through their visits. God used Christian and non-Christian friends' supportive words, prayers, provisions of food, phone calls, encouraging cards, and practical assistance. I experienced Him through the medical staff, home care support, volunteer drivers, and many circumstances. God orchestrated everything that blessed and fortified our hearts. I constantly prayed, thanking God for the many little perks that brightened my day.

Earlier in the day, Tanya's sensitivity and self-reflection moved me profoundly. She apologized for being snappy and demanding and asked me to forgive her. How could she ask me for forgiveness? She had such a gentle, caring spirit, aware of the welfare of others, yet was repentant for her perceived errors. I prayed that I would always follow the example of Jesus's love in action that she lived daily. I accepted her apology and asked her to forgive me as I repented of my inadequacies, which she, too, forgave.

Deanna called and when we spoke about experiencing God in diverse ways, we focused on repentance. John the Baptist paved the way for Jesus through a message of repentance. We come to the Cross through repentance. Sometimes repentance was neglected in church messages as the venue to knowing and experiencing God. From the time they were preschoolers, my life with Tanya and Eric had been filled with my repentance and their forgiveness. I knew I was flawed. They knew I was flawed. Tanya also repented freely and asked for forgiveness whenever she felt convicted. It broke my heart that as desperately ill as she was, she thought she had been snappy and demanding and had asked for my forgiveness. I experienced Tanya as a sweet, long-suffering angel. I experienced God through her humility reflected in her meek, submissive attitude. Many stories of Tanya's childhood came to mind of how we experienced God through each other.

She had allowed herself to be transparently vulnerable from early childhood, speaking openly without reservation. There was a time when Eric's hospitalization had been extended due to setbacks. I remained with him while Tanya lodged with friends. By the time he recovered and we resumed family routines, spring break was upon us. We had been planning a vacation to Florida that had thrilled the children. Solemnly, Tanya spoke privately to me. "Mom, I have hardly had any time with you since Eric needed you in hospital. I want some special time to go with you to Florida without Eric."

"Special time" was a term I had introduced to the children when they were preschoolers. It meant that the child having the "special time" could choose any activity and enjoy my undivided attention for a designated length of time, and then I would repeat the same with the other child. Both children respected "special time" because they knew their turn would come. Tanya's request was unprecedented because "special time" for a week in Florida was quite different than an hour at home. I promised Tanya I would pray about her request and speak to Eric about it. When I approached the subject with him, I asked, "Eric, who have I spent the most time with lately, you or Tanya?"

Without hesitation, he beamed, "Me!" I agreed that his health challenges had warranted my undivided attention, and now Tanya would like to have 'special time' with me over March Break in Florida. Eric's initial response was a question. "Does that mean that one day I will get 'special time' with you in Florida?" I assured him that he would receive the same, but when that would be couldn't be predicted. He was happy to stay with friends while Tanya and I enjoyed many activities and adventures in Florida. Our 'special time' helped her to feel special and secure. Years later, when I was again planning a trip to Florida for the Christmas holidays, Tanya insisted that she stay at home with her best friend's family so Eric could have his Florida 'special time' with me. Eric was so thankful to Tanya for her generous heart, and he and I had a wonderful vacation. We celebrated Christmas with my cousins, visiting Disney World and the beach together. It was gratifying for me to appreciate the extent to which my children experienced God through the gift of each other.

Later the same day, another couple from church dropped by with food, another gift and an opportunity to express indebtedness and gratitude to our church family and our heavenly Father. Tanya's elementary school friend phoned with news of her pregnancy, announcing the baby due in September. As Tanya related excerpts from her conversation, she was filled with joy about her friend's maternal future.

The telephone was Tanya's connection to her many friends. She phoned Marah, another high school friend who had promised her a manicure. Tanya informed her that the upcoming trip to Toronto was a same-day return, so they rescheduled for a later date. Another loyal friend from school, Portia, phoned and chatted at length on many topics that helped Tanya to feel included in her life. Tanya was moved with gratitude for friends that kept her in the loop of their lives. So much activity. Later, Dr. T and his lovely wife, Angel, dropped by with food. God was lovingly present as He drew us to Himself, and we experienced Him increasingly each day through our friends and church family.

The next day, Tanya was very tired but still welcomed company. The sound of chatter and laughter was a happy sign of life. When the guests had gone and Tanya and I were spiritually reflective, we decided to watch more of the third video depicting the Gospel of Matthew.[23] Watching the video series of Matthew brought the reality of Jesus to life for us as we followed His journey on this earthly sod. The visual seemed plausible with the script verbatim from the Bible's New International Version, confirming that our hope for a miracle was realistic.

After Tanya and I discussed the message and had a lovely time of prayer, we thanked God for his Word and prayed for our church, friends, doctors, nurses, volunteers, medications and treatments.

Friday, March 12, 1999, just before Tanya's ambulance to Toronto arrived, Reverend David Mainse's [24] secretary returned our call. Tanya spoke boldly about standing with God, believing for the manifestation of healing. The secretary invited Tanya to be a guest on 100 Huntley Street to share her testimony when her healing was completed, assuring us that Reverend Mainse would receive the message that she needed ongoing prayer. Another experience of God!

---

[23] Shepard Design, director, "Matthew, The Visual Bible NIV," Dallas, TX: Visual International and Visual Entertainment, Inc. 1997 Four Volumes, VCR.

[24] Rev. David Mainse, Founder of 100 Huntley Street, 1977

Upon arrival at the hospital, Tanya received a blood transfusion followed by intravenous CPT11 chemotherapy. A lengthy wait for an ambulance followed by several stops to pick up more patients delayed our trip home. We finally arrived at 8:00 p.m. What a long, tiring, day!

Even though the trip to Toronto for chemo had been exhausting, the next day, Tanya's friend, Dennis, invited her on an outing, and she eagerly anticipated his arrival. I was thankful that God had given her enabling grace to live life to the fullest. When she returned home, she vividly recalled the highlights of her mini-adventure.

She still had energy, so we then watched the fourth and final video from the Matthew series.[25] This graphic depiction of the betrayal and crucifixion of Jesus was disturbing and humbling as Jesus's suffering and death were vividly portrayed, reminding us of the incredible price He paid for our salvation. We wept, moved by the intense anguish and pain that our beloved Saviour suffered for our sins and the sins of the world so we could be reconciled to God and receive the gift of eternal life. *"See what great love the Father has lavished on us, that we should be called children of God! And that is what we are!"* (1 John 3:1a).

Following the video, discussion, and prayer, Tanya slept until Marah, a buddy from high school, arrived and delighted her by painting her fingernails blue and burgundy. Tanya had told her to *go wild,* and she did! I heard ripples of laughter as the two girls chatted and giggled for several hours. Once again, I thanked God for such a sanctuary of joy for Tanya through the love and attention of friends. Immediately following this friend's visit, two more caring young adults dropped by with a lasagna dinner, salad, and bread. We were still eating Angel's tasty shepherd's pie, so we tucked the new dish in the fridge for our next meal and thanked God for the uplifting visit and prayer time. After they left, Tanya and I were still drawn to further prayer about ways God could use us to minister to others. *"Freely, you have received; freely give"* (Matthew 10:8b).

Another Sunday arrived, but again partial paralysis bound Tanya to a wheelchair. We couldn't attend church. In past weeks, I had regularly kept the pastor informed so he could update the congregation during Sunday services. Many had indicated that they appreciated knowing our struggles, and praying for Tanya had drawn them closer to the Lord. After I sent the email, Karin dropped by unexpectedly, and I thanked her profusely for her visit and help. She phoned later to check in with me, and I thanked her again for her ongoing,

---

[25] Shepard Design, director, "Matthew, The Visual Bible NIV," Dallas, TX: Visual International and Visual Entertainment, Inc. 1997 Four Volumes, VCR.

practical, spiritual and emotional support. I suddenly realized that I had been relying on her prayers and kindness and wondered if she had felt *used* during my crisis. I was trying to be sensitive. She reassured me that she was happy to help and knew what it was like to be ill and come home from the hospital without food or staples, and she also understood what it was like to receive support with strings attached. Her motivation to support me was without any hidden agenda.

IT HAD BEEN eight days since the neurooncologist in Toronto had prescribed an experimental chemotherapy treatment, tamoxifen. It had been a successful treatment for breast cancer but hadn't been tested for brain cancers. Since he had no other options to offer, he suggested a high dose of this drug in addition to the CPT11, which was chemotherapy treatment for colon cancer. The hope was that combining the two drugs would work on brain tumours also. The dose for breast cancer patients was one tablet daily, but he prescribed 12 tablets by increasing the dose in increments until she reached twelve. When Tanya reached eight tablets (160 mg of tamoxifen), she started menopause with hot flashes and tearful mood fluctuations. To further complicate the cocktail of drugs, he had previously doubled Tanya's decadron, morphine, dialantin, naproxen, zantec, and clobazam. So many drugs!

Propped up in the wheelchair, she was slumped over like a rag doll. I often encouraged her to hold on until we reached the other side of this horrible storm and that we must keep our eyes on Jesus sleeping on a cushion at the stern (Mark 4:35–41). She feebly whispered, "Mummy, the other side is heaven." Her body was imprisoned in sickness and suffering while her mind remained free with thoughts of heaven. I wasn't prepared to let her go.

With tears in her eyes, she lamented, "Mum, I want the miracle of healing so badly that I'm afraid I won't get it. Mum, are you frustrated to watch both your children die?"

I couldn't even imagine that as a possibility. I broke the silence, redirected her focus, and reminded her of God's truth in His Word. "Tanya, never give up or lose sight that the other side is healing." I pleaded with her.

Barely audible, she bemoaned, "Mum, I have told you before. You must listen and understand; the other side is heaven. I will make it to the other side, with Jesus, and that is heaven."

"What about your professor's words of encouragement that you are destined to impact genetic science?" I searched for reasons to instill hope.

"Mum, I will impact genetic science with all these experimental drugs. I just never thought I would be doing it through my death." She replied in her practical analytical style. I refused to grasp the magnitude of what she was saying. She was my only living child, and she loved God more than life itself. I wanted to share our walk with God together in years to come.

I reminded her, "What about our cruise to glorify God and to celebrate His miracle of healing?" This had been a long-range plan that she and her friends had made when they visited her in hospital. Her pain and weakness blocked her vision.

Exhausted, she restated her observations with a whisper, "Mum, I am a science student. Can't you see my body is dying?" My denial was steeped in hope for healing, and I couldn't fathom that hope crumbling. I understood the analytical part of Tanya's mind. Even as a child, she had always been logical.

Another story about Tanya's teen years that shows her analytical character drifted into my consciousness. It seemed that every Friday night, she asked me for the car keys so that she and her girlfriends could go 'cruising.' One Friday night, teasing her, I withheld the keys and asked her why should she get the car every Friday to entertain her friends?

"Convince me that I should give you my car," I playfully challenged.

She chuckled and met my challenge, confidently stating her case. "Well, Mom, by Friday, the car is littered with gum wrappers, and the tank is on empty. My friends and I put gas in your tank and clean out your car every week." Our eyes met with delightful humour as I handed the keys to her and thanked her. She reciprocated with a smile and trotted off, jingling the keys. That was Tanya. So logical. So practical.

I begged her to bypass analysis, logic, and the evidence of her imminent death and instead, rely on the unseen healing and restoration found in God. "Tanya, please keep your eyes on Jesus and His promises for a long life. You aren't like Eric. You won't die. You have plans to finish your master's, get married, and adopt children." In past conversations, she articulated that she hadn't finished her work on earth. I reminded her of God's promises in His Word, imprinted on my heart, which supported a plan of hope for her future (Jeremiah 29:11–13). She listened silently.

Tanya became increasingly lethargic and other than a few brief exchanges, she barely spoke the next day. Speaking took too much energy. She received phone calls from the Toronto research scientist, Cherri, and out-of-town friend, Vivianna. Though weak, she spoke with clarity. Also, the clinical trial nurse in Toronto phoned and informed her that her next CPT11 chemo would be Thursday instead of Friday. I wondered, as her strength declined, if she could make the trip to Toronto. Patti phoned, and when I poured out my ardent desire for Tanya's healing, she offered me supportive prayer. I appreciated her timely words and consistent faithfulness.

While Patti was still on the phone, six church friends arrived. Tanya drifted in and out of sleep as they chatted at her bedside. All but Cori left, and Tanya seemed more alert than she had been the entire day. Cori wondered if Tanya had enough energy for a Bible study. She perked up and responded, "Yes, let's have a Bible study! Let's study Hebrews 11!"

Tanya knew Hebrews 11 from memory, the chapter known as the faith chapter. Multiple tumours crowding her brain couldn't crowd out her memorized scriptures. It was settled. Cori would organize the event. More encouragement arrived as two more church friends popped in with lasagna. Later, Karin arrived with mouthwatering stir-fry rice and chicken. Our fridge was overflowing with delicious meals. Karin's friendship was a source of strength and comfort. She never tired of being ever-present in our life. I appreciated her far beyond what I could ever say. What would I have ever done without the generous help of the body of Christ? Indeed, God was present daily.

I anointed Tanya with oil, as I did every night, and fervently prayed for healing. We had previously committed to speak at the Baptist church the following Sunday regardless of our circumstances, as a step of faith believing God would supply a miracle. The church leader needed a commitment from us as they prepared the bulletin with our names as guest speakers. If God was calling me to glorify Him before we saw the evidence of Tanya's healing, I wanted to obey. Tanya had already prepared most of the message on prayer, and I felt strongly about unity between us, so I asked for her input. Should I be the guest speaker at church on Sunday? Tanya explored my emotional resources insightfully, "No and yes. I think you should do it, but I am worried you will feel stress." I reassured her that God's grace would be sufficient. We joined our hands and prayed again. With wisdom, Tanya directed me, "Tell the leader yes and no about speaking this coming Sunday." I asked Tanya to explain her response, and she said, "Tell her, yes, you will speak, but no, not this Sunday." Her answer resonated with me. I phoned the church leader and explained that I would have to postpone speaking on Sunday. Tanya and I had planned to speak together—we would speak after her miraculous recovery.

Tanya's relationship with God remained transparent and submissive, and prayer time was filled with raw passion. She prayed, "Heavenly Father, I need more faith and grace to walk this path. There is a battle going on in my head, a struggle to just blackout, and it would all go away, and a struggle to keep fighting. Dear God, my subconscious wants to just blackout and my conscious wants to keep fighting. Please help me to follow You." I directed her to keep fighting even as I knew her heart to follow Jesus was the right response. She was incapacitated, weak, and frail as eight tumours consumed her brain and multiple cancers assaulted her body.

Early the following morning, Tanya apologized profusely for waking me up the second time around 4:00 a.m. I tried to reassure her that it was alright to wake me up any time, and I felt sorrowful and brokenhearted that she had suffered so much. I resolutely clung to God for a miracle. Our only vision was Christ.

Even in her anguish, Tanya found occasions to laugh; we cherished our humorous interludes. She reiterated an hour-long phone call she'd had a few days previously with a long-time school friend, now living in British Columbia, who jokingly teased she would find Tanya a male match. Tanya found it humorous and chuckled as she recalled the details from the conversation. Her short-term memory sharpened even as her body weakened. Brief windows of light-hearted humour were treasured relief amid unfathomable agony.

Her discouragement grew as the tamoxifen dose increased. I tried to reassure her that we would get to the other side, but she moaned, "The other side is an illusion." Then she corrected herself and said the other side was heaven. I told her God had a good plan for her life, and she interjected, "Maybe it's fulfilled." I asserted that I needed her, and she replied, with a faint hint of humour and sarcasm, "Why? To turn on the computer? You'll learn." She was so discouraged. I told her I would call Mama and Papa Blessings to pray with her, and she emphasized that if she didn't have a miracle that night, she would go into a coma. She bemoaned that she was so tired and just wanted to sleep. I wept, my heart aching beyond words, and prayed with Mama and Papa Blessing. They prayed with Tanya and nurtured her with scripture from Exodus that the battle was the Lord's, and she should rest in Him. Afterward, I wept again with Tanya; I repeated over and over that I wanted her to live.

A short time later, two church members, accompanied by high school youths, dropped by and encouraged Tanya with cards and appreciative words for her involvement at church. The first card was a message from a young teenager telling Tanya how she had profoundly impacted her life, and the second card wished her wellness. I used the words written on the cards to encourage Tanya to a greater purpose here on earth that would augment the lives of others. Again, we sealed our love with tears. As darkness overtook our day, and I blessed her with a good night and see you tomorrow, she whispered, "If tomorrow comes." Earlier I had anointed her with oil on all the parts of her body suffering pain and prayed again for her healing. I surrendered all to obey God. I sensed God carrying us in our suffering and our struggles.

By March 17, Tanya's decline was startling. She slept the entire day. I woke her at 6:00 a.m., and she went back to sleep until 4:00 p.m. She drooled, had mucous in her throat, a rattle in her lungs, and couldn't sit upright.

Our doctor phoned, alarmed because Tanya's anticonvulsant medication levels were dangerously high. The recommended range was 40–80, and Tanya was at 120. One effect of this was that Tanya couldn't support her head and had to lay horizontally.

The pastor and his daughter made a brief visit, and Tanya thanked her for the card. Chatting with an adolescent helped Tanya to imagine assisting others with her life. Then two friends from her university genetic class called, but she was too weak to speak. Later, she lamented about her high school friend Tori, who needed to see a miracle to believe in God again, and sadly she wouldn't see it in her. Her mind and thoughts were coherent and lucid. Earlier, she asked me to look for nail clippers to trim her toenails. I couldn't find them anywhere. She whispered, "Go downstairs to my bedroom. Look in the white basket on the floor beside the far wall, and you will find the clippers." I followed her directions, and sure enough, I found her clippers exactly where she said they would be. Her long-term and short-term memory were intact. She could recall conversations from the previous day, detailed information, telephone exchanges, contents of letters and notes, despite the tumours and cancer, and the side effects from chemotherapy drugs and massive doses of tamoxifen. God had preserved her mind, and I believed and hoped that He would restore her body.

We had an early morning ambulance to Toronto for another CPT11 chemotherapy session. I spoke to the clinical trial nurse about the extremely high levels of anticonvulsant medication causing severe muscle weakness that had incapacitated Tanya. I explained that she had regained the strength to hold her head up with a reduced dosage. I added that the tamoxifen dosage had resulted in severe depression and hot flashes that lasted for hours. She empathized with my concerns. In the meantime, Tanya felt low emotionally, and nothing I offered could boost her morale. The day was long and taxing.

We arrived home at 8:00 p.m., and as I helped Tanya shuffle into the house, she tearfully lamented, "I'm not going to be healed. Mom, look at my physical handicaps. My body is paralyzed on one side and weak on the other. I can't hold my weight. Can't you see my body is deteriorating and I am dying? I know about science. With eight brain tumours dividing and multiplying, the amount of space in my brain will run out. Isn't that enough evidence for you that I am not going to be healed? Mom, I feel so sorry for you. You are in such denial."

I couldn't let myself hear her words, so I recorded them on paper. I thought it was the depression speaking, so I spoke the scriptures to redirect her attention to God. Tanya joined me and poured her heart out to God. Before bed, she prayed, "This is my prayer, Jesus. I need grace and mercy. Have mercy on me please. I need a sign that You are here. Dear Jesus, You seem so far off," she whispered.

I also felt alone at times, but I reminded myself and reminded Tanya of God's Words, *"...Never will I leave you; never will I forsake you"* (Hebrews 13:5). Both Tanya and I had cried out, *"Lord, don't you care if we drown?"* (Mark 4: 38).

That was the security of our relationship with Jesus. We could expose our raw vulnerabilities and know that God still loved us even as we searched for Him with all our hearts.

Shortly after her prayer, her friend, Elle, came by with a casserole. Tanya had asked God for a sign, and Elle spoke to Tanya about taking hold of her healing as she promoted the Word of God. As Elle spoke, Tanya was more alert than she had been in weeks. It felt like a miracle, an uplifting visit from God. Later, when Tanya prayed, the depression was less intense. She seemed more content that God was still in control. I recalled the many times during her university years she had instructed me to be content in the Lord, "Mom, to be content in the Lord Jesus, do not let your expectations exceed your reality." Her wise words reverberated in my thoughts many times, and I cherished them as if they had been spoken afresh.

Friday, March 19, Tanya wept frequently. I embraced her, tried to console her, and reminded her that the devastating drugs caused her depression. On my way to the kitchen, I asked if she wanted anything. With desperate tears, she cried, "Mom, I want to be healed, but I'm not getting it." The deep places in my heart were filled with silent grief, but on the outside, my words only pointed back to faith in Jesus for healing. I prayed for wisdom.

Tanya was so downcast in Peterborough that she wanted to move back to London to have Dr. C as her neurooncologist, hoping a new treatment plan would reverse this horrible disease. I was concerned because her support system of school and church friends was in Peterborough. Nevertheless, she called the doctor, and his care plan wouldn't differ from the Toronto oncologist. He also spoke with me privately, explaining that he wanted his role to be Tanya's friend that she could phone and vent on, not her oncologist. He had had a more personal connection with her through her past volunteer position at the London Cancer Regional Centre when she had studied at Western and his brief involvement when Eric had been first diagnosed. He empathized with Tanya's frustrations, and his compassion was comforting.

Later, the clinical trial nurse called and told Tanya they required a negative pregnancy test for Tanya to receive the thalidomide that Dr. C in London had recommended. While I was still on the phone, a church member came to the door with food. Talk about God's perfect timing! Barbara worked at the clinic, so I asked if she would be willing to pick up the material for the urine test and take the sample directly to the lab. The clinical trial nurse had a deadline for faxing the results to the drug company. Otherwise, it would mean waiting another week. Barbara was pleased to help us. Only God orchestrated and coordinated the timing and availability of people for the continued, ongoing, amazing support. We were indebted to the many people God had placed so strategically in our lives.

Our family doctor made a house call and advised us to check her anticonvulsant levels in a few days now that the dose had been reduced. Shortly after the doctor left, Tanya had a seizure. It started with her left hand twitching, and it moved up to her elbow. I began to pray in the Spirit and increased the Christian music volume. As Tanya focused on Jesus, the intensity of the seizure subsided. She slept. My darling daughter remained weak with debilitating cancer. When she awoke, disoriented, she cried in frustration and discouragement. Just at that precise moment, Mama and Papa Blessings called, and I asked them to reassure Tanya, which they did with prayer. Later, when Tanya and I chatted about God's faithfulness, I suggested, "Wasn't Mama and Papa Blessing's phone call our Father God's perfect timing?" She wholeheartedly agreed.

Tanya couldn't understand why God hadn't healed her completely. Our scripture reading that night was in Luke, about the man with the shrivelled hand that was healed (Luke 6:6–11), the widow's boy raised from the dead (Luke 7:11–17), the centurion servant healed, all when Jesus spoke a word (Luke 7:2; 7:10), and the woman who wet Jesus's feet with her tears, poured on perfume, and dried his feet with her hair. She loved much because she was forgiven much

(Luke 7:44–50). We asked the Lord again for forgiveness and to reveal any hindrances in our lives that would block Tanya's healing. Her eyes pooled with tears as she repented, probed her heart to determine any shortcomings in her attitude that impeded God's healing power. *"Search me, God, and know my heart; test me and know my anxious thoughts. See if there is any offensive way in me, and lead me in the way everlasting"* (Psalm 139:23–24). I, too, repented, as I had been doing for months, looking to God to reveal any wrong in me. I trusted that He would show us clearly if we were defiant or were blinded with tunnel vision. I believed that God had given Tanya a crystal-clear mind for a reason. Although aware of her dire situation, she ultimately rested in the grace and promises of God. I anointed Tanya and prayed desperately for healing. My urgent prayers ascended to heaven and rebounded with a deafening silence.

On Saturday, March 20, we had a day trip to Toronto for CPT11 chemo and a scheduled follow-up appointment five days later to start thalidomide therapy, with an exorbitant cost of $1,500.00 a month. Even though I was unemployed, I had confidence God would provide, just as He had faithfully provided a fridge full of food.

Surprised by a visit from a couple bearing food, we talked about the goodness of God, exalted His Name, and cherished God's unending love. Later, Tanya's friend, Selena, dropped by, and we invited her in to join us for dinner to share the abundance of food God had provided through the church. I rented a comedy video, and another friend from church popped in for an impromptu visit. I snuggled Tanya on her bed while Cori sat in the wheelchair and Selena on the high-back chair, and we watched this mindless comedy, revelling in the silliness, savouring every breath of laughter. We needed this laugh-filled interlude to offset the deep sorrow and ongoing agony of the disease. The girls left, and Tanya rested, exhausted from the eventful day. Later, she recalled details from the movie in casual conversation, which redirected our attention to a trivial, nonsensical dialogue. Selena phoned later and arranged another small-group visit. Two more friends called and scheduled a visit. A busy day, notably marked by the love of God, expressed through His loving, caring people.

Our journey was *with* God and *to* God. Our life, our thoughts, our readings, and our conversations revolved around God. With every detail, God was with us. Some days seemed more memorable than others, but none compared to Sunday, March 21, 1999. What an unfathomable day! Tanya exploded with clever comments, cracked jokes, and made comeback statements to my playful teasing. During our morning worship, I again anointed her, read scripture, and we celebrated the Lord's supper. We broke bread while mindful of Jesus's body broken for us, and the juice representing Jesus's shed blood given up freely for our sins, our forgiveness, and redemption. What a mighty Saviour! We prayed passionately, thankful for the sacrifice of our Lord Jesus and for the gift of so many wonderful believers He had placed in our life.

Tanya prayed fervently, "Please, Lord, don't tarry, and let your healing be manifested." I wondered if healing would be soon since Tanya remained alert and articulate all day. Her sharp memory amazed me; both her short and long-term memory were astounding, with no change in her cognitive ability. I repeatedly observed this phenomenon. With malignant and rapidly advancing tumours in the brain, one would expect a cognitive decline. But Tanya had none! That was the major evidence that convinced me that God would heal her. She had such a sound mind!

SEVENTEEN
Hebrews 11: The Beginning of Healings

TANYA EXCITEDLY ANTICIPATED the evening Bible study all day. Right on time, the college and careers group of ten young adults arrived and crowded into her tiny bedroom to study the faith chapter that she had requested: Hebrews 11. To introduce the Bible study, we sang praises to the Lord with a harmonic, angelic chorus of youthful voices. We read Hebrews 11 aloud followed by a verse-by-verse discussion of its meaning and application. Tanya digested every word for spiritual nourishment. She savoured every moment with eager participation for three full hours. The young adults concluded in prayer and conversed over goodies and treats. The Bible was precious and filled with miracles that led us closer to knowing Jesus.

Later, Mama Blessings phoned and prayed the Psalms, specifically the psalm of David, that Tanya would *"...see the goodness of the Lord in the land of the living"* (Psalm 27:13). I told Mama Blessing that was the verse Tanya had recited as she clung to life. We had celebrated Holy Communion that morning with the expectation of healing through the Body and Blood of Jesus Christ. Mama and Papa Blessing revitalized us with their ongoing prayers, words that pointed us only to Jesus. Words! Healing Words!

God's Words were crucial to our spiritual existence, and words were respected in our family. I raised my children on positive words, and Tanya had become a person true to her word. I taught both Tanya and Eric that their word was the most significant thing they could give to me. Do what you say and say what you do. Do not use words flippantly. Words had power! My children weren't permitted to use words to hurt themselves or others. It was understood that you would not speak words that you didn't mean. When you lived with many life and death health crises, you did not waste words; you didn't sweat the small stuff. Words were spoken to encourage, to build up and support one another. Words were spoken to point each other to Christ. Life was too precious to speak idle words. My children could count on my words, and I could rely on theirs. Words were like a tool to accomplish great things for each other and in each other.

I recalled when Tanya was a teen and purchased her first road bike, twenty-one speeds, with handlebar brakes, the Cadillac of two-wheel mobility. My bike was antique, becoming obsolete. To stop, you back-peddled hard and up steep hills, well, you walked the bike. Riding Tanya's new bike was pure delight. And Tanya was exceedingly generous. "Mom, you can ride my bike anytime I am not using it." I asked to ride her bike often, and she happily granted me permission. Well, back to words.

One Saturday, I nonchalantly handed her my car keys and announced that she could use the car, and I would be taking her bike to run my errands. It was a bright, sunny day, and I was eager to feel the cool breeze kissing my cheeks, my hair blowing in the wind. She popped my euphoric bubble and explained she had a bike ride already planned with her friends. I tried to persuade her to use my car, but she simply restated her intentions.

She reiterated her earlier promise, "Mom, I said you could use my bike anytime I wasn't planning to use it, and today I have plans."

I pulled out a "no, no" card from my subliminal manipulation deck to deepen my persuasion. "Tanya, why won't you let me use your bike? Look at all I have done for you, and you would deny me the use of your bike?"

Her response was gentle but on point. "That's a guilt trip, and I'm not travelling there. I agreed to allow you to use my bike anytime I wasn't planning to use it. Today, I have plans. Why don't you buy yourself a new bike? Be good to yourself, Mom; you are worth it!"

With that, she hugged me and left. I was wounded. I called my friend for sympathy and prayer, but she agreed with Tanya. My daughter had been true to her promise, and I couldn't refute that. So, with Tanya's kind words echoing in my ears, I walked to the bike shop, bought a mountain bike with 21 gears, and excitedly peddled home. Tanya was pleased with my decision and even more pleased that we could cycle together.

I was amazed that Tanya had remembered the previous day's events with precise detail, especially the playful exchanges of words and humorous banter she had had with her friend Dennis during a telephone conversation. As we chatted, she moved her toes slightly at will, and we rejoiced that God had released her paralysis. She felt stronger than the previous days, less lethargic and sleepy. Amazingly, she had steady balance, and she bore her weight when she shifted from the bed to the chair and decided to remain there for the two hours of our daily praise and worship time.

Patti arrived with her guitar. Karin and her two adult children, Lara and Mark, came, too. Lara played Eric's keyboard, and Mark played his guitar. Eric's elementary teacher, Linda, joined us in worshipping God and celebrating His faithfulness. After weeks of being too weak to speak above a whisper, Tanya's exuberant voice and ability to stay alert were a definite miracle. Steps toward wellness had begun.

The next few days brought additional healing on our journey with God. While I prepared Tanya's breakfast, she watched the morning news and wept. She transitioned into singing, her voice strong, "My God is an Awesome God He reigns; in heaven above...."[26] Praise God! God is so good! I heard her sing the chorus over and over as she worshipped. Tanya explained that she wept because she felt drawn to become a foster parent to help distressed children. In the moment, her sensitive affection was directed toward homeless children that she longed to nurture with the love of God. Throughout her childhood, she had been kind and sensitive to her brother's trials and had taken him into her care, attentive to his struggles and as his loyal supporter. Now, she needed to chase her dreams to help others, and I believed God would illuminate her path to achieve them! Tanya's heart for others had been a consistent theme throughout her life and reminiscing about her past brought joy and edified me.

Tanya's high school years reflected her growth and maturity. She was involved in many clubs and activities helping others. She had a vision for her future that she pursued with diligence. She had declared, "I want to be a physiotherapist."

My commonsense response was, "That's a great career choice. Perhaps volunteering might help refine the scope of that field that is of most interest to you."

She readily adopted my suggestion, began volunteering at the Sports Injury Clinic at the college and later at the Five Counties Children Centre in physiotherapy. She was eager to learn and was reliable, applying her knowledge with professionalism over several years at the college and the Children's Centre. The latter segued into a summer job as a camp counsellor and coordinator. Tanya was competent, single-minded, and conscientiously implemented her commitments and responsibilities passionately. I recalled times during her years growing up that I had prayed, "Thank you, God, for the remarkable daughter you have loaned to me to raise."

[26] Rich Mullins, "Awesome God," *Winds of Heaven, Stuff of Earth*, Producer Reed Arvin Label: Reunion, Album, 1988.

After she graduated from high school, her teacher wrote a beautiful letter of recommendation. The following excerpts from his lengthy letter aptly described Tanya:

"Tanya helps others willingly, whenever and wherever the need arises, often sacrificing her own personal, social and work time. Her courtesy, manners and sense of responsibility are beyond reproach and serve as a wonderful role model for both her peers and the younger students with whom she works in various clubs and organizations. I am the staff advisor of the school service club, The Court of Leo; Tanya has been an active member of this club for nearly three years, and throughout this time, I have been impressed with her initiative, responsibility, and diligence. She is willing to try new ideas, takes on duties cheerfully, and follows through on her obligations to successful completion. She is currently Vice-President of the club. In discussion with other teachers, I am told that Tanya has demonstrated the same kind of dedication with the Kids Helping Kids Club for the past three years, the Science Fair Committee for the past two years, set painting for our drama/musical productions for three years, and currently, works on the school play production. Each year, Tanya took on more obligations as her interests continued to grow and diversify. The partial listing which follows is just an example of this growth and is in addition to the various activities already discussed. Tanya was a member of the ISCF during her first two years at high school, then joined the Outdoors Club in grade 11, added the ECOS club in grade 12, and in her final year has joined the Lion's Roar (school newspaper) the Science Club, the School Formal Committee and the GWME organization which performs perfecting functions at various school social functions as well as organizes various other activities in the school. Throughout the five years, Tanya has been an active participant on the school Track Team as well… Tanya measures her own success against a realistic standard that she establishes for herself, and whether it be in sports, academic effort, or in social situations she abides by these standards. Her ability to offer encouragement when spirits are down and to support others when they need help are well known and appreciated. Socially, she has numerous friends who respect her and enjoy her company…. I appreciate the opportunity to write on behalf of such a well-rounded individual with so many superior qualities. She amply illustrates the best in our youth today." (Excerpts from her high school teacher's reference letter)

As her mom, I knew that Tanya wasn't perfect, but she certainly was the perfect daughter for me.

Fast forward. We watched 100 Huntley Street, and the guest speaker spoke about those in Jamaica's ghettos. Tanya and I instantly prayed earnestly for the many children presented, and as I held her limp, paralyzed left hand, she squeezed it and shocked me! I interrupted my prayer and asked her if she had squeezed my hand? Smiling with a twinkle in her eyes, she squeezed again, and we praised our Lord for the evidence of healing! My heart pounded with great delight and leaped with joyful thankfulness! I could barely contain my elation! All day, Tanya continued to lift her once paralyzed arm from the shoulder and wiggle her toes at will. We prayed without ceasing, thanked and worshipped God for the healing that had begun. Eagerly, I pushed the wheelchair to the bathroom for her shower, and while she balanced on her stronger right leg with my support, she lifted her previously paralyzed left leg into the tub. We were exuberant with gratitude to God, brimming over with joy unspeakable!

Around noon, she announced her intention to walk from her bed to her wheelchair, about six steps away. I held her waist lightly as she put one foot in front of the other, all the while excitedly praising God for her remarkable transformation! After so many weeks of paralysis, Tanya's healing had begun. I phoned many people who glorified God with me in tearful thanksgiving. Tanya's voice was strong; her energy was back! When the home care nurse arrived, she was flabbergasted by the sudden improvement in Tanya's health. When Tanya squeezed the nurse's hand with her previously paralyzed left hand and moved her left foot, leg, and toes at will, the nurse continued to be incredulous at her remarkable recovery. We directed the nurse's attention to Jesus, the healer.

Meanwhile, Tanya invited Dennis and Selena for a visit, and just before they arrived, she asked me to watch her walk to the bathroom—a lot farther than the six steps she had taken earlier. I was a little hesitant since her legs hadn't fully supported her body weight for some time. I positioned my arm around her waist for minimal support, and she stepped one foot forward and then the other and walked the distance. Praise God! We thanked Jesus, declaring, "You are faithful! You are Healer! You are Awesome!" When Dennis and Selena arrived, they were astonished as they watched Tanya walk.

Dennis brought a celebratory pie, and for three hours, the young adults chatted, ate dessert, and prayed, brimming over with thankfulness. I phoned more friends and my father, bursting with worship and gratitude to Jesus! I called Deanna and my friend in Dallas and many others. It was hard to imagine it would have been nearly three weeks earlier that the Toronto neurooncologist had given Tanya the bleak prognosis of two weeks to live, with one of those weeks in a coma before death.

Tanya phoned the clinical trial nurse that afternoon and asked if she could have a baseline MRI before starting thalidomide the following week. The oncologist nurse couldn't believe it was Tanya speaking to her; she was shocked to hear a strong, confident, healthy voice. Tanya and I couldn't stop praising God for His healing power manifested in her body! Later, she talked on the phone with Elle for hours after sunset, alert, her voice resilient and definite with no evidence of fatigue.

We phoned Mama and Papa Blessings with ecstatic joy. Just minutes before, they had been praying for us. What perfect timing! We celebrated, worshipped God with praise and prayers of thanksgiving for this evidence that Tanya's healing had begun. They said they would call the American television ministries that had been praying to give the praise report and would continue to pray for her full recovery.

During our evening Bible time, Tanya prayed ardently. She had been praying for days, "Please Lord, do not tarry, manifest your healing please," and tonight with great energy and fervour, she thanked our Lord God for not tarrying; again, I anointed her with oil as I did every night, and I prayed passionately with gratitude for Jesus's healing; we had the oil of joy, for our mourning was past and rejoicing had come.

"Mom, do you remember Eric always wanted to be a missionary?" Tanya asked. "Do you think we are to fulfill his calling?" Her words gripped my heart with absolute agreement. My new desire wasn't in the classroom teaching. I wanted to do God's will and serve the Lord on the mission field. Elated with new direction and purpose, Tanya and I yearned to obey God wherever He would send us.

I prayed, "Dear Father God. You are so faithful, so faithful, so faithful! All praise, honour, and glory are Yours! You are so wonderful I scarcely have words to express it, and while I hold my breath that perhaps I'm dreaming, I know I am living in You and Tanya's healing isn't a dream. It is hers because of Jesus's stripes that He suffered for us. Thank You, Jesus, for Your Word, Your promises, and Your faithfulness to Your Word. In Jesus's Name, Amen."

In the following days, Tanya's strength improved, and words of gratitude spilled continually from our lips. We talked extensively to anyone who visited about the Lord's love and goodness. We had a welcome surprise visit from the young adult pastor with his two preschool boys, who spread a bouquet of energy and laughter into our home. The little children represented growth and the surprises of life. Things seemed to be getting better and better.

After the children and pastor left, Tanya suddenly had a mild seizure. As before, we sang Christian choruses, relaxed, and refocused on Jesus until the seizure subsided. I felt perplexed because seizures might interfere with her progress. My thoughts returned to a more pleasant focus.

Some of her friends dropped in unannounced, and Selena and the others diverted her attention from the seizure with a comedy movie. They hooted and hollered over humorous scenes, their voices rising above each other. I relished the joy, basking in the waves of laughter that rippled through our home. Her friends concluded their evening with prayer.

It had been a full day. In the quiet before bedtime, Tanya and I reflected on God's intervention during the day. Earlier, God had protected us while we were oblivious to danger that could have cost us our home and even our lives. Tanya had asked for tea, so I filled the kettle, turned the stove on high, and fell asleep snuggled with her while we waited for the water to boil. When a beeping scream pierced the silence, I thought it was the oxygen machine malfunctioning, so I ignored the beep until I realized it was the smoke detector and the kitchen was engulfed in smoke. The kettle had melted like butter, fused to the glowing burner. God had awakened me in time to avert a tragic house fire.

When we arrived at the hospital on March 25 for Tanya's chemotherapy, the clinical nurse had tears in her eyes, astonished at Tanya's remarkable recovery. Tanya startled her by using her previously paralyzed hand to give her a squeeze. Hardly noticing her transformation, the neurooncologist was impressed that Tanya had been able to tolerate such a high dose of tamoxifen. He commented that most patients with breast cancer tolerated one tablet while Tanya was taking twelve. This treatment came with horrific side effects: drug-induced menopause, deep depression, mood swings of tearfulness, and hot flashes that lasted for hours.

A drug from the USA, thalidomide, arrived, and since it wasn't licensed or approved in Canada, the cost would be $1,500.00 out of pocket. The neurooncologist was pessimistic about its effectiveness but ordered it upon request. Dr. C in London had suggested it at a time when Tanya's health had been failing. Now, with her miraculous recovery, Tanya decided to hold off from taking it, and the oncologist agreed, reassuring her that he would keep the drug in the event she changed her mind.

Following our appointment, Tanya called her grandfather, who arrived with food she had requested. They had a pleasant visit, chatting about her improved health because of Jesus's healing touch. He was impressed with Tanya's sudden recovery but still skeptical. The attending nurse remembered us from the previous week in daycare chemo; now, she noted Tanya's ravenous appetite and asked about the bruises on her calf, which I attributed to the high doses of decadron. When I told her that Tanya was on 64mg of decadron, she insisted that I must have made an error since no one could tolerate that much and still function. I showed her Tanya's prescription. She referred to her pharmaceutical dictionary. The ceiling dose for palliative care was 30mg daily, and Tanya was taking more than twice that dose. I consulted the attending pharmacist, who also expressed grave concern that Tanya's dose was much too high. The pharmacist listed life-threatening and adverse side effects, many of which Tanya was experiencing. I would investigate the side-effects on the Internet later and found startling information that concurred with the pharmacist. What was the meaning of this? I determined to believe that God would reverse these worrisome side-effects with His continued healing.

The next day, Friday, March 26, we were back home. Every word I spoke was praise and thanks to God. Tanya moved her fingers, toes, and feet easily. We phoned the Christian television ministry in Toronto and reported God's healing miracle and asked her to relay it to those who had prayed.

We had no sooner hung up the phone when the family doctor dropped by. Tanya walked from the bedroom to the living room with minimal assistance. She waved her fingers and lifted her hand to her eyes. The doctor was astonished and filled with joy. Tanya and I praised God and shared a synopsis of our faith journey with God. We took every opportunity to give God glory.

After the doctor's visit, Tanya called the pastor and invited him to come and see the beginning of God's healing. When he arrived, his expression widened in surprise. He brought up the scripture where Jesus made the blind to see and the lame to walk. I thought of the blind as unbelievers whose eyes were opened to see Jesus, and the lame who walked was Tanya. Perhaps God had planned to use our testimony of healing to bring souls to Christ.

Every day when my father, Sharon, Patti, Karin, Selena, Dennis, and Vivianna called, we excitedly declared our thanksgiving to our Lord Jesus. They called often. Tanya's frail body was steadily healing as she was being restored to health and strength.

Now that she no longer needed the wheelchair, Tanya requested that I put the bathroom door back on the hinges. The college and career young adults came soon after to watch a movie. I so enjoyed hearing the sounds of carefree young adults in group discussions as the movie played. The energy in the room was contagious, reminiscent of a normal life for a young adult, and Tanya was part of it. After her friends left, I anointed her with oil and prayed a lengthy prayer of thanksgiving for the gift of God's healing and the daily progress of strength and improvement. We submitted ourselves completely to God, available to be used in any way to glorify Him.

The weather was balmy with a hint of spring as March ended. Tanya sat outdoors for hours, chatting on the phone, watching her dog play. Then she spoke with my friend, Carolyn, in joyful anticipation of fulfilling God's will for her life.

The following days were all amazing! Glory to God in the highest flowed from our lips constantly! Tanya awoke during the night, walked to the bathroom, and excitedly showed me that she could lift her left arm and grasp the trapeze on the hospital bed. Every day her hand and arm became stronger. I could barely contain myself with thanksgiving to God with the excitement of witnessing hourly improvements. She squeezed my hand tightly with her left hand, and as she moved her left hand into mine, she squeezed tightly again. It was splendid to celebrate God's goodness over and over!

During the afternoon, I was looking for the mop to wash the outdoor deck in preparation for her barbeque party but couldn't find it in the crowded garage. Tanya piped in that she had secured the mop on nails under the deck last summer, and sure enough it was there. Later, when I planned a bike ride, I realized I didn't have a lock, so I borrowed hers, and without hesitation, she said her lock combination was 1563, which was correct. She hadn't ridden her bike in over a year but hadn't forgotten her combination. The frailty, lethargy, weakness, feeble whispers, discouragement, and pain of a few weeks ago seemed like a distant nightmare.

Tanya sat outside on the patio with her friends, and together they enjoyed their first spring barbeque. It was sunny and a pleasant sixty-five degrees. She had a wonderful visit and checked her biceps for fun, noticing the muscle bulge improving. Tanya gave God all the credit for healing. Her chatter and chuckles were evidence of her recovering health as she and her friends enjoyed the afternoon. Father God had healed my daughter, my child! My heart was exploding with gratitude! While Tanya entertained her friends, I went out on my bike for the first time to welcome the spring season. He had given Tanya back to me! As I peddled, my mind drifted to some of Tanya's cycling events, and another time when I had to let her go.

So many stories about Tanya were imprinted on my memory. She loved to cycle and was drawn to adventure. One summer, she and her girlfriend decided to cycle over fifty kilometres with camping gear on their backs to Lovesick Lake for a few days. After they arrived and settled at their camping site, they invited me to drive up for a visit and enjoy their campfire culinary skills. I complimented their courage and desire to explore and discover their strengths.

I had always felt close to Tanya. Back when she was preparing for university, I couldn't bear the thought of being separated from her, so had encouraged her to apply to the local university rather than the one she had chosen, which was 300 kilometres away. It would have been cheaper to have her live at home while attending classes in our city. She saw through me. "Mom," she replied sweetly, "you have taught me the skills to live independently, and I want to try my wings." So, she had left for school while I suffered empty-nest syndrome—I called daily to check up on her. I asked many mom questions until she gently asked, "Mom, have I ever gone anywhere or done anything that has ever caused you pain or distress?"

"No, of course not," was my emphatic reply.

"Mom," she gently coaxed me, "trust me to God and let go. I don't need you as a mom right now, but I do need you as a friend."

"Tanya, I know how to be a mom, but I don't know how to be a friend." I was out of my element.

"Mom, I will teach you. If I need a mom, I will say so plainly and ask for your advice when we talk. When I need a friend, I only want a listening ear, a sounding board, and not your solutions. God will show me the solution."

She guided me into this new way of communicating, and it deepened our relationship. She never distanced herself or broke relationship, and my role as a listener became more crucial as our closeness grew. She had a relationship with God, and He was her best friend. I trusted her to God and let her go as she requested, but she was never gone.

After her friends left, our evening prayer time was exuberant with thanksgiving; as Tanya and I committed ourselves to the Lord's service anew, she proclaimed, "God is awesome! I only want to glorify God with my life." In His grace, God had preserved her mental and emotional faculties despite the extensive brain malignancies.

En route to the hospital for a blood transfusion, we were nearly there when a focal seizure began, causing her arm to jerk severely; she opened the window, focused on Jesus in worship, and practiced deep breathing while I prayed. We praised and thanked God when it was over! While hooked up to the IV a few hours later, she had another seizure. She asked for more anticonvulsant medication. Seizures were still active, and I was puzzled that the healing wasn't overcoming them.

Later in the day, Tanya tackled the stairs. She was always careful to walk backwards down the stairs holding the handrail while placing her initial weight on her stronger right foot. On her way to the patio the day before, she almost collapsed when she mistakenly put weight first on the previously paralyzed left leg.

Tanya still took many phone calls, and her robust, sunny disposition energized the house. It felt like illness was a thing of the past and a testimony for our future. When I anointed her with oil and prayed for her continued healing that evening, we concentrated on what God had already accomplished.

Tuesday, March 30, 1999, we were so happy and content in the Lord. I couldn't have asked for anything more when God lavished more love upon us. A school colleague phoned to say the staff had an Easter gift. Thinking it was flowers, I wrote a thank you note to the staff praising God for Tanya's recovery. The teacher arrived bearing only a card from my coworkers. When I opened it, I was stunned to discover an uplifting message of Christian love along with $1,120.00 cash tucked inside! Wow! Incredible! To use Tanya's frequent praise, "God is awesome!"

The same day the cable TV installer came, Tanya negotiated a reduced rate before he installed the system! The substantial discount pleased her and enabled us both to watch a wide variety of programs. Her church friend, Dennis, dropped in, and we invited him to join us for lunch. While he visited with Tanya, I took a walk around the block. On my return, I raved to Tanya about the beautiful weather. She was tempted to go out in the wheelchair with me, but the novelty of the new access to cable TV won over, so we enjoyed the new variety of programs instead and even received scriptural nourishment from our pastor's televised sermon.

Sandwiched into our busy day, Barbara phoned with a number for the healing service at the Airport Church in Toronto since Tanya's healing hadn't been completed, and we were willing to go wherever God led us.

Later in the evening, Tanya had a seizure, and the few minutes' duration seemed forever. I prayed in the Spirit, and we both stayed calm and focused on Jesus. Her left hand was so weak after the seizure that she couldn't move it. It was paralyzed again. All that progress was lost. Before this seizure, she had been able to raise her left hand above her head, wave her fingers, and touch thumb to finger. I anointed Tanya with oil and prayed as we did every night, asking God for wisdom and guidance to resolve this plague with seizures. She had been doing so well. Why this setback? I suggested that she might go back to using oxygen more during the day as a preventative measure. She agreed.

Tanya and I reflected on how we had spent the day—how the warm, sunny wheelchair walk for pizza had felt carefree. Since she had craved cinnamon rolls, I stopped to buy some along with fruit. We had such pleasant conversations as we strolled to our various stops. The phone rang just as we returned. Devastating news! Tanya had been inadvertently exposed to chickenpox, and the risk of getting shingles again because of her compromised immune system was troubling. A few days after the young adult pastor had visited the previous week, the children broke out with telltale spots. The pastor and I prayed for God's protection.

After the call, Tanya hobbled to a chair, bent over at the waist, and laid her head on the adjacent stool and wept. One more battle, one more anxiety to cast on the Lord. *"Cast all your anxiety upon Him because he cares for you"* (1Peter 5:7). It seemed never-ending. Her left hand hadn't fully recovered from the previous day's seizure, and this threat of shingles added more discouragement.

Tanya sobbed, deeply concerned that she was a burden to me. Even when I held, comforted, and reassured her of my unconditional love, she continued to lament. I felt helpless, sad that she suffered so much and even more because she thought she was a *burden*. Oh, how I wanted to carry her burdens. I refocused her vision on Jesus. Oh, how I wanted her to cast her burdens on Jesus. Now she had to deal with the prospect of getting shingles again. "O Father God, we surrender all to You and trust You to keep her focus on You and not on her circumstances. We cast all our cares upon You." This had been my constant prayer.

Tanya wrote a contract, requested my signature, and in it was the promise of servitude. She regretfully repented that she had been difficult, ignoring my assurance that it was the devastating disease and drugs that had discouraged her. I signed it as she requested to give her control.

"I, Tanya Rebecca Williamson, prepare this mini-contract to remind myself and Janet Cecile Williamson what retribution she will receive when I am totally and utterly healed. PTL** This house will be cleaned fully from roof to basement. I will explain the computer programs that she will need to utilize, especially in the fall. I will do my best to have supper on the table every night by 5:30. These are for payment of her coping with a very difficult person who has been disagreeable and just terrible at most times. As well as being demanding. Please forgive me. Sign Tanya Rebecca Williamson March 31, 1999, * I know that you love me as I do you, though most of the events are totally uncalled for, and in my thinking can neither be justified."

Tanya was so hard on herself and wouldn't allow herself any excuses for what she perceived to be unacceptable behaviour. In reality, she had always been humble, gentle and patient, and never difficult or demanding. I explained that I thought she understood cognitively that much of her tears and depression were the side effects of decadron and tamoxifen. I was exceedingly grateful that she hadn't experienced the side effect of personality change or psychotic behaviour that often accompanied these drugs. Thank you, Jesus, for that!

Tanya remained emotionally sweet even in her catastrophic condition. No changes in her kind, giving heart, and that was a miraculous gift! She prayed faithfully and shared her feelings transparently with meekness and sincerity. She held nothing back, knowing that God loved her with all the emotions she brought to Him. She knew that I loved her unconditionally. She had never blamed me or God or projected her pain on me—but only courageously endured. Who could cope any differently with chronic pain and the horrific effects of debilitating drugs?

Preparing the outside barbeque was an effective distraction from the concerns about chickenpox. As Tanya focused on the beautiful evening, the sound of chirping birds and our light generic conversation improved her mood. Later, I anointed each body part with oil and prayed for healing. Again, Tanya paraphrased Mark 4:35–41 in her prayer. "Even the disciples cried out and He responded by calming the storm." Tanya prayed earnestly, "Lord please do not tarry. Complete the healing."

EIGHTEEN

Faith, Hope, Determination, and Prayers for the Journey

THURSDAY, APRIL 1, I anxiously awoke at 3:00 a.m. feeling sleep-deprived. I cast my cares upon Jesus and tried to rest. I finally staggered out of bed at 6:00 a.m., lugged the backpack and portable oxygen cylinder into the volunteer driver's car, helped Tanya get in, then slid in beside her. She rested her weary head on my shoulder. At the Toronto hospital, they had overbooked treatment schedules because of the upcoming Easter weekend. We had to wait three hours. We used the extra time with the clinical trial nurses to share stories. They erupted with bursts of laughter when Tanya described her home as a prison and how she plotted her escape for a haircut and nail manicure—but Mom restrained her with a collar and leash. Her dramatization and dry humour spurred us to more laughter when she reenacted how she had recently debated with the TV cable company over the exorbitant rates until they reduced the fee by 50%.

I piped up with a story about her accomplishments and described her success at the Canada Wide Science Fair during her last year of high school. Her project on "Brain Dominance and Learning Styles in High Schools" was extended beyond the competition, with an invitation to present her data and findings to science department leaders from a number of high schools. As her chauffeur to her speaking engagement, I casually suggested she might like to review her notes. Chuckling, with a twinkle in her eye, she had confidently assured me that she knew her topic thoroughly and didn't have notes. She delivered her presentation brilliantly and eloquently. She professionally reviewed her research for her audience while referring to her handouts and overheads, all without a cue card, hesitation, or a glitch. The teachers were intrigued with her research and asked questions that she competently and scientifically answered.

Entertained by my stories, the nurses coaxed me to share more. I talked about Tanya confidently defending her university thesis on "The Molecular Pathway of Colorectal Cancer" in her honours genetic year and receiving an excellent grade. The conversation was lighthearted and full of humour during our long wait for chemo. Tanya delighted the nurses with her bright optimism, and we both credited God for answers to prayers. After chemo and a long, exhausting fourteen-hour day, we were homeward bound!

The next day was Good Friday, and Tanya made her last audio journal entry as she commemorated fourteen years since her Good Friday surgery for colon cancer at age eleven. The day was significant because it was all about Jesus and what He had done for us. We reflected on the Lord's agonizing journey to the Cross for our sins and His gift of salvation; we read the scriptures about the events leading to Jesus's suffering, death, and resurrection, and celebrated communion. Tanya and I prayed, grateful for the people Jesus had placed in our lives and for the grace to suffer courageously. She had stubbornly faced her challenges yet bravely battled frequent episodes of tears through the day.

My dear father arrived for Easter. We cherished his presence, his daily phone calls, and his ongoing support and interest in Tanya's health. His willingness to help in constructive ways was greatly appreciated. Along with her grandfather, the faithfulness of her friends had been paramount. She leaned on her close high school friend Portia who phoned and offered a sympathetic ear as Tanya wept with raw vulnerability while sharing her deep desire to be well. Portia cheered Tanya with the anticipation of a visit from more high school friends the next day. Shortly after the phone call, two church friends and Selena arrived and engaged her in light conversation. I was forever grateful to Jesus for all the people He had brought into our lives at crucial times who laughed, chatted, and supported Tanya in her times of anguish. Friends lightened her otherwise dark moments.

Even with the uplifting times with friends, Tanya's physical limitations were disheartening. My hands on her hips steadied her gait as she shuffled to the next room. The strength she had had in her left hand to raise it, wave, and move her fingers freely, had almost vanished. She had to concentrate intensely to move her fingers slightly, and now it was even more pronounced. She was upset to realize she was losing ground. She started to seize again while eating dinner—she didn't want me to fuss over her, so I prayed in the Spirit and sang worship songs. I felt helpless. There was nothing I could do to relieve her ongoing suffering. She asked weakly, "Mummy, has God forgotten me?" I held her close, confused, and unable to speak.

I, too, was asking, "Where are you, Lord?" It was unbearable to watch my daughter suffer so. I couldn't understand why her recovery progressed so quickly at first, yet now she was regressing. I clung to God's promises that *"...he who begun a good work in you will carry it on to completion until the day of Jesus Christ"* (Philippians 1:6).

Shortly after the seizure subsided, Patti from church called and directed our attention to God's faithfulness. Then Cori from church phoned and chatted with Tanya, followed by Mama and Papa Blessings in Dallas; they strengthened us with their prayers. Only God could have strategically placed so many believers in our lives to encourage us with the same message—keep our eyes on Jesus and remain firmly rooted in God's faithfulness.

The next day, Tanya was overcome with tears, annoyed at herself for her many physical limitations. She had an intense desire to be healed, to get on with glorifying God, do His Will, and serve Him all the days of her life, but the weakness and disability seemed insurmountable. Several times during the morning, her tears flowed; she repented, humbly and earnestly confessed her wrong attitude as sin, and pleaded with God and me for forgiveness. She perceived herself as demanding and impatient because of her tears. I reassured her again and again that she had a sweet, humble spirit, and her perception of herself wasn't mine and was tainted by her pain. She courageously endured intense suffering from the unpleasant side effects: the toxic mix of drugs, decadron, tamoxifen, experimental chemo as well as multiple metastatic cancers all assaulting her body. Her logic and ability to analyze were perspicacious, beyond the natural, but the circumstances were beyond her emotional capacity.

Tanya's outlook improved later when high school friends Portia, Sonya, Marah and Elle arrived together. Her mood brightened; this was exactly what she needed. I snapped a photo of the group smiling as if high school carefree days were back and life was copasetic as it should be. The picture revealed that the drug decadron had caused extraordinary swelling in her face. Tanya was aware but not disturbed by the changes in her appearance. She had come to terms with the adverse effects of the drugs.

I recalled when she was still physically fit, athletic, and strong before the debilitating limitations of cancer and side effects. She was in high school when she applied lessons of life not taught in a textbook. Tanya's athletic school team had won championships in many competitions. She had a collection of track and field medals from competing at COSSA (Central Ontario Secondary School Athletes) events to remind her of success. A particular track meet comes to mind where I anticipated another victorious meet for Tanya and the team. I was in the stands with the other parents, eagerly cheering for their offspring as they lined up for the short distance race. She could sprint effortlessly and would typically quickly surge her way to the lead where I could easily spot her. The gun sounded, and the runners dashed from the starting line. Moments later, the gun cracked again. I thought it was a false start. There was a long pause. Then the race resumed. Through the tightly compacted cluster of athletes, I searched for Tanya to come bursting through the pack as usual, but I couldn't find her. I must have missed her. Most of the runners had sped past my view and were approaching the finish line when I glimpsed a lone athlete limping her way to the end. It was my Tanya. I dashed to the finish line—seeing her scraped face, shoulder, and arm oozing blood and receiving medical attention.

Her coach told me what had happened. The gun had sounded, and the crowded heat of runners collided with each other, accidentally tripping Tanya, who fell and skidded across the tarmac, scraping her face, arm, and shoulder. Her coach had urged her to seek immediate medical attention, but she refused, saying that she had started the race and was going to finish it. Wounded and bleeding, she ran, knowing she would lose. She told me it wasn't about winning another race but more about trying and doing her best. It wasn't about bringing home a medal as a souvenir of accomplishments but rather inspiring her team. It would have been perfectly acceptable for her to step away from that event, but she wanted to finish to boost team morale. Her teammates affectionally dubbed her 'Skid' and continued to perform even more diligently to make their school proud.

It was Easter Sunday, and the death and resurrection of Jesus was foremost in our thoughts and prayers as we contemplated the Bible passages and worshipped God with hymns. My father stayed overnight, and together we were blessed to worship via TV church. While the pastor was preaching, Selena and Dennis arrived for a visit. Tanya listened to most of their conversation and, despite fatigue, enervated by the disease she made efforts to chat. When her visitors left, I snuggled her close, and we both slept until the phone woke us up. My loyal friend Sharon, who called almost daily to support us, wished us a Happy Easter.

Still weary, Tanya warmly greeted another visitor, Cori, and thanked her for the cheerful yellow mums that had brightened her room and day. Although they visited, a very drowsy Tanya didn't contribute much to the conversation. Other people phoned to extend Easter greetings, like Tori, a high school friend from another church who was struggling with her faith and who didn't know that

Tanya had relapsed. And Bonny and Carolyn called, CFNI Bible college friends, and we reflected on Jesus's resurrection and saving grace.

Wen, a friend who had survived breast cancer and attended a neighbouring church in our community, called and told us about a guest speaker with a healing ministry at their church whom she hoped would visit us. That boosted our faith as we eagerly anticipated this possibility—aware of a buzz around our city about some believers who had received healing through this ministry. Perhaps God would use this ministry to complete His healing?

I hadn't given up hope for healing! Wen and her husband dropped by in the evening to keep Tanya company while I attended her church which had an evening healing service. I waited until 11:00 p.m. in the prayer line, and after all the believers had received ministry, I pleaded with the preacher to come to my home, but he responded regretfully that he couldn't. When I returned home alone, Tanya wept, feeling abandoned. She had also anticipated that he would come and pray for her. Leaning over her, my friend's husband laid his hands on her and prayed fervently for healing. It was nearly one o'clock in the morning when this sweet couple left. Though weary and disheartened, Tanya still wanted our special prayer time which bonded us closely to God and each other.

Tanya felt many waves of despondency that we attributed again to drugs. With all the horrible side effects of tamoxifen, she had no memory problems and no personality change. The depression had made her weepy and sad, but she was still the same sweet Tanya as before. When I spoke to Wen, she said her treatment for breast cancer was one twenty-milligram tamoxifen tablet daily, and she had plummeted into such deep depression she had to discontinue its use. Wen was alarmed when I told her that Tanya took twelve tablets daily, 240mg, and although it was an experimental procedure, there were no survivors to endorse its effectiveness. We trusted God that Tanya would be the first to survive and be healed. I knew she was at her limit. We continued to clasp the hem of Jesus.

During my dad's weekend visit, we let him know how much we appreciated his listening ear and the attentive ways he helped. Tanya loved her grandfather dearly, and his affection for her was reciprocated, displayed by his presence and willingness to serve, run errands, and engage in small talk. My father wasn't a big talker, but his actions spoke louder than words.

The beginning of the week, Monday, April 5, was much the same. Tanya was still discouraged that her healing was taking so long. I phoned a television prayer line and left a message for someone to call us to pray. Just as Tanya's feelings of defeat threatened to overwhelm her, a woman from the prayer team called and prayed at length with her. Tanya immediately recognized that the timing was of God.

My memories are an oasis in the desert of painful reality. Tanya had battled other surgeries and challenges but forged through with determination and triumph. The summer before she started university, she had been hemorrhaging. To determine the severity, exploratory surgery was necessary. The surgeon explained that the bleed could mean either that the internal intestinal pouch needed minor repairs or required a major overhaul. The former would be a speedy recovery—in time to start university in the fall—but the latter would be a long operation, and recovery time could be up to six months. Tanya was determined to start university with her peers and gave consent to the minor repair surgery. However, if the exploratory surgery revealed that the internal pouch needed total reconstruction, the surgeon was instructed to close her up—she would return for the major operation after she completed her first year. Tanya reasoned that the bleeding was manageable, and she had been living with it before her diagnosis. An hour into the operation, the surgeon appeared in scrubs and said that she had closed Tanya up, as she had requested because the extent of damage to her pouch required major surgery.

As planned, Tanya started university in the fall and fell in love with her course studies and university life. She was in her element. She completed all her assignments and mid-term exams, but she called me just before the first semester final exams, concerned that she had been hemorrhaging more profusely. She called the surgeon in Toronto, and within a few days, was on the operating table. She was discharged in time for Christmas but with complications. Because of an abscess, the incision remained open and required the home care nurse to pack it daily until the infection healed from the inside out. Tanya recovered and was able to have the second surgery to close the temporary ileostomy on Good Friday and thus test the durability of the rebuilt pouch. It was nearing June when she recovered her energy to resume her daily routines.

As we pensively reflected on the six months of recovery time, I asked Tanya why she thought God had allowed her to start university, knowing she would lose her year and have to forfeit all the money for housing and tuition. She was optimistic. "Mom, God knew that I needed a taste of university so that I would be motivated to recover thoroughly to return to my studies in the fall. If I'd had this operation before starting university, with all the recovery struggles, I would never have started." So true. It was the vision of returning to her studies that propelled Tanya forward with hope for recovery. Repeating the first year with a depleted energy level wasn't tedious, and since she was familiar with all the course material from the previous year, she felt confident. Studying was her forte; thrilled, she blossomed.

Now, as she struggled with the effects of cancers and drugs, she also lacked the energy to cast a vision for her future. I knew it was up to me to inspire her to look forward. Later in the afternoon, we went for a three-kilometre wheelchair marathon, joyfully basking in the fresh air, fortified with humour, and invigorated by her quick-witted jokes and comebacks. We enjoyed a peaceful and happy day, cheerfully focused on having fun, yet discouraged when discussions turned to her physical decline.

Back home, we nestled on the couch and prayed at length. We spent prolonged periods in prayer. It seemed that God had given us a vast measure of grace to pray constantly and to praise and worship Him frequently during the day. Nevertheless, we needed God's physical intervention soon. We were literally dependent on Jesus for dear life. Tanya prayed, "Lord, the disciples woke up Jesus, and although Jesus reprimanded them, He did calm the storm, and they continued their journey to the other side on still waters." Tanya and I were crying out in unison, "Lord, don't you care if we drown?" We were physically weak.

Her hopelessness, coupled with extreme hot flashes, left her feeling depleted. We went for a drive to get her mind off confinement and limitations... and to fulfill her cravings for Greek food. We ate lunch outdoors, ran errands, and enjoyed a successful outing.

NINETEEN
Precious Memories and Disappointments

TANYA AWOKE THE following day with her whole body in a hot flash, feverish to touch, but her temperature normal. Dolefully, she endured it for hours. She wept inconsolably because God hadn't completely healed her. She was so frustrated she wanted to throw something, so I gave her pillows and a tube of hand cream. I felt deep sorrow that I was unable to relieve her suffering. I, her mom, was helpless. My love for Tanya was inexhaustible, but I couldn't protect her from this incapacitating disease nor alleviate her agony. All I could do was pray!

Our pastor made frequent calls for updates to give at the next Bible study. I asked him to invite church members who had been praying for Tanya to phone to let us know this because such calls encouraged us. He agreed.

Dennis came by again, but after he left, Tanya was tearful. I wanted her to have control over her day—she was so downcast. I asked her what her heart's desire was.

She pondered a moment then responded, "Get my hair cut and a manicure at the mall!"

I called the hair salon, and they were open to doing the hair but no longer provided manicures. That was fine with Tanya, so I helped her dress in blue jeans and a sweater, put the wheelchair and oxygen in the car, and off we went. She had to wait about ten minutes, so we wheeled into the music shop, where she bought two comedy videos and a movie soundtrack. Pleased with her purchases, she asked me to leave her alone for the half-hour while getting her hair cut, so I went shopping for a hands-free telephone headset. Her short hairstyle boosted her morale, and we celebrated her new look with an epic wheelchair walk, some five kilometres and two hours over cracked sidewalks, all the while engaged in stimulating conversation. Tanya repeatedly apologized for being difficult and depressed, and I reassured her that she wasn't and that I loved her unconditionally. She was aware of her depression and felt sad that she hadn't exercised control over her tearful mood swings.

Growing up, Tanya hadn't been an excessively emotional child. She approached her challenges with reason, rationale, and in manageable chunks. So now, on our walk, what she deemed as inappropriate and overly emotional, I regarded as normal responses to abnormal circumstances. We enjoyed our time together, an answer to my prayers that God would lift her spirits.

Shortly after we returned home, she received a call from a close friend who was feeling ill. Tanya attentively listened to her struggles. Then another of her friends called and chatted at length, telling her about a product to improve the immune system. It was later in the evening than I realized after Tanya's two chats. I was prepared to cancel the rest of our outing because of the late hour, but she was ready to go. Tanya insisted we drive to our selected restaurant for a late dinner. It helped her to be allowed to make decisions and have a sense of control. When we arrived, we were seated at the perfect table that accommodated her wheelchair nicely, away from the traffic of incoming guests. We had a wonderful meal, and our conversation highlighted meaningful discussion about her life, past, friends, and commitment to God. Her heart was vulnerable and tender towards the Lord. On the way home, we stopped for treats at her request. It was the perfect ending to a wonderful day—a beautiful memory, a precious gift from God for us to treasure in the days ahead.

Early the next morning, Tanya convulsed with a grand mal seizure. She directed me to sing in the Spirit with intermittent whispered prayers. When the seizure subsided, exhausted, I cuddled with her, then packed up the car with the portable oxygen and headed to the Peterborough hospital for our 9:00 a.m. appointment with the neurooncologist, Dr. West. The Toronto oncologist had arranged for her to get her chemotherapy locally.

Dr. West introduced himself with the statement, "So you just won't give up!" It was an opening for Tanya to boldly share her testimony of faith in God, who enabled her to persevere. Her knowledge of genetics impressed him, especially when she discussed her disorder, a genetic condition unfamiliar to him. The CPT11 treatment was cancelled due to her low blood count, so we decided that a fun activity was in order for the day. Tanya suggested we drive up the winding Otonabee River Road to Lakefield, a hamlet we frequented for their famous ice cream, but first, she wanted a cold drink to quench her thirst and cool the unrelenting hot flashes. Before I could enter the store, a seizure came on that lasted for several minutes. At her request, I silently prayed, and she sang worship songs with her entire being to divert the energy from the part of the brain experiencing the seizure to the opposite hemisphere engaged in singing. As always, worship helped.

As we drove the twisting road close to the banks of the river, our stimulating conversation about memorable childhood events and experiences with her brother and friends brought smiles and unforgettable laughter. She painted the canvas of her childhood memories with vivid, detailed rainbow colours of diverse experiences, expressed with a cheerful dramatic flair. We reminisced about Eric's childhood antics and adult maturation when he lived with her in London, always grateful for their close sibling bond.

She narrated cherished stories from her childhood that were etched in her memory, joked about our driving vacation to Expo 86 in British Columbia, and the many detours I took as I got lost on route. She reflected on her determination to learn new skills: ballet lessons, tap dance, swimming lessons, and horseback riding. She recalled cycling over 50 kilometres with her girlfriend to Love Sick Lake. She went on to replay other treasured moments—the fun of living in Dallas, Texas, stomping in the deep, flooded waters in the parking lot after a torrential rain, her antics at school, her track-and-field competitions and accomplishments, volunteering at the Sports Injury Clinic and the Children's Centre in physiotherapy, and her walk with God throughout her youth and adolescence. She had so many treasured experiences. She repeatedly expressed that she had been a contented child even with life-threatening cancers beginning at age eleven and again at fourteen, followed by complications. Overall, we had an outstanding day reviewing cherished memories!

As a single parent raising my children, my life was atypical because of all the health challenges they faced. Tanya wasn't a typical child growing up. Rebellion or disrespect was never part of my parenting experience. She was autonomous and strong-willed in the best ways. When Tanya graduated from elementary school, she educated me about the life of her peers. She said, "Mummy, do you know that kids get grounded?" I was naïve and asked for clarification. She explained, "It's when a kid doesn't come home when they say they would; the parents would take away privileges." Puzzled, she asked, "Why would a kid not come home when they said they would?" Tanya was such a person of her word that she would never change her plans without informing me.

I recalled another time when she had started high school and had announced, "There is no such thing as peer pressure. Nobody can make you do something you don't want to do." That was how Tanya lived. She marched to the beat of her faith and not her peers.

When we were nominated Family of the Year in 1992, primarily because of our family involvement in volunteer services, the front page of the city newspaper was entirely our family picture. The reporter interviewed my children with me, and the newspaper article quoted their words verbatim.

An excerpt from the Peterborough Examiner, Monday, October 6, 1992, written by staff writer Susan Clairmont, with Tanya's words combined with mine, read: "Whenever we have supper, we always have really good conversations,' says Tanya, and Janet agrees. 'We're a very talkative family. We do a lot of heavy-duty talking,' Janet says." The staff writer concluded her report with words that reflected our family, "And a strong faith in God is what ties all of the other family elements together for the Williamsons. 'We have a real strong faith and belief in God as a strength and support in our life,' Janet explains..." (Excerpt from Peterborough Examiner Monday, October 6, 1992, Examiner Staff Writer Susan Clairmont)

Now, even with her most dire suffering challenges, we were still "heavy-duty talkers," and God was still the hub of our life, the glue that cemented us in unity.

Back at home, Tanya sat at the kitchen counter while I prepared her lunch; she seemed pensive and took the pen and paper on the counter and appeared to be writing a message. I didn't interrupt, question, or disturb her concentration. After she wrote her piece, we talked about how it was alright to own her feelings and that God heard her surrendered heart filled with love and compassion for her. These were her words:

"Lord, please do not tarry and continue with the tangible manifestation of my full healing so that I can glorify your Name and encourage the body of Christ. I am feeling frustrated and as though you are not here; your presence is not sensed. Have you forgotten me? From my human perspective, it totally feels as though you have. But at the same time, please forgive me for boxing you into what my expectation was for this healing."

Humbled, she surrendered all her expectations. She had confessed her feelings of abandonment, only to recognize that her feelings and desires had placed God in a box. She opened the box, asked for forgiveness, and then laid it on the altar again with no expectations. If only I had learned to do that. She had often reminded me, "Mom, to be content in Christ Jesus, do not let your expectations exceed your reality." She hadn't instructed me not to dream big, but rather to remember God was ultimately in control—when our reality doesn't match our expectations, God was still in control even if we had boxed Him in. Recognizing that I had a "human perspective," as Tanya had, was liberating, not condemning.

But her desire was to be healed to serve God. Her prayer that she felt forgotten was from her heart. It wasn't to change God but to submit to Him. God understood her heart. She was real and vulnerable with Him. She recognized that she had expectations. She recognized that she had lived her life in contentment where she hadn't let her expectations exceed her reality until now. And to get back on track, she had asked God to forgive her. Yes, repentance was the only way to get back into right standing with God. It would be some time later before I realized that my expectations for Tanya's healing had boxed God in, and I needed to repent.

I phoned my friend, Deanna, and we prayed and talked about holding firm to our beloved Saviour. Tanya had said many times during the day, "I just want to be healed. I just want to be healed and be normal again." I wanted that for her too and couldn't give up on her or God.

As the day progressed, Tanya's depression increased along with her desire to die, wanting to overdose on morphine. The pain was too great! I reminded her that it was the depression, suffering, and drugs speaking, not her. I served lunch in the dining room, hoping a change in surroundings would lift her spirits. It did for a while until discouragement and frustration filtered into our conversation, and she drifted off to sleep.

Suddenly, she opened her eyes with emphasis. Very coherently and articulately, Tanya mourned, "Mom, I feel sorry for you. I feel sorry that you are in denial and not facing reality. I'm not going to be healed. I just want a bottle of morphine and to go into a coma and sleep." Every fibre in her body exploded with pain. Her voice trailed off to a gentle mumble. At other times, she whispered when I encouraged her to hang on until we got to the other side, "Mom, getting to the other side is heaven. I will get there." I repeatedly told her during the day that it was the depression speaking, the tamoxifen, and not her. She would only repeat, "Mom, you are not facing reality. Mom, you're in total denial. Wake up and face reality. Can't you see my body is dying? The cancer cells are dividing and multiplying at a rate that my body won't be able to accommodate." Her tone was matter-of-fact, scientific. I wouldn't let them penetrate my heart. I changed the subject.

Fortunately, I convinced her to let me take her for a walk in the wheelchair to the restaurant. She leaned heavily to the left, her eyes closed, while I pushed the wheelchair. Even though she seemed to be drifting in and out of sleep, she always had a sharp and on-target answer for everything I would say casually or in response to my questions. It was crowded at the restaurant, but we were seated at a quiet and isolated table. We both ordered Greek salad and manicotti, and even though her eyes were shut and her head and shoulders slumped as she chewed, she made relevant comments. The outing created another fond memory, which I tucked into my journal for the future.

Over the coming days, her health steadily declined. Every day and night, I read scripture, anointed her with oil, and prayed for healing. I didn't even know how to pray anymore. The words were a cry from the soul, a pleading that transitioned into surrender. I was exhausted, but I refused to let go.

Tanya's friend, Willow, her closest university companion from London, called and tearfully spoke to me that she hadn't realized how serious Tanya's condition had become. Tanya recalled Willow's tearful words later, "You're so strong. You're so strong."

Tanya bemoaned, "I don't feel strong, Mom." Her voice was a weak, tender whisper.

Willing to try anything, I felt like I was grasping at a fleeting vapour when I ordered a product to build and repair the immune system. I was willing to try any innovative potion that might arrest these cancers. If she continued to go downhill, I thought I would contact the neurooncologist in Toronto about the thalidomide drug he had placed on hold for her. We were fighting against time. Every day, every hour, Tanya grew weaker. I knew that God must interrupt this deadly decline soon. I knew that nothing was ever too late with God. I prayed all the time. Perhaps the following day, at the Toronto Airport Church healing service, would be God's time to intervene and raise her to health.

TWENTY
Another Grasp at Healing: Hebrews 11 Again

SUNDAY, APRIL 11, 1999, started with a sleepless night. I awoke suddenly at 1:00 a.m. I knew Tanya's health was failing, and I strained to hear her laboured breathing. Resounding silence prevailed. Alarmed, I sprung to her side and with my ear to her nostrils, I waited for her to exhale and listened to the rhythm of her shallow breaths as her frail chest rose slightly. My whispered prayers ascended to heaven. I stroked her forehead. I still couldn't sleep all night. I wondered if she had stopped breathing and worried that I wouldn't be with her if she needed me. I strived to focus on Tanya's healing manifested miraculously at the upcoming healing service. When I glanced at the clock, I was aware of the hours that slipped by, restlessly praying, tossing and turning.

Before breakfast, Tanya prayed a beautiful, powerful prayer of thanksgiving, blessing the food and praying against the harmful effects of the drugs. She prayed for wisdom and God's guidance to share her testimony of a faithful God with her friend, Willow, who would be attending the service. She prayed that Father God would help her trust Him more so that her expectations wouldn't exceed her reality in order to stay content in the Lord. After her prayer, I again reminisced on the many times when Tanya had studied at university, and she had instructed me, "Mom, to be content in the Lord, do not let your expectations exceed your reality." Now she was praying her own words of wisdom. She asked God to show her clearly at the healing service if she should go forward for healing or stay in her pew and let God's power heal her there. Her thoughts were coherent, strong, and quite like the old Tanya, without the depressing repercussions from drugs and chemotherapy.

After prayer, Tanya slipped in and out of bouts of depression and hopelessness. She repented many times and asked God for forgiveness, even wondering if she had committed the sin of backsliding. I frequently reassured her that her heart was tender and submissive to Jesus. I stressed that Father God had her cocooned in the palm of His hands—her repentance was evidence of her closeness to God. Her discouragement was the voice of drugs, pain, and depression.

Portia phoned, prayed with Tanya, and pointed her to God's love. What an authentic friend she was to Tanya! My father called, and Tanya instantly spoke of God's faithfulness and healing power, hoping her testimony might draw him to Jesus. He remained guarded. In the midst of depression, she embraced every opportunity to glorify Father God. I believed that only the gift of God's grace and faithfulness could do that!

The young adult pastor phoned to explain that insurmountable obstacles were preventing him from taking us to the Toronto Airport Healing Service that evening and asked if we could postpone it until the following week. I replied passionately, "No!" It was alright if he wasn't able to drive us. I had instant peace that God would enable us to manage alone. Tanya's depression, excessive sleepiness, and struggle to walk alarmed me more and more as time passed. Next week held no certainty if her health deteriorated further. It was this week or no week, our last attempt to touch the hem of Jesus's garment for healing.

Meanwhile, Willow had offered to support Tanya at the Toronto church, and that filled Tanya anew with joy, thrilled that her closest university friend would bolster her. Later, during a lengthy chat with another friend, her voice trailed off. Her speech slurred, mingling with mumbled words as she fell asleep during the conversation. It reinforced the urgency to attend the healing service that evening. I couldn't understand God's ways, but I knew God was orchestrating events so that our trip would be possible. After I resolved to drive alone, the pastor called and confirmed that he and church member, Matt, would take us after all. My heart overflowed with deep gratitude, and I repeatedly thanked him. God was so good! About the same time, both Patti and Karin called to bid us a safe journey and covered us with prayer.

When we arrived at the Toronto Airport Church, Tanya was still in excruciating pain but masked it with a smile when she greeted her friend. The healing service began with a scripture reading. God ordained Hebrews 11 as the passage. Hebrews 11, the same chapter Tanya had studied with the Young Adult Group a few weeks before. It was what I read aloud to Tanya in ICU after surgery. Hebrews 11 was what Tanya read to her brother before he died. What were the chances of that? Only God could have selected this particular scripture reading. Truly God communicated in ways that we understood. God never ceased to amaze me!

After the service, she had to wait an incredibly long time for prayer. With increasing back pain, a comfortable sitting position was difficult to maintain in the wheelchair. When her turn for prayer arrived, while folded over at the waist in unfathomable pain, she confessed her feelings that God had forgotten her and had overlooked her great desire for healing. The minister reminded Tanya of the love of God shown to her through all the people surrounding her to support her. Tanya received a tangible peace as she recognized again that the body of Christ was the evidence that she hadn't been forgotten. God placed a multitude of people, friends, church members, and believers from all over the country by her side to bring God's words and the comfort of Jesus. I recognized God's peace beaming on her face.

The next day, a peace beyond understanding permeated every fibre of Tanya's core, but it hadn't relieved the excruciating pain. Very coherently, Tanya lamented again, "Mom, I feel so sorry for you. I feel sorry that you are in denial and not facing reality. I feel sorry that I'm not going to be healed. The pain is unbearable. Please let me go." It was agonizing to witness her despair, but I couldn't let her give up.

At times during the day, she would sigh when I encouraged her to hang on until we got to the other side, "Mom, getting to the other side is heaven. I have told you so many times, but you are in denial. Wake up and face the truth!" I kept telling her that it was the depression, the tamoxifen speaking and not her. She was too exhausted to refute my blindness. She would only repeat gently, "Mom, you aren't facing reality. Mom, you are in total denial. Surely you see my body is dying. You need to let go." She was deeply immersed in suffering and wanted relief, but I was not letting her give up. She was my only child. I was cleaving to God. I was cleaving to her life.

Suddenly, out of the blue, she felt energized; she perked up and said she was bored. She mustered up strength, and with pen and ink, she doodled on her leg, then phoned her grandpa and encouraged him to get his income tax receipts together so she could fill out his tax return. She said that she needed something intellectual to stimulate and challenge her brain. She hadn't shown any changes in her cognitive ability since her disease started. Her intellectual strength confirmed to me her imminent healing; the initiative she took was evidence that she was going to be restored. I imagined it to be impossible to endure eight glioblastoma brain tumours and be astute. Wasn't that God's intervention and grace that had sparked her energy? Who could do that apart from God?

Sandra, Tanya's childhood friend, now living in Vancouver, phoned—although Tanya's voice was weak and it took effort to converse, she chatted for over half an hour. Her mind was clear, and after the phone call, she shared incredible details that invigorated her.

She whispered weakly, "Sandra told me that her fiancé's brother is single and only a year younger than me. I do want to get married one day and adopt children. Sandra's fiancé's brother is adopted." I wondered what God might have in store for Tanya's future. She had renewed hope. So did I!

Tanya's pharmacist friend, Jesse, also phoned and talked with Tanya for over an hour. It was good for her to receive so many phone calls. She seemed less depressed but sleepy. Her weakness had overpowered her depression.

I repeatedly tried to block out her soft whispers that echoed in my head, "You are in denial. The other side is heaven. God isn't going to heal me. It's obvious. Mom, you need to let go." I responded to the invasive thoughts adamantly; I will not let go! My son's death was still a deep well of sadness and now she was all I had. Although I had God, I experienced Him through Tanya's love and devotion to Him.

The following day, she fell asleep in the middle of conversations and sentences. Dennis and Selena came by for an hour, and we watched a comedy. Tanya was so lethargic; she barely participated in the conversation. Later, she spoke again to Willow for two hours on the phone and recalled details from their chatter.

I reminded her frequently that she must live and not give up. I needed her here. She had a job to do for God, the cruise, her master's, so much... "Mom," she replied, "I have fulfilled all I have been called of God to do." Her words pierced my heart. I saw her tangible peace and felt it. But I couldn't accept it.

She took the initiative and phoned another university friend in London, requesting her cheesecake recipe. Then she called her grandfather and mustered up the energy to remind him of her love, her appreciation for him, and her desire for his salvation. It would be her last call to her grandfather.

Then she phoned another friend and invited her over and asked her to bring a blender. The girls chatted and made chopped ice to cool Tanya's hot flashes. It was as if Tanya had a list of people she wanted to speak to and say goodbye.

The doctor informed Tanya that her low haemoglobin and white-blood-cell count necessitated another blood transfusion, so her CPT11 chemo was cancelled. With the blood work report so low, she may have dozed off several times while her high school friends visited due to this anaemia. I called the oncology nurse and wondered if it might be wise to start the thalidomide treatment since she had missed chemo for two consecutive weeks. I recalled the neurosurgeon pressing us to be aggressive with treatment. The nurse reassured me that introducing another drug wouldn't conflict with her low white blood cell or haemoglobin count—the only side effect would be sleepiness, so Tanya should take it just before bed. Tanya suggested that we ask Grandpa to bring it to Peterborough since he lived near the hospital in Toronto. My father, pleased to help, agreed to deliver it to us the next day.

Tanya recalled previous conversations with her pharmacist friend, Jesse, and her university friend, Willow. Her short-term memory was intact, and her memory for details outstanding. I still held firmly that God would heal her. Much later, I would understand that Tanya's cognitive ability was indeed a miracle and a direct answer to her prayers back in July, before brain surgery when she had asked God to preserve her intellect.

Our Abba Father continued to provide Christian friends that offered to do what we most desired, that was to sing praises and worship. Patti, her husband and two young children, came over to worship the Lord with us. This beautiful family buoyed us in the Lord continually. Patti played praise and worship songs on her guitar, and we lifted our voices heavenward in love and adoration to God. Tanya made a remarkable effort to sing even though she fell asleep at times. Her depression had lifted. She glowed with God's peace; the hub of her heart was focused on Jesus alone. Singing praises with Patti and her family helped lift our hearts and spirits to the Great I Am. We had experienced a deep sense of His presence and unconditional love through this wonderful family.

For the remainder of the day, Tanya frequently declared that we worshipped an awesome God! She sang with all her being, "Our God is an awesome God, He reigns... from heaven above...."[27] That was the theme song of her heart, our God is an Awesome God, Psalm, 68:35. Tanya loved the hymn "Blessed Assurance," and the lyrics spoke of her story with God. "Blessed assurance, Jesus is mine; oh, what a foretaste of glory divine! Heir of salvation, purchased of God, born of His Spirit, washed in His blood. This is my story, this is my song, praising my Saviour all the day long..."[28] That was indeed Tanya's story.

---

[27] Rich Mullins, "Awesome God," *Winds of Heaven, Stuff of Earth*, Reed Arvin Label: Reunion, Album, 1988.

[28] Fanny Cosby, "Blessed Assurance." (music by Phoebe Knapp)1873 Wikipedia: httmi:// en.m.wikipedia.org/wiki/Blessed_Assurance).

Willow called again, and Tanya thanked her for the beautiful plant basket she had received from her three university friends, Willow, April, and Larcey. She mentioned on the phone that the prayer plant in the flower arrangement reminded her to pray for Willow and her family. The three friends had planned a visit, and to satisfy Tanya's craving for her favourite dessert, they said they would bring cheesecake. Tanya told me how much she had appreciated the kindness of her friends rallying around her supportively.

TWENTY-ONE
Healing Of a Deeper Kind

TANYA STARTED THE next morning with a debilitating headache with pain increasing behind her eyes, left temple, and the top of her head. I phoned the doctor who suggested I give Tanya two additional teaspoons of morphine at intervals, and by noon I had given her ten more teaspoons over and above her morning dose of 60 mg, yet the pain prevailed. I called the oncologist in Toronto, who suggested another 180 mg of morphine.

To determine Tanya's pain level, the home care nurse asked, "On a scale of 1 to 10, with 10 being the most severe pain, how would you rate your pain, Tanya?"

"13.5," Tanya whispered firmly.

I knew Tanya's pain had accelerated beyond belief. I was even more alarmed when her nose bled spontaneously. It would clot then bleed again without provocation. Her face was beet red, roasting hot to touch. Her forehead sweated profusely, with drops of perspiration sprinkled on her upper lip. Her temperature was an alarming 39 Celsius. I called 911!

"Do you know who we are?" The paramedic's booming voice aroused Tanya.

"Yes, you are ambulance attendants," she feebly whispered, attempting to open her eyes.

Tanya started to seize in the ambulance, but she verbalized to the paramedic how she could interrupt it. She explained, "I just have to set my mind to Jesus, relax and reduce the adrenaline flow, and the seizure will stop." It did.

At the hospital emergency, the doctor examined her immediately; then IV antibiotics were started. My friend's husband, Bill, a paramedic, who happened to be in the hospital at the time, dropped by to pray, and he kissed Tanya's forehead. This was now the second time. He seemed like an angel sent by God to connect Tanya to her heavenly Father. She recalled a previous visit when he had kissed her forehead. After he left, Tanya stirred and whispered that when Bill kissed her forehead, it felt like Father God had kissed her again, securing her in His love, wrapping her in His arms. She felt protected and comforted.

My father arrived from Toronto with the thalidomide and sat with me until the examining doctor returned. After the doctor finished his examination, I read the Bible aloud to my sleeping child, lying motionless on a narrow stretcher.

From the emergency department, she was transferred to a floor with a comfortable bed. Bill returned and prayed again, gently kissing Tanya's forehead. Even though he was wearing a mask, Tanya was instantly aroused from sleep.

"That kiss means a lot to me." Her voice was weak but clear. She was speaking to Bill but also to God.

It again reminded me of a few months before when Bill appeared to pray over Tanya and had kissed her forehead. It meant so much to Tanya to be treated in a fatherly way. Many times thereafter, she had said it was as if her heavenly Father had kissed her forehead. It seemed that God had sent Bill, a godly man, a kind father with children of his own, specifically to the hospital at that precise time to again kiss Tanya's forehead as a gesture of Abba Father's comforting presence. God said He would never leave us or forsake us, and it was true!

Again, I read scriptures aloud dear to her: the Psalms, Mark 4, Hebrews 11, and the book of Luke. I constantly prayed, wrapped in a bubble of God's love and care.

The oncologist in Toronto requested that the Peterborough hospital take a CT scan and deliver the results to Toronto. After I read the CT report, I wept softly. For the first time, I talked to Tanya openly about dying. She had been telling me for weeks that I was in denial, and I refused to listen. I was distraught with regret. I asked Tanya to respond to my questions by squeezing my finger once for yes and twice for no. My eyes were swollen from stinging hot tears. I asked her if she was going to see Jesus and her brother Eric soon, and she responded with a nod. I sorely repented and asked her to forgive me for promoting only healing, even when she had tried so often to talk honestly about her deteriorating health. She forgave me. I talked about forgiving herself for expectations she had for healing, and she did. Concerned, and for my benefit, I enquired if she might have harboured unconscious resentment or disappointment toward God for not healing her. I talked about forgiving God and urged her to repeat a prayer of forgiveness after me, and she clearly articulated, "I forgive God." I knew that those words were to ease my guilt and agony, knowing it was well with her soul. She had repented of any hidden sins so many times as her sweet spirit prevailed despite her suffering.

A peace that passed all understanding radiated from her quiet body. Her actions never demonstrated anger towards God, not even after last Sunday's desperate attempt for healing at the Airport Church in Toronto. Now, she was no longer seeking healing and had an implausible peace, resting in the Lord. She just wanted the suffering and tortuous pain to stop! This hospital room permeated with forgiveness and healing of a deeper kind as the warm sun streamed in through the window, casting dancing shadows on the bed.

The physician brought me to the radiologist's room and displayed the CT scan. I gasped in disbelief, my jaw ajar! I couldn't comprehend that my eyes were looking at the brain scans of my dear, darling daughter. Tanya's entire brain was a huge mass of tumours.

I profoundly regretted I hadn't permitted Tanya to speak about dying. So often, she had tried to talk to me, but I wouldn't let her. I always steered her back to a discussion about life. Discouraging thoughts were deflected as I convinced her it was the horrible side effects of tamoxifen, chemotherapy, the decadron drug, and depression speaking. I was convinced that with her astute cognitive ability and no change in personality, it was a sign that God would heal her. I was presumptuous! I was wrong! I had projected what I had wanted onto God and erroneously claimed what I wanted as a word from God. The test that God had spoken was in the evidence of the desired outcome. God hadn't spoken she would be healed physically. Those words were mine, not His.

Tanya had told me so often that she felt sorry for me because I was in denial and not facing reality. She told me often to *wake up and face truth.* I couldn't imagine losing two children in less than nineteen months.

I left the CT scan room, broken with the vision of the massive tumours covering her entire brain as an indelible memory. Back at Tanya's bedside, I begged her to wake up, to squeeze my finger. I prayed. I repented. I cried and pleaded with her to communicate with me. She did not.

Two special teachers in Tanya's life arrived, and for a few hours, reminisced about Tanya's high school achievements, her dogged determination, her kind regard for all people and her walk of truth throughout her secondary school years. Her science teacher said he had never before nor since entrusted any student with his car and grandchildren as he had done with Tanya when she babysat for him in high school. Mrs. H. remembered the hug and goodbye Tanya had given her in January. That was when Tanya had designed and taught a unit on genetics to the high school students. Her teacher said she would try to obtain Tanya's Science Fair project, still hanging on the school wall five years later, as a keepsake for me. Tanya had won first place at the Canada Wide Science Competition, and that had honoured her school.

After her teachers left, Tanya stirred. I crawled into bed beside her and drew her close. She squeezed my hand upon request. I asked her many yes-and-no questions. I needed to know without a doubt that she felt God was with her every second. Before I fell asleep while embracing her still body, I read aloud Mark 4 and Hebrews 11, and when I awoke the next morning, I read the same scriptures again.

Her breathing was laboured and intermittent. When Willow and Tanya's two university friends from London, Larcey and April, entered her room, Tanya raised her hand to greet them, her last gesture to acknowledge someone. That would have taken an exorbitant amount of strength and concentration. She tried to open her eyes but couldn't; her eyelids trembled. She was responsive to the voices of her university friends with an occasional grin. More friends visited, including a special friend whom she had met when they were camp counsellors for children with cancer. Later, my faithful friend, Patti, brought her guitar, and many church friends packed her room. Together we lifted our voices heavenward and sang worship songs to Jesus. What a beautiful gift Patti had given, worship with song, knowing that Tanya, even in a coma, was singing with us in her heart.

The ambulance arrived in the evening and transported us to the palliative care facility across town. The driver was the father of Tanya's close friend, Portia, who had faithfully supported her throughout her illness. God had again surrounded us with Christian support. Tanya started to have a seizure with the change in position, but I asked for a moment for her to adjust her thoughts to focus on Jesus. With that, she subdued the seizure and prevented it from progressing. In the ambulance, Portia's father prayed for us. His prayer was like the voice of our Abba Father wrapping His arms of love around my dear daughter and me.

Tanya was soon settled in her room, and I sat beside her, listening to her steady breaths. I asked her to allow me to be with her every moment and to know I would never leave her, and Jesus would never leave her. I repented again and asked Tanya and God to forgive me for selfishly wanting Tanya's life on earth for my benefit. She had been a blessing from the day she had been born and all the days of her life. I read aloud from the Bible, prayed, and openly spoke to God and Tanya that I released her to be with the Lord as I sang, "Turn your eyes upon Jesus. Look full in His wonderful face, and the things of earth will grow strangely dim in the light of His glory and grace."[29]

I had slept on the cot holding her right hand all night. The nurse administered a needle that brought relief whenever her breathing was laboured and her lungs filled with mucous.

Early in the morning, I crawled into bed and snuggled her, resting all day from 8:00 a.m. until 7:00 p.m. Cuddling closely, I could hear gently spoken words and prayerful whispers fill the hollowness of the room, as Karin monitored the number of people coming in to pray over us and say goodbye. There were Tanya's grandfather, church friends, school friends, my friends and many people God had placed in our lives to walk with us at the end of this earthly journey.

In the evening, I prayed again Mark 4:35–41 and Hebrews 11. I wept oceans of tears when I read about all the great saints of old who had great faith but never received the promise; they only saw it at a distance, like my Tanya (Hebrews 11:39). She had never received the promises the way she had expected, the way I had expected. I recalled Tanya's words of wisdom, "To be content in the Lord, do not let your expectations exceed your reality." I remembered the letter she wrote asking God to forgive her for her expectations for this healing. Truly, her deepest expectation was to walk with God and talk with God all the days of her life, no matter the cost. Her expectation was to remain in Christ Jesus. And she had! Her expectation did not exceed her reality because God granted her the fulfillment of her expectation—to love and know Him.

Again, I gave Tanya permission to return to the Lord and Eric. I reminded her of the words she had spoken to Eric, "Save me a front-row seat, and I'll see you in heaven." And now I was asking her to save me a front-row seat for that moment, beyond time, when I would be reunited with her and Eric in heaven. With the Lord, a day is as a thousand years and a thousand years is as a day (2 Peter 3:8).

I asked Tanya to please not leave me while I was asleep snuggled beside her and to allow me to be awake. I asked her again to forgive me for my inadequacies, for all the needs I had failed to provide. I remembered how when she was a child, I would regularly slip into her bedroom at night while she slept, crouch down on the floor beside her, take her relaxed little hand in mine, and pray over her, asking God to forgive me for the mistakes I had made that day, and to bridge

---

[29] Helen Lemmel, "Turn Your Eyes Upon Jesus." *Glad Songs* collection, 1922, and *Gospel Truth in Song* American collection, 1924. Public domain.

the gap between what she had needed and what I had in resources to give her. Now, I couldn't repent enough to correct the wrongs I felt I had done. I had asked her for forgiveness over and over even though she had squeezed my hand on Thursday to communicate that she had. Holding her quiet body, we rested in the Lord.

God's hands and feet were the body of Christ, the church. If it weren't for the body of Christ, I don't know where I would have been. God surrounded me with incredibly strong, faithful Christian friends. In the evening, eight of Tanya's loyal church friends from the College and Career Young Adult group gathered around her bedside. I could only imagine that Tanya felt included as they chatted. I was convinced Tanya was aware of their presence, evidenced by her steady, relaxed, and quiet breathing. Patti strummed her guitar; Karin and the group worshipped in song with me. We sang the scriptures taken from the Song of Songs 1:3b *"… your name is like perfume poured out,"* Psalms 119:105, *"Your word is a lamp to my feet and a light to my path,"* and Isaiah 43:4a, *"Since you are precious and honoured in my sight, and because I love you…"* These were all scriptures dear to Tanya, so we sang the song as a prayer, "Jesus, Jesus… Your Name is like honey on my lips…"[30] I remembered that we had sung that particular "Jesus" song early one morning at 3:00 a.m. on our way to the hospital, focused on Jesus to ward off an impending seizure. Now we were singing it again as Tanya was saying goodbye to the world and hello to heaven.

Later Saturday evening, Tanya could no longer squeeze my hand, but when I read scripture, prayed, spoke to her, and stroked her cheek, I knew she heard me and understood. She would deliberately change her breathing rhythm at my request, speeding it up and then adjusting it back to normal. She was communicating with me! One more gift from God!

I slept soundly, my body wrapped around hers. Throughout the night, her breathing remained stable and her lungs cleared. I gently stroked her hair, repeating how much I loved her and how much God loved her. I reminded her that it was okay to go to the Lord, but I wanted to be awake when the Lord carried her to heaven. I slept peacefully beside her. I awoke just before 10:00 a.m. with a fleeting thought. Tanya had been born on a Sunday, and I wondered if the Lord would take her home on the Lord's Day. I quickly dismissed the thought, observed her steady, rhythmic breathing, and wondered if Tanya would continue in this peaceful state for weeks. Her vital signs were stable.

---

[30] John Barnett, "Holy And Anointed One." Wow Worship/ Mercy Vineyard Publishing, Vineyard Music USA, 1988.

Five minutes after ten o'clock in the morning, on Sunday, April 18, 1999, with her grandfather and me by her side gazing at her radiant face, and while holding her hand and surrounded by God's love and my eternal love, Tanya gently slipped from my earthly arms into the heavenly arms of Jesus. My torn heart flooded with tears of grief as I let her go on her new journey with God.

TWENTY-TWO

Love Letters from God

THE NEXT DAY, there was torrential rain when I went to the funeral home, downcast and despondent. I spent hours praying and talking to Tanya. She would make her last journey with God to London the next day to be buried beside her brother, Eric. Her funeral service would be a few days later in Peterborough. How could I say goodbye? I whispered *until we meet again* since there were no *goodbyes* in Jesus. Like my only son, Eric, my only daughter, Tanya would forever be the love of my past and the love in my future until I joined them in eternity. When I walked out of the funeral home, it was both sunny and drizzling. I felt a warm embrace from above and a prompting to look up, but my heart-rending anguish prevented me. The essence of my heart had been totally shattered beyond repair. Perhaps I felt I could never look up again.

Later, I received a letter from a dear Christian friend, Irene. She spoke about the double rainbow she had seen that melted on the horizon toward my house at the bottom of the hill. A double rainbow! How could I have missed it? Many people saw it and told me about it. Did I not feel a prompt to look up but was swallowed up with despair? I was too grief-stricken to look up, so God found someone else to do it and to describe for me what God had painted on the sky. He was with me even now in this fresh sorrow. Eric had said, "When I die, I am going to ask God to turn me into a rainbow. Then every time you see a rainbow, you will think of me. The job of a rainbow is to help people, and you are one of them, Mom." Eric was always in tune with my heart's cry. Now the double rainbow would always be a symbol of God's Love… Eric and Tanya… both with Jesus.

PART FOUR

Epilogue

A SYNOPSIS OF TANYA AND ERIC'S DIAGNOSIS:

THROUGHOUT OUR STORY there are numerous references to my children's genetic condition. When Eric was four years old, diagnosed with a grade 4 glioblastoma brain tumour the size of a grapefruit, neurosurgeons at the Children's Hospital said that this degree of brain tumour malignancy was rarely seen in children. There was no diagnosis at the time. When Tanya was eleven and diagnosed with colon cancer, also rarely seen in children, it was then that they were diagnosed with Turcot syndrome which results in an increased risk of colon cancer, polyps, and brain cancer. In addition, both children had "cafe-au-lait-spots" which were spots on the skin characteristic of Turcot syndrome. As time unfolded and more scientific understanding was added, my children were also diagnosed with an associated inherited disorder called Hereditary Nonpolyposis Colorectal Cancer (HNPCC), which is also known as Lynch syndrome. People with HNPCC and Lynch syndrome are vulnerable at a younger age to colon cancer, and it is characterized by inherited mutations in genes and a DNA mismatch repair deficiency. Another diagnosis my children received was Biallelic Mismatch Repair Deficiency (BMMR-D) which is characterized by gastrointestinal tumours, and brain tumours with a repair gene deficiency.

Additional Reflections

MYSTERIES ABOUT GOD are part of our journey with God. We suffered many challenges that we didn't understand; however, the scriptures comforted us, particularly Proverbs 3:5–6. Our limited human understanding would have boxed God in and nullified the mysteries of an almighty God who created us. Instead, we chose to trust that God would keep us on the straight path that always led back to Him. And He did!

Nevertheless, suffering was on that path, too. Joy and humour were on that path. Thanksgiving and gratitude were on that path. Peace and grace were on that path. Above all, God was on that path, leading us on a journey with Him.

God didn't take away our pain. But He gave us peace, grace, and strength to go through it. God revealed Himself to us in ways that we understood. He was with us and would never leave us or forsake us. God is faithful! We declared His faithfulness at the beginning of our journey, and we declared it at the end. God gave us the grace to read His Word, grace to worship Him, grace to pray without ceasing, grace to love Him and walk and talk with Him all the days of our lives. He taught us lessons. He answered our prayers. How God was able to do that remains a mystery to me.

At first, I expected God to answer my prayers the way I prayed them. I was taught to be specific when I prayed to God. My specific prayer was for physical healing. But God knew a lifelong prayer that extended over twenty years. "Lord, please do not let my children's suffering cause them to turn away from You. That would be more that I could bear." He answered that prayer. God chose to shape my life through suffering. That remains another mystery. Many times, I asked the Lord, what are You trying to teach me? What am I to learn? I learned to be thankful and to see the goodness of the Lord in the people and events that unfolded. I learned to live life to the fullest, to love and live one day at a time, and to laugh and be filled daily with the joy of the Lord as my strength. My children and I learned that everything that happens in life is to draw us closer to Jesus, especially when suffering is great. Both Eric and Tanya said it well. Eric said, "The devil can put cancer on me, but the devil can't take away my love for Jesus." And Tanya said it well in her newsletter. "It isn't so much what happens to you in life that really matters, but rather it is what you do with what happens to you that is really significant." When we took one step toward Jesus, He had already taken ten toward us. It's like stepping out of the boat and walking on water, keeping our eyes on Him, so we don't sink. And we didn't!

The reader might conclude that my children did not get their prayers answered because both my children died. That remains a mystery. Did God answer my children's prayers? Since a preschooler, Eric loved scripture, and God gave him an amazing memory for the Word, despite having a damaged left hemisphere and a damaged right hemisphere at age twenty-one.

Tanya wanted to be healed, but then she overrode my prayer, beseeching God for healing and to pass this cup of suffering from us, intercepting my prayers with, "Lord, not mine, but Thy will be done." That is part of the mystery of God's grace. I understood with my finite mind that I was praying for healing, but God understood our heart's prayer far deeper than words. Tanya prayed that after her brain surgery, she wouldn't lose cognitive ability. God answered her prayer right up to the end of her life; she was cognitively astute despite eight brain tumours.

God always answered my prayers, but I needed to ask myself the question, "What did I really pray for?" Did I pray that I wanted bodily healing at any cost, or did I pray that I wanted my children and me to love God, walk and talk with Him all the days of our lives, no matter the cost? I always prayed for my children that no harm would come to them. However, I also prayed—should struggles come their way, the Lord would help them keep their eyes on Him. The Bible says, *"In this world you will have trouble. But take heart! I have overcome the world"* (John 16:33). My prayer wasn't just to shield them but to equip them to turn to God in their struggles—through prayer and the scriptures. Only in Him would they overcome the world.

I can't imagine what it would have been like in the midst of suffering to be without God. His grace carried us through the most difficult times. The Apostle Paul knew it well and declared it boldly—His grace was sufficient (2 Corinthians 12:9). In fact, it is by grace we are saved (Ephesians 2:8). We can grow in grace (2

Peter 3:18). Grace belongs to God alone, and we can share in it (Philippians 1:7). Grace can be expressed in our conversations (Colossians 4:6). Grace is given to us in our time of need (Hebrews 4:16). Everyone gets a portion of grace (Ephesians 4:7). Grace was consistently a vital ingredient on our journey with God. Many times, I prayed for a larger portion of grace and received it. I often confessed that the will of God would never take me where the grace of God couldn't keep me. And His grace was and is truly sufficient.

I can't imagine what it would have been like if God hadn't given us His peace. We walked in the peace that surpassed our understanding (Philippians 4:7). I am thankful that we learned to access this peace, releasing our anxiety through prayer, presenting our requests to God with thanksgiving (Philippians 4:6). In our experience, anxiety became a conduit to peace. It was a useful emotion when it took us to the Lord in prayer and brought us closer to God. The Holy Spirit taught and redirected us when we were off course. To receive this direction that brought His peace, we needed to listen in prayer. For Jesus Himself is our peace (Ephesians 2:14). Our God is the God of peace (Philippians 4:9). Not peace, as in the absence of struggles, but rather peace in the midst of struggles.

I can't imagine what it would have been like if God hadn't mixed a portion of joy into His peace. The Bible teaches us that we have peace and joy in the Holy Spirit (Romans 14:17). And that the Holy Spirit gives us joy (1 Thessalonians 1:6). Many encouraging scriptures point us to joy. The God of hope fills us with joy and peace (Romans 15:13). God anoints us with the oil of joy (Psalm 45:7). Jesus gives us His joy (John 15:11). No one can steal your joy (John 16:22).

What's more, the joy of the Lord is our strength (Nehemiah 8:10). James encouraged believers to find joy even in their trials (James 1:2). Trials aren't joyful, but you can find nuggets of joy in them. Eric had this joy. He taught me how to "look at the bright side of things." What a legacy of joy he left me when he repeatedly expressed that he only wanted me to remember 'positive words.'

I can't imagine what it would have been like if God hadn't given us a heart of gratitude and thanksgiving. The scripture taught us to present our petitions to God with thanksgiving (Philippians 4:6). The Psalms tell us that we are to give thanks to God in song (Psalm 28:7). Even Jesus gave thanks before He broke the loaves and fed the five thousand (Matthew 14:19). Jesus set the example, *"give thanks in all circumstances; for this is God's will for you in Christ Jesus"* (1 Thessalonians 5:18). A thankful heart helps us see God in our circumstances and the silver lining in life. A thankful heart enabled me to see God through the body of Christ, prayers, prepared meals, cards, support systems, volunteer services, and all the kindness that was showered on us during our time of need.

I can't imagine what it would have been like if God hadn't given us forgiveness for repentance. "All have sinned and fall short of the glory of God" (Romans 3:23). "If we confess our sin, he is faithful and just and will forgive us…" (1 John 1:9). We come to Jesus through our repentance and His forgiveness.

On my journey with God, I made errors. I was wrong to project healing onto my daughter at the end of her life. I was wrong and failed to let her talk about dying when I had allowed her brother to do so. Even with my errors, God was faithful, and my children loved me and honoured me. The reader will judge the many times I erred. But most importantly, I hope the reader will recognize that our life together as a family was saturated with forgiveness. I am thankful to God for the gift of repentance and forgiveness, both from Him and my children.

I thank God that on this journey He has been the hub of my family wheel, and we have been the spokes. He guided us with the Bible, the light to our path (Psalm 119:105). He kept us focused on Him, for the scriptures pointed us back to Jesus. He promised that when we prayed, He would listen and that when we sought Him, we would find Him (Jeremiah 29:12–13). As we prayed, God worked out His plan in us. Eric, Tanya, and I held our hope for a future firmly in Christ, trusting His eternal purposes. Our job was to seek and love God with all our hearts, to cast our burdens on Him, and then rest in Him (Matthew 11:30). Eric and Tanya's lives continue to teach me how to "Seek God's Face and not His Hands," love Him, yoke myself to Jesus, and rest in Him.

"Don't forget to write our stories" were the last will and testament of my children as their earthly journeys ended. My daughter wanted to encourage the "body of Christ," the church, and my son wanted "to help people." I hope that their stories and mine will encourage both believers in the church and those searching or not yet searching. I hope our stories will help people. There may be those that wonder what happened after my children died and how did I cope on a new journey without my children? That will be the next story of "My Journey with God Through Grief."

I had two constant prayers to God all the days of my children's lives. The first was, "Lord, please do not allow my children's suffering to cause them to walk away from You. That would be more than I could bear." God answered that prayer! My second prayer was, "Lord, please give us the grace to love You, know You, worship You, serve You, and walk and talk with You all the days of our lives, no matter the cost." God answered that prayer, too! In addition, He poured out His love to us. I hope my story glorifies God and that my experience of Him as *God of the Valleys* through the *Mysteries Along Life's Journey* encourages you on your own journey with Him.

Special Memories

I FOUND A poem Tanya had written to praise God in the midst of her suffering a few months before she died. I decided to use it in the funeral service bulletin to encourage the body of Christ, which was her heart's desire.

"Official What? Official Glory to God Giver;
God is a great God
Dwells in the heavens
And also amongst us sinners
I yearn to see His Face, to
Fully know and understand what
His plans are for my life,
In all His power and might, He separated
Night and daylight; ocean and dry land
As well as man from animals.
How much more does He not want us
To be separated from His love, mercy, and grace.
We only have to reach out our hands and
Allow Him full reign in our lives
For nothing can separate us from the love of God.
Psalm 27:8 "My heart says of you, 'Seek your Face!'
Your Face Lord I will seek."
October 31ˢᵗ, 1998.

The Books I Read Aloud to Eric during his end-of-life days: Genesis, Exodus, Deuteronomy, Judges, Joshua, Ruth, Esther, 1 Samuel, Psalms, Isaiah, Luke, John,

Acts, 1 Corinthians, 2 Corinthians, Ephesians, Philippians, 1 Peter, James, 1 John, and Revelations.

References

Barnett, John, "Holy And Anointed One." Wow Worship/ Mercy Vineyard Publishing, 1988.

Chisholm, Thomas, O., "Great Is Thy Faithfulness." Hope Publishing, 1923. Wikipedia: en.wikipedia.org>wiki>Great_Is_Thy_Faithfulness Cosby, Fanny, "Blessed Assurance." (music by Phoebe Knapp) 1873 Wikipedia: htmm:// en.m.wikipedia.org/wiki/Blessed_Assurance)

Clairmont, Susan, "Family of the Year named." *Peterborough Examiner*, October 5, 1992.

Davis, G., "We Are Standing on Holy Ground." Meadowgreen Music Company/ Songchannel Music Co, admin. by Capital CMG, 1983.

Deasy, Mike, and Mcguire, Barry, "Bullfrogs and Butterflies." *Bullfrogs and Butterflies*, Alpha Omega Publications, 1978. Wikepedia en.m.wikpedia. org/wiki/Agap)

Hayford, Jack, "Majesty, Worship His Majesty." *Hayford Ministries,* 1986 Wikipedia en.m.wikipedia.org/wiki/Jack _W._Hayford

"Holy Bible, International Children's Bible." New Century Version: Sweet Publishing Ft. Worth Texas, 1986.

Lemmel, Helen H., "Turn Your Eyes Upon Jesus." *Glad Songs,* 1922, and *Gospel Truth in Song,* 1918.

Mainse, David, 100 Huntley Street, (Founder of 100 Huntley Street, June 15, 1977) All references to Rev. D. Mainse and 100 Huntley Street used with written permission)

Matthew, The Visual Bible NIV, directed by Shepard Design, Dallas, TX: Visual International and Visual Entertainment, Inc., 1997.

Moen, Don, "God Will Make A Way." *God Will Make A Way*, Hosana Music, Integrity Incorporated. 1997.

Mullins, Rich, "Awesome God." *Winds of Heaven, Stuff of Earth*, Reed Arvin Label: Reunion Album, 1988.

Parks, M. et al. "He Is the Bread of Life." *Bread of Life, New Dawn*, Singspiration Division of The Zondervan Corporation, 1978.

Pollard, Adelaide A. and music by Stebbins, George C. "Have Thine Own Way Lord." *Northfield Hymnal with Alexander's Supplement*, 1907. Wikipedia: en.m.wikipedia.org/wiki/Have_Thine_Own_Way Public Domain.)

Sellar, M., Kristofferson K., and Wilkins, M., "One Day at a Time." *One Day at a Time*, California Label: Mega Records, 1974.

Smith, Michael W., "I'll Lead You Home." *I'll Lead You Home* Deer Valley Music, Universal Music, Brentwood Benson Songs, Magic Bean Music, Capital CMG Publishing, Union Records, 1995.

Spafford, H. and Bliss, P., "It Is Well With My Soul." 1873.

Vega, Hose, MD PhD. "An Overview of Frontal Lobe Damage." *Brain and Nervous System Very Well Health*, October 14, 2020 www.verywellhealth.com/the-brains-frontal-lobe3146196.

About the Author

JANET WILLIAMSON'S STORY is about a unique journey with God as a single parent, the voices of her children heard through pages of dark valleys, mingled with joy, hope and humour, while grappling with the mysteries of things not understood. The Scriptures, worship, prayer, church, friends and the community were sources of strength and comfort as this family put their faith in God, while yearning to grow spiritually. Studying Early Childhood Education was her parenting foundation to understanding child development and moving the family to Texas to attend Christ For the Nations Bible Institute anchored them in trusting God. Back to Canada, she worked as a teacher assistant and as a child and youth worker that equipped her to support her children emotionally and academically. Attending evening courses at Trent University, she earned a Bachelor of Arts degree, followed by a Bachelor of Education at York University which opened the door to elementary teaching. Additional courses at Queens University equipped her with a Specialist in Special Education. Later, she attended Tyndale University and earned a Masters in Divinity majoring in counselling and at the Toronto School of Theology, she completed the Chaplaincy Program at The Scarborough Hospital, Grace Division. Janet continued to work in education and volunteer counselling until she retired in 2013 and recently moved with her Akbash dog to Vernon BC Canada, anticipating the next chapter of her journey with God.